Constructing Eschatology

Constructing Eschatology

Rethinking the Prophecy in Isaiah

NIXON DE VERA

foreword by Mark R. Lindsay

WIPF & STOCK · Eugene, Oregon

CONSTRUCTING ESCHATOLOGY
Rethinking the Prophecy in Isaiah

Wipf & Stock
An Imprint of Wipf and Stock Publishers
199 W. 8th Ave., Suite 3
Eugene, OR 97401

www.wipfandstock.com

PAPERBACK ISBN: 978-1-6667-0222-4
HARDCOVER ISBN: 978-1-6667-0223-1
EBOOK ISBN: 978-1-6667-0224-8

DECEMBER 9, 2021

I dedicate this book to those affected by COVID-19.

CONTENTS

FOREWORD

by Mark R. Lindsay

SINCE THE INITIAL OUTBREAK of the coronavirus pandemic in early 2020, much of what we have taken for granted has been called into radical question. Patterns of wealth distribution, access to affordable health care, the capacity of governments and statutory agencies to be agile in their responsiveness to ever-changing epidemiological realities, the critical importance—and forms—of community engagement, the role of faith networks, and the vulnerability of culturally and linguistically diverse peoples have all been highlighted and challenged by the global impact of COVID-19. In this context, religious traditions have been amongst those social groupings whose very purpose has been questioned and disrupted. What does a faith community look like if it cannot meet together? How are religious rituals and liturgies performed—more pointedly, how are *sacraments administered*—if that performative administration is limited to virtual spaces? Such are just some of the questions that have been asked by church and other faith leaders over the course of the pandemic. And so, it is not surprising that even more provocative questions have also been asked, including those that touch upon God's role in, and accountability for, the current health crisis. It is against this backdrop that Nixon de Vera has produced this volume.

Taking seriously the immediate context of crisis and disaster with which so much of the world is still confronted, de Vera takes with equal seriousness the scriptural and (Christian) theological affirmations of God's sovereignty. How, he asks, can both be true? If God is sovereign, and has freely determined himself to be with and for us, how do we account—Christianly—for current and historic catastrophe? De Vera's response is to ask, and then seek to answer, this dilemma by recourse to the prophetic visions embedded in Isaiah, and the Revelation to St. John the Divine. His solution is as disconcerting as the question it seeks to address. By identifying what he refers to as the "striking-healing" motif, de Vera argues that the superabundance of God's love for all creation not only permits, but indeed requires, a "striking"—divine punishment, if you will—*in order for* a subsequent and universal divine healing to be wrought. Forms and forces of natural evil—including the current coronavirus pandemic—are thus capable of being interpreted not as moments of evil but rather as mediations of God's mysterious, but ultimately inexorable, grace towards all things.

Such a claim makes for uncomfortable—some might even say *intolerable*—reading. In his study of Isaiah's prophecies, for example, de Vera does not shy away from naming Israel's sin. Israel's "arrogance" brought them to inevitable "shame and destitution"; God "had to" humble the Hebrew people, in order that they might be cleansed; even God himself is described as the "bringer of plagues," and the "organizer of ethnic cleansing." Can such language really be employed after the *Sho'ah*? Yet all of this, suggests de Vera, is for the final realization of God's glory and humanity's restoration.

One cannot help but ask, as others have asked of such claims before: could God not have authored a different path to salvation? Does this not render evil the necessary corollary to good, as both Leibniz and, before him, St. Thomas argued in their various ways? Does it not make God's benevolence dependent upon a prior hurt and harm—and if so, is this really a God worth worshipping? To paraphrase the Jewish theologian Steven Katz, despite the final good to which God is faithfully shepherding his people, is not such a form and means of redemption infinitely more barbarous than the sins for which it is meant to provide cleansing?

No doubt, these are questions to which there are no really satisfying solutions and about which debate will continue. There is also little doubt that any moment of trauma and disruption is likely to force such issues into the forefront of consideration. Whatever one may think of Nixon de Vera's conclusions, he is to be much admired for having the courage of faith to ask the most vexing of questions. The state of our world, and the role that faith communities and leaders have within it, requires nothing less.

The Revd Professor Mark R. Lindsay
President of the World Conference of Associations
of Theological Institutions (WOCATI)
Deputy Dean and Academic Dean, Trinity College Theological School
June 2021

ACKNOWLEDGMENTS

I AM DEEPLY INDEBTED to the LORD God for helping me understand who he is and what he intends for my life. It has been an honor to have Rev. Prof. Mark Lindsay write the foreword, something well worth celebrating. I am grateful to (Pastor) Dr. Mel Baga for his proofreading assistance in the introduction, despite his workload, and to the rest of my batchmates at Philippine Union College for serving as constant reminders to explain my thoughts as simply as possible. My appreciation extends to Rev. Dr. Jason Goroncy and Rev. Dr. Robin Parry for casting an eye over this manuscript. Also, it is surprising to get the endorsement of Prof. David Bentley Hart—a keepsake indeed. I owe gratitude to my colleagues for their helpful feedback during my presentation of a paper at the Australian and New Zealand Association of Theological Schools (ANZATS) 2021 conference. As always, cheers to the staff of Wipf & Stock for processing the requirements for publication, especially to Dr. Rebecca Abbott for copyediting the manuscript. Above all, I am blessed to have my wife Methyl for her continued support in my passion for completing this work. And of course, thanks to my daughters Zenji and Yuji for the inspiration they have given me.

ABBREVIATIONS

CD	*Church Dogmatics*
CEV	Contemporary English Version
NASB	New American Standard Bible
NKJV	New King James Version
NRSV	New Revised Standard Version
NT	New Testament
OT	Old Testament
PG	Patrologia Graeca
SECB	*Strong's Exhaustive Concordance of the Bible*
THOTC	Two Horizons Old Testament Commentary
TOTL	The Old Testament Library
TNICOT	The New International Commentary on the Old Testament

INTRODUCTION

WHEN WE CONSIDER THE VIRAL PANDEMIC, with the surging new variants and vaccine problems, we cannot help but wonder: what is the cause of COVID-19?[1] Is it from humans, from the devil, from God, or from elsewhere? Christian churches have to admonish people to stay positive amid the outbreak, but rarely is optimism construed from the *character* of God. The doctrine of God is considered or reconsidered in light of the pandemic. What is God's role in the pandemic? These are some of the reactions from different worldviews (in hyper-, quasi-, or semi- forms): Calvinist—"God knows best, do not ask further"; rationalist— "God is in control, do not worry"; Arminian—"God has nothing to do with it, blame humans"; Stoic—"God allows it for a reason, get on with it"; utilitarian—"God is not responsible for it, but he would use it for his purpose"; altruistic—"God's part in it is irrelevant; do what you can to help"; apocalyptic—"God uses it to signal his return. Get ready!"; activist—"God is angry with the destroyers of the earth. Stop it!"; and fundamentalist—"God is punishing humanity for its perversion. Change now."

Whatever appeals to you is valid in one way. In another way, the issue presents itself in the human conditioning of God. It is critical to assess what God thinks of us, to reassess who God *is* and who God is *not* in relation to pestilence and disasters (for example, the coronavirus). If God is responsible for this pandemic in the first place, then we have to take its implications seriously. If this were true, church leaders should rather appeal for members to pray for enlightenment concerning God's purpose. Consequently, the members will find solace in it, rather than

---

1. COVID-19 stands for coronavirus disease 2019.

finding ways not to be affected by it. I am not saying that people should be desensitized to COVID-19. Of course not. God is not insensitive, which would be nothing short of antipathy for the victims. N. T. Wright is correct in suggesting that instead of rushing for answers, we need to restrain ourselves and lament, groan, and cry with grieving families, sympathizing with those struggling with isolation.[2]

This project approaches the virus threat from the standpoint of God's self-determination towards humanity. The best way forward is to know God and what he can do in the world. No matter how much we wonder what caused COVID-19, or what its cure might be, the wonder would lead nowhere if we fail to link the threat first to God. One might ask: which God are you talking about? I am referring specifically to the Creator God of the Bible who had a human face—Jesus Christ.[3] Such a reference will not misrepresent God, let alone tarnish his glorious image. In fact, it is quite the opposite. The key here is to consider the doctrine of God given the devastating circumstances.

Pondering on the havoc of the coronavirus, we have to understand divine providence *within* foreordination. Foreordination means that God planned for creation even before creation itself. In the eternal past, God had determined the actions and events in the affairs of humankind and its surroundings. Now one might probe the extent to which foreordination applies. I think all that concerns God's majestic blueprint for humanity is covered.[4] In the Isaiah narratives, wasting diseases, calamity, drought, and anything often associated with natural evil come from God.[5] It is equally true that these serve the Lord's purpose for the ultimate good. Here, this study undertakes to explore divine goodwill alongside chaos, death, and destruction. The prophecies in Isaiah are indispensable in highlighting the unchangeable God in uncertainties.

OVERVIEW OF ISAIAH

The steadfast God in a wicked world is the main figure in Isaiah, but this thought does not come easily in considering the material itself. It is an ambitious task to navigate through labyrinthine writing addressing a vast

2. Wright, "Tom Wright," video, 14:10. Also see Wright, *God and the Pandemic*, 4.

3. Heb 1:3.

4. Isa 46:8–10.

5. Isa 31:2; 45:7.

period. Isaiah is a very long prophetic text about ancient Israel, and its shape and structure are somewhat difficult to comprehend.[6] For now, let us first break Isaiah into two intelligible halves in order to discuss God's treatment of Israel.[7]

The first half tells of impending punishment for Israel.[8] The prophet Isaiah ben Amoz is mentioned in quite a few places in the pre-exilic era.[9] He spoke in the first person in these instances, specifically where he saw the worship of the LORD God (*Yahweh Elohim*) by strange heavenly creatures.[10] The timeframe is within the last decades of 700 BCE (the latter period of the Northern Kingdom of Israel). The focal point is Jerusalem (capital of Judah, the Southern Kingdom), where Isaiah had lived.[11] Judah was insignificant compared to Assyria, since Assyria was on the rise to becoming a formidable empire in the ancient Near East.[12] The Jews in Judah were careful how they reacted to this superpower after the Assyrians conquered the Northern Kingdom in 722 BCE. That kingdom's loss and the dispersal of the ten tribes of Israel throughout the Assyrian Empire were consequences of the Northern Kingdom of Israel's

6. Williamson, *Isaiah 1–5*, 1–2. Isaiah has sixty-six chapters whereas other OT major prophetic texts have far fewer; namely, Jeremiah has fifty-two chapters, Lamentations has five, Ezekiel has forty-eight, and Daniel has twelve.

7. The name Israel has 125 yields of sure masculine depiction. Israel is not considered a woman. In avoiding the distortion of biblical thought, this study uses *he* for Israel but *she* for Jerusalem and Zion. Judah's gender, however, is more flexible, thus it is referred to as *she* henceforth (Hildebrandt, *Interpreting Quoted Speech*, 77–78n83). See also Schmitt, "Israel and Zion," 20–22, 28–30.

8. Isa 1–39. This study centers on God's paradoxical treatment of his people—punishment and restoration. The notion of punishment is frequent in Isa 1–39, and 40–66 exemplifies the notion of restoration.

9. See Isa 7, 20, 36–39. In Isa 7, the prophet talked to King Ahaz of Judah about the war with King Pekah of Israel. In Isa 20, the prophet walked around naked for three years in Jerusalem. And then in Isa 36–39, he advised King Hezekiah to trust God when King Sennacherib of Assyria attacked Jerusalem.

10. Isa 6, 8.

11. Samaria was the capital of Northern Israel. The United Kingdom of Israel and Judah split around 930 BCE during the reign of Rehoboam (son of Solomon). The northern state was called the Northern Kingdom (Israel) and the southern state was called the Southern Kingdom (Judah). The modern State of Israel constitutes the ancient two kingdoms, having land borders with Lebanon and Syria to the north and northeast, the Palestinian territories of the West Bank and Gaza Strip to the east and west, Jordan to the east, and Egypt to the southwest.

12. Assyria, to the northeast of Israel, is composed of present-day northern Iraq, southern Turkey, northwestern Iran, and northeastern Syria.

unfaithfulness to the LORD God.[13] That is why the Southern Kingdom of Judah's own pride, lack of social justice, and, worse, idolatry became the target of Isaiah's rebuke.

Isaiah served as God's messenger to Judah in performing the necessary judgment if the corrupt leaders continued their wicked ways. He condemned the people for their unwillingness to repent and return to God. God summoned the empires of Assyria and, later, Babylon to correct Jerusalem if she persisted in serving Bel and Nebo and oppressing the poor.[14] Such warning, however, was combined with a message of hope through the divine initiative. These encapsulate the first half of Isaiah.

The second half tells of a sure restoration for Israel.[15] The prophecy of judgment is in tandem with a promise of better times ahead. God, in the future, would consummate the covenant made at Mount Sinai by sending a Davidic king from David's line to establish the indestructible kingdom of God.[16] The Davidic figure would lead the people to the covenant, so the blessing of liberty would flow to Israel and likewise to all nations, just as God had promised Abraham.[17] The series of lyrical poetry about salvation, predictions for the original readers' era, is comforting. It underscores the efficiency and sufficiency of divine sovereignty. God indeed is highly active in foreordaining things. Whatever God foreordains shall be accomplished.[18] In one respect, God used heathen nations to punish Israel; in another respect, God also punished those pagans for their arrogance and cruelty.[19] We can see the punishment motif as God disciplines Israel. The Babylonians conquered the Southern Kingdom circa 587 BCE.[20]

Another important facet is the Messiah prophecy. God raised Cyrus the Great (king of Persia) to accomplish the divine decree.[21] After the Babylonians had laid waste to Jerusalem and brought several Jews to

---

13. 2 Kgs 17:6–12.

14. Isa 3:14–15; 46:1. Bel (or Ba'al) and Nebo are Babylonian deities.

15. Isa 40–66.

16. Cf. Exod 19; 2 Sam 7.

17. Cf. Gen 12.

18. Isa 41.

19. Isa 44.

20. Babylon was in the east of Israel, now Iraq.

21. Isa 45. Persia was in the east of Israel, now Iran.

Babylon, Cyrus became Israel's hero.[22] When Cyrus conquered Babylon, he freed the Jews as part of his foreign policy.[23] In fulfillment of the decree, the Persian king and his successors permitted many Jews in exile to rebuild the temple; this is the account traced in Ezra and Nehemiah.[24] Such a trajectory is pivotal in Isaiah, where it spotlights the salvific message for *all* nations. It is against this eschatological hope that the provocative declaration is viewed. That is substantially the core of the second half of Isaiah.

With a refreshing sense of the covenantal decree, Jerusalem embodies the eschatological promise. Nonetheless, we have the kind of language where the promise does not seem to match reality. The reason given has to do with Israel's response or lack thereof, not with God's commitment. On the one hand, Israel is condemned by ignoring admonition. On the other hand, he finds hope in the future by repenting. Furthermore, given the contrition, Israel will serve as a beacon of hope for all nations. This is so because Israel will introduce the LORD God to the heathens, and they will worship this God.

COMPLEXITY OF ISAIAH

Aside from Isaiah's lengthy and perplexing content, its material intricacy (complicated literary design, written almost entirely in rhythmic form) adds to its complexity. Scholars recognize that Isaiah can be partitioned into three strata of Israel's history.[25] The first part refers to the time of the prophet, about 150 years before the end of the Southern Kingdom.[26] It is usually known as the "negative prophecies."[27] The second part speaks

22. Even if Cyrus the Great is referred to as God's "shepherd" and "anointed," he is not the promised messianic king. See Isa 44:28; 45:1. The topic is in ch. 4.

23. For the discourse about the possibility of Cyrus as the Messiah, see Oswalt, *Holy One of Israel*, 12.

24. See Ezra 5:13–17 and Neh 2:5–8.

25. In the conventional parsing of the text, the authorship shapes the two halves (1–39, 40–66), whereas the epoch shapes the three parts (1–39, 40–55, 56–66) (Berges, "Farewell to Deutero-Isaiah," 575–77; Eriksson, "From Genesius to Childs," 13–15; Petersen, *Prophetic Literature*, 47–48).

26. Isa 1–39. This part, known as Proto-Isaiah or First Isaiah, contains the actual words of the prophet from the eighth century BCE (Lemche, *Old Testament between Theology and History*, 18).

27. Sommer, *A Prophet Reads Scripture*, 59.

about the end of the Jewish exile in Babylon, exclaiming a message of salvation often called the "positive prophecies."[28] The third part pertains to the future of Israel, and likewise to the future of humankind, generally accepted as "apocalyptic prophecies."[29] Scholars also admit the challenge posed by the hanging components in the third part—that is, the seemingly unfulfilled eschatological promise and the period where it is applicable.[30]

It is noticeable in the first part that the sections seem to echo what comes towards the third part, suggesting that it is quite unsystematic.[31] Some scholars hold that this is evidence of at least three writers in different periods, coalescing into one book. Other scholars assert one voice— the prophet Isaiah.[32] Because there are accounts in the first part similar to the third part, it is rational to assume that later writers took the prophet's earlier predictions and deliberately bound the writings together in one manuscript.[33] For instance, if you take Isaiah 1:1–9, it reads like the Assyrian siege of Jerusalem—evident in Isaiah 29:1–4—but is attentive to the unfaithfulness of the Jews. Furthermore, the stipulated reconciliation between God and his people in Isaiah 1:26–27 is almost identical to the presentation in Isaiah 60:21–22. So, one might be tempted to conclude that Isaiah 1 was intentionally designed as an introduction to the three parts, to guide the reader. The pressing concern emerging from the facts above is the improbability of a *unified* message in a diachronic text—given the several voices addressing different situations in various periods.[34]

Another issue running through Isaiah takes shape as the reader continues to ponder: is the prophecy about Israel also applicable to the present? Even though we live in an entirely distinct situation with diverse priorities and preoccupations, it is viable to see thought patterns or lines

28. Sommer, *A Prophet Reads Scripture*, 46.

29. Collins, *Oxford Handbook*, 32. This part is the heart of theo-philosophical exegesis.

30. Gowan, *Theology of Prophetic Books*, 60. This project will attempt to close the loop concerning the hanging components in the third part of Isaiah.

31. For example, Isa 2:2–4; cf. 66:18–20 and 11:12; cf. 56:8.

32. The majority of OT scholars think that Isaiah was written by several people relating to their immediate situations. See Childs, *Isaiah*, 4–5, for the suggestion of multiple writers; for the assertion of just one writer, cf. Tomasino, "Isaiah 1.1—2.4," 81–98; Carr, "Reaching for Unity in Isaiah," 61–80.

33. Broyles and Evans, *Writing and Reading*, 1:187–88. In this project, what is crucial are the situations addressed by the prophecies, not the issue of authorship.

34. This project favors a steady message in Isaiah which will be explained shortly.

of interpretation agreeable to forming a consolidated proclamation that can be taken into the twenty-first century. For example, in Isaiah 1, social justice was a big issue, where the prophet Isaiah criticized his audience for exploiting the poor and weak. The Jewish courts were so debased that graft and corruption had become rampant. The true owners of properties were being taken advantage of, widows and orphans were open to abuse, small-time laborers and traders treated unfairly, and many other malpractices were perpetrated by the rich and powerful.[35] The people in the position to effect reform had neglected to utilize their status to help the ostracized and disenfranchised.[36]

The messianic content in Isaiah 1 is another important yet puzzling material to consider for its imageries of judgment *and* restoration. The "Holy and Mighty One" is the Judge as well as the Restorer of Israel.[37] It seems that the means of punishment of God's people outweighs the outcome, which is their renewal. This is a subject of contention in interpreting the ethics and theodicy of Isaiah. The direction of the narratives points to Israel's inadequacy for the task. Nevertheless, the periods of adjudication involved here call for a decisive response from Israel, so that acquittal and rejuvenation may be made.[38] If not, the outcome shall be devastating—that is, being burned up like fire, which is depicted in the ending verses of Isaiah.[39] Overall, cogently, Isaiah 1 might serve as a sort of summary of the whole manuscript.

The second part of Isaiah gives attention to national identity, monarchy, and legal courts.[40] It deals with the descendants of the Jewish slaves who were in the Persian Empire. These Jews lacked two things: freedom and a monarchy, because Achaemenid kings had been ruling over them. But in one of the accounts, a *unique* emissary will bring forth justice and

---

35. Isa 3:13–15; 5:23; 10:1–2.

36. This project asserts several concerns in Isaiah that resonate with our present setting. For instance, the practice of justice *and* righteousness is always necessary for following God. (The terms justice and righteousness are used together about eleven times in the first half of Isaiah).

37. Isa 1:4, 24.

38. Isa 1:26; 66:12–13.

39. Isa 1:31; 66:24.

40. Isa 40–55. This part, known as Deutero-Isaiah or Second Isaiah, is believed to be the work of an anonymous author during the Jewish exile in Babylon in sixth century BCE (Lemche, *Old Testament*, 19).

righteousness to the people of God.[41] Again, scholars are baffled as to its application—whether it is exclusive to Judah alone or universal, concerning all nations.[42] The territory of the unique emissary somewhat bridges the lacuna mentioned.[43]

The servant entity is another enigma with which to wrestle. Remarkably, this figure is depicted using royal-like language of a king whose domain encompasses not merely Judah or Israel but beyond.[44] With that in mind, the Servant-King's renewal of Zion foreshadows the legal courts' enforcement of social justice worldwide.[45] Whether the return of the Jewish exiles from Babylon typifies the return of humanity to God is worthy of investigation.[46]

In the third part of Isaiah, the gap between the powerful and the powerless is shored up again.[47] It communicates that the theme of justice and righteousness is continually applied through different political settings. The prophet's witness of heavenly worship might not be appropriate to the contemporary standard of political correctness, due to the hierarchical structure implicit in the vision: the king ruling over his subjects.[48] Of course, God is right on top, yet this God is also depicted as a Servant.[49] The Servant-King is a suffering Lord. Hence, God being on top is at the same time being on the lowest level.[50] Such dialectical rendition of God, portrayed by the Messiah, is yet another facet to review in light of the prophet's predictions.

The Servant-King is the opposite of the lords of Israel, local and foreign. God as angry with the proud and merciful with the humble is a

41. Isa 42:1–4.

42. Alexander, *Commentary on Isaiah*, 128–31.

43. Isa 40:17; 43:9; 49:22; 52:10. This project will prove that God's justice and righteousness shown to Judah are extended worldwide.

44. Isa 49:7; 55:4–5. In Isa 40, all flesh will witness the Messiah's glory; this account is also evident in other parts of the book.

45. Isa 42:4; 51:4.

46. This project posits that the return of the diaspora typifies the return of humanity to God. People who ignore God will eventually come back to him; also, people who do not know God will, in time, know God and accept him.

47. Isa 56–66. This part, known as Trito-Isaiah or Third Isaiah, was written, most likely, by Isaiah's disciples during the post-exilic period around the end of the sixth century BCE (Lemche, *Old Testament*, 20).

48. Isa 6:1; cf. 57:15.

49. Isa 61:1–4.

50. Isa 63:8–9.

recurring motif in Isaiah. In this insight, trees, mountains, fortresses, and all kinds of lofty elements are pictured as being flattened by God.[51] God's arm will be at work in full force, "so that his own personal power will do the job, overthrowing Babylon and rescuing Israel."[52] In other words, the LORD God brings into account rulers and kings who make themselves gods. God sets a day of judgment to ensure the condemnation of the oppressor and the protection of the oppressed. God has his way of ordering the Jewish society and other societies too through the suffering Lord. The concept of the suffering Lord finds its epitome in self-sacrifice. The Servant-King will die unjustly but will come back to life and be glorified.[53]

That speaks about the restoration and exaltation of the victims of injustice as well as those guilty of it. This is another motif indispensable for the treatment of God's affinity with the sufferers, whether in this life or the afterlife.[54] Whether or not it would follow logically that the Isaianic prophecy hints at the final restoration of all is a concern demanding thorough inspection.[55]

This project challenges the claim that there is no unifying motif in Isaiah simply because the book is a collection of writings. J. J. M. Roberts, for instance, has "deep reservations" on any assumptions of underlying coordination of parts in Isaiah.[56] However, it is probable to formulate a steady message out of Isaiah, despite its complexity of authorship and scope. The key is in the God who maneuvers things concerning Israel.[57] As laid out in the overview, God's treatment of Israel and the surrounding nations is the lynchpin subject for the prophet. The viable unifying message is God's striking and healing of people.[58] Of course, other major

51. Isa 57:7–12; 64:1–3.

52. Wright, "Fifth Gospel," para. 8.

53. Karl Barth has similar notions, namely, "the Lord as Servant" and "the Servant as Lord" (Barth, *CD* IV/1–2, ch. 14–15).

54. Granting that the wicked are forever tormented in hell, yet due to God's eternal compassion, I posit, "There is no wicked kept any moment longer in hell because of the mere pleasure of God." A revision of Jonathan Edwards's statement: "There is nothing that keeps wicked men at any one moment out of hell, but the mere pleasure of God" (Edwards, *Sinners in the Hands*, 2).

55. Restitution and glorification are platforms in discussing the redemption of all in and through Jesus Christ—the Servant-King—and so tackle Christian universalism.

56. Roberts, *First Isaiah*, 2.

57. Becker, "Book of Isaiah," 38.

58. Isa 1:24–26; 4:4; 10:24–27; 11:4–5; 15–16; 19:22; 38:15, 21; 48:9–10; 49:8–10; 53:5; 54:7–8; 57:18–19; 58:8,11; 60:10b; 63:4.

themes, namely, the coming of the Messiah, God's sovereignty over world kingdoms, and the surety of the final judgment are candidates,[59] but the striking-healing motif carries them all. Because this study asserts the undergirding theme of the discipline of Israel, God's method of striking-healing is in light of God's love. God's supreme love for his people is paramount in the talk of foreordination.

Regardless of its anthological and cryptic characteristics, the overall shape of Isaiah is established.[60] This is over the fact that Isaiah is known for having "perfectly harmonious" parts devoid of literary blunders, which so make it astonishing in "literary grandeur."[61]

FRAMEWORK OF THE STUDY

The study will focus on the following: first, God, the revealer and implementor of prophecy in Isaiah; second, the negative and positive prophecies of Isaiah; third, the apocalyptic prophecy on Israel; last, the final state of humanity.[62] The issue of the authorship of Isaiah will not be dealt with in depth.[63] Rather, this study will exhaust the Isaiah collection that has direct relevance to end-time events—the circumstances before, during, and after the final judgment of God.

Note that *Isaiah* (without the preceding *prophet*) primarily refers to the book of Isaiah. When it refers to the person, *the prophet* is most often used, depending on the context. The name *Israel* pertains to the descendants of Jacob, hence, the constituents of the United Kingdom of Israel and Judah. The study differentiates Zion from Jerusalem to highlight Israel's paradigmatic transition from insurgence. Although *Zion* and *Jerusalem* both refer to Judah's capital city, the former signifies the spiritual distinctiveness of Israel (internal aspect), while the latter signifies Israel's

59. McKinion, *Isaiah 1–39*, xlii–xliii.

60. The concerns inherent in the complexity of the scope of Isaianic prophecy, namely, fulfillment of the promise, unified message, implication of Judah's renewal, the role of the Messiah, the political and ethical correctness of God's punishment, and the present application of justice and righteousness are addressed in the chapter synopsis.

61. Stromberg, *Introduction to Study of Isaiah*, 97; Oswalt, *Book of Isaiah, Chs. 1–39*, 3.

62. For insights concerning the eschatological significance of Israel to the future of humanity, see Dumbrell, "Purpose of Book of Isaiah."

63. Despite the crisis in authorship, attempts have been made to read Isaiah "as a unified whole" for over three decades (Couey, *Reading the Poetry*, 201).

universal role as a spiritual hub for the entire world (external aspect).[64] In other words, Jerusalem is the place where the spirit of Zion "penetrates the inner life of distant peoples."[65]

The term *eschatology* refers to the vision of the new era relating to the vision of the past era.[66] The new era indicates the outcome of the final judgment of humankind, while the past era indicates the judgment of Israel. In this respect, Israel stands as a type of the human race. Whenever *universalism* is mentioned, it is understood strictly in the Christian context. Through Jesus Christ, all people of all generations are guaranteed the inheritance of the New Jerusalem and the habitation of the new earth.[67]

In the search for the real author of Isaiah, the criterion in this enterprise is to rigorously examine the internal evidence.[68] Let us take for example Isaiah 40 as it raises a big question: who is talking here? The voice proclaiming the words of hope has the perspective of somebody who had lived in the post-exilic period. It happened in the time the prophets Ezra and Nehemiah described, disqualifying Isaiah to have written this section, since he died 150 years before this period.[69] So to make sense of this puzzle is truly an intellectual challenge. Some scholars suppose that it is still the prophet speaking in his day but prophetically transported around two hundred years into the future.[70] In that case, he is said to speak to future generations as if the exile had passed.

The manuscript itself, however, renders clues that something else (most probably) is taking shape. In Isaiah 8 and 29–30, we can see that after the leaders rejected the prophet Isaiah, the prophet wrote and sealed up in a scroll the declarations of judgment and hope. It is also understood that he entrusted this to his disciples as a witness for later generations.[71] It appears that when the exile was over, the prophet's disciples revisited

---

64. Kook, *Ein Ayah*, 385.

65. Kook, *Ein Ayah*, 385. For an alternative view, "Zion was the church, Jerusalem was the state" (Calvin, *John Calvin's Bible Commentaries*, 109).

66. Everson, *Vision of Prophet Isaiah*, xvii–xviii. For more insights on the meaning of eschatology in Isaiah, see Goldingay, *Theology of Book of Isaiah*, 143–44.

67. Jang, *Particularism and Universalism*, 3, 99.

68. The concerns inherent in the complexity of the authorship of Isaiah are slightly tackled here.

69. Rebuilding the Second Temple (Ezra 3, 6), and the walls of Jerusalem, and the reading of the Mosaic Law to the people (Neh 3, 8).

70. For instance, see Oswalt, *Book of Isaiah, Chs. 40–66*, 19–20.

71. Thompson, *Isaiah 40–66*, xix–xx.

the scroll and began applying his messages of hope to their situation.[72] Whichever view makes sense to the reader, one thing finds consensus: the entire manuscript signals a promising future, and at the epicenter, God consummates the eschatological hope.[73] In this respect, it has become plausible to read Isaiah as a composite whole.[74]

Content-wise, there is a more manageable way to navigate through the varied aesthetic-predictive declarations well suited for this study, that is, to divide Isaiah into six sections, which make the six chapters of this book.[75] This division reframes the prophetic messages according to the universality of foreordination. The main theme for each chapter is not the outstanding subject matter in each designated section; however, the identified theme is implied in the talk of God concerning Israel, namely: God's identity, intention, operation, and purpose.

The main schema of chapter 1 (Isa 1–12) is about God as overall in charge of Israel's destiny, in light of God's love. The sovereign love for God's people is paramount in rendering foreordination. Of course, one could argue that the unfaithfulness of Judah, the judgment upon God's people, the fall of Zion, or the humbling of the proud are a better fit for the section. Although the argument is valid, the overarching thrust in this project is to extract the doctrine of God from Isaiah. Instead of attending to the plight of the people, the concentration is on God and his decree. Accordingly, each chapter bears a theme that coheres with the entire project, albeit such a direction does not order the discourse in Isaiah. The project still recognizes the way Isaiah is structured according to the writers' intent, hence below are the sections based on the original layout of Isaiah.

Isaiah 1–39 contains three large sections that develop the warning to Israel and culminate in the fall of Zion and the exile of the Jews to Babylon. The first three chapters of the study pursue the development of the theme by understanding how God's love, power, and grace can

---

72. It had been a practice in translating the Bible that scribes interpreted old texts "in light of their own historical circumstances" (Mackie, *Expanding Ezekiel*, 29).

73. What is incontestable is that Isa 1–39 seems to deliberately show that the prophet is a true messenger of God, because his prediction of the Jewish exile to Babylon happened.

74. Evans, "On Unity and Parallel Structure"; O'Day and Peterson, *Theological Bible Commentary*, 209.

75. In sequence: Isa 1–12; 13–27; 28–39; 40–48; 49–55; 56–66 (Dumbrell, "Purpose of Book of Isaiah," 123).

be related to judgment. Correspondingly, the first section is dedicated to presenting God as sovereign. The second section deals with God as Creator. The third section is aimed at expositing God as Sustainer. There is also a message of hope after the exile. It had been prophesied in Isaiah 40–66, explained in three large sections, too, that the promises would all be fulfilled and that eschatological hope developed. Here, the message of hope is in light of the eternality, suffering, and glory of God. In this respect, the fourth section is dedicated to expounding God as Elector, the fifth section discusses God as Redeemer, and the last section is intended to showcase God as Glorifier. These are the set parameters in considering the final status of humanity in the apocalyptic condition of Israel.[76]

This undertaking is distinctive. Recent monographs on how universalism can be derived from Isaiah (in a way that reformulates the final judgment in Revelation) are lacking.[77] In other words, the negative prophecies are taken to serve the apocalyptic prophecies to effect an optimistic end. In that regard, I endeavor to critically evaluate the notions of foreordination and theodicy, given the prophet's messages, and systematically dialogue with Karl Barth, P. T. Forsyth, David Bentley Hart, and Robin Parry on the final reinstitution of all humankind that is hinted at, but not explicitly stated, in Isaianic eschatology.[78] The divine discipline, such as invasion and exile, could be a precursor to divine healing.[79] This might serve as an antidote to the misappropriation of God's involvement in human affairs. I shall argue that in his enigmatic outworking, God not only is but can be seen beyond reproach.

---

76. Here, Isaiah's apocalyptic vision of Israel is studied in conjunction with the apostle John's apocalyptic vision of the church. Henceforth, Revelation (first letter capitalized) refers to the book of Revelation.

77. Almost all studies of Isaiah that, to some degree, engage with the concept of universalism are journal articles; most were published more than thirty years ago. See Simkovich, "Origins of Jewish Universalism"; Kaminsky and Stewart, "God of All the World"; Whybray, Second Isaiah, 63–64; Gelston, "Universalism in Second Isaiah"; Lindars, "Good Tidings to Zion"; Van Winkle, "Relationship of Nations to Yahweh"; Davidson, "Universalism in Second Isaiah"; May, "Theological Universalism in Old Testament." To date, the only recent material is Blenkinsopp's "Second Isaiah—Prophet of Universalism," in Essays, 50–62.

78. These theologians are chosen specifically not because of their discussion on Christian universalism as they read Isaiah per se but due to their conception of the eschatological role of the Messiah in the outcome of humankind. Thus their reading of Isaiah could be foundational as well as peripheral to their discourse.

79. Young, Book of Isaiah, 42.

Theological exegesis is applied to present philosophical-theological arguments that presuppose Christian universalism.[80] In doing so, we have to examine the contributions, but not exclusively, of the mentioned theologians on the matter.[81] Furthermore, the system of study is thematically cognizant (per section) of the eschatological glory predetermined for humanity.[82] The end-time projection of Isaianic prophecies is evaluated alongside the eschatological events in Revelation. The latter, however, is reconceived in light of the former.[83]

WHY READ ISAIAH THROUGH REVELATION?

More than any other prophet in the OT, Isaiah is quoted about sixty-one times in the NT.[84] This fact makes Isaiah very relevant historically, more so in dealing with eschatology.[85] Around six direct quotations from Isaiah in Revelation could pertain to the end.[86] Both manuscripts speak of God as "the first and the last," show God to possess "the key of David" (a symbol of absolute authority and supervision), portray God as "the light" in the renewed world, signal that God "will wipe away tears" in the new Zion, announce that the righteous "shall not hunger or thirst anymore," and report the forthcoming "new heaven and new earth."[87] These are visions of God and God's achievement at the eschaton.

Surprisingly, John the Evangelist utilized probably about one hundred twenty-three Isaianic references to write what he had seen in a

80. The majority of the manuscripts in n77 are biblical expositions. The lexical study, nonetheless, is employed in building a formidable argument on certain points.

81. Barth, CD I/2, 178–96; IV/3, 579–81. See also Gignilliat, *Karl Barth and Fifth Gospel*, 63–104; Forsyth, *Descending on Humanity*, 197–203; Hart, *That All Shall Be Saved*, 68–94; Parry, *Lamentations*, 162–68.

82. McCruden, *Solidarity Perfected*, 9.

83. For example, Isa 2:1–4; 66:18–20; cf. Rev 19:19–20; 20:7–10.

84. Isaiah is quoted about twenty-one times in the Gospels, twenty-five times in the Pauline epistles, six times in 1 Peter, six times in Revelation, five times in Acts, one in Hebrews. For the significance of Isaiah in the NT, see Moyise and Menken, *Isaiah in New Testament*, 1–7.

85. Hulse, "Eschatological Dimensions of Isaiah," 33.

86. Rev 1:17; 3:7; 7:16; 21:23. Steve Moyise, however, observes that there are only allusions (no explicit quotations) to Isaiah in Revelation (Moyise, "Isaiah in New Testament," 538).

87. Isa 41:4—Rev 1:17; Isa 22:22—Rev 3:7; Isa 49:10—Rev 7:16; Isa 25:8—Rev 21:4; Isa 65:17—Rev 21:1; and Isa 60:20—Rev 21:23.

vision.[88] The similarities are sometimes astounding. When one who is familiar with Isaiah reads Revelation, one cannot help but see numerous thought patterns shared in both accounts. That is evident in *every* chapter of Revelation.[89] For example, both books showcase the Lord's power to subdue world kingdoms.[90] Another example is when the two describe the wrath of God against his enemies.[91] One of the closest links indicates the irretrievability of the past in the world made new.[92] After all, Revelation 21 contains the most cross-references with Isaiah.[93] With this insight, the

88. These are words, phrases, thoughts, or thought patterns in Isaiah similarly found in Revelation. They have common motifs/themes or references illuminating a particular verse or passage in Revelation corollary to complete or extend the thought (Ellison, *Nelson's Complete Concordance*).

89. Rev 1:4—Isa 41:4; Rev 1:5—Isa 55:4; Rev 1:8—Isa 41:4; Rev 1:16—Isa 49:2; Rev 1:17—Isa 6:1, 41:4, 44:2, 6, 48:12; Rev 2:8—Isa 44:6; Rev 2:12—Isa 49:2; Rev 2:17—Isa 56:5, 65:15, 62:2; Rev 2:27—Isa 30:14; Rev 3:7—Isa 22:22; Rev 3:9—Isa 45:14; Rev 3:12—Isa 62:2, 65:15; Rev 4:2—Isa 6:1; Rev 4:7—Isa 6:2-3; Rev 4:9—Isa 6:1; Rev 5:1—Isa 29:11; Rev 5:5—Isa 11:1, 10; Rev 5:6—Isa 11:2, 53:7; Rev 5:9—Isa 42:10; Rev 5:10—Isa 61:6; Rev 5:12—Isa 53:7; Rev 6:13—Isa 34:4; Rev 6:14—Isa 34:4, 54:10; Rev 6:15—Isa 2:10-11, 19, 21, 24:21; Rev 7:2—Isa 41:2; Rev 7:16—Isa 49:10; Rev 7:17—Isa 25:8; Rev 8:7—Isa 28:2; Rev 8:9—Isa 2:16; Rev 8:10—Isa 14:12; Rev 9:20—Isa 2:8, 20, 17:8; Rev 9:21—Isa 47:9, 12; Rev 10:3—Isa 31:4; Rev 11:2—Isa 52:1, 63:18; Rev 11:8—Isa 1:9; Rev 12:2—Isa 26:17, 66:6-9; Rev 12:3—Isa 27:1; Rev 12:5—Isa 66:7; Rev 12:12—Isa 44:23, 49:13; Rev 12:14—Isa 40:31; Rev 12:15—Isa 59:19; Rev 13:4—Isa 46:5; Rev 13:8—Isa 53:7; Rev 13:10—Isa 33:1; Rev 14:5—Isa 53:9; Rev 14:8—Isa 21:9; Rev 14:10—Isa 51:17; Rev 14:11—Isa 34:10; Rev 14:13—Isa 57:2; Rev 14:19—Isa 63:2-3; Rev 15:4—Isa 66:3; Rev 15:8—Isa 6:4; Rev 16:1—Isa 66:6; Rev 16:6—Isa 49:26; Rev 16:10—Isa 8:22; Rev 16:12—Isa 11:15-16, 41:2, 25; Rev 16:17—Isa 66:6; Rev 16:21—Isa 1:21; Rev 17:2—Isa 23:17; Rev 17:15—Isa 8:7; Rev 18:2—Isa 13:21-22, 21:9, 34:11-15; Rev 18:3—Isa 48:20, 52:11; Rev 18:6—Isa 40:2; Rev 18:7—Isa 47:8-9; Rev 18:8—Isa 47:9; Rev 18:17—Isa 23:14; Rev 18:18—Isa 34:10; Rev 18:20—Isa 44:23; Rev 18:22—Isa 24:8; Rev 18:23—Isa 23:8; Rev 19:3—Isa 34:10; Rev 19:4—Isa 6:1; Rev 19:8—Isa 61:10; Rev 19:11—Isa 11:4; Rev 19:13—Isa 63:3; Rev 19:15—Isa 11:4, 63:3; Rev 19:20—Isa 30:33; Rev 19:21—Isa 24:22; Rev 20:4—Isa 26:14; Rev 20:11—Isa 6:1; Rev 20:13—Isa 26:19; Rev 20:14—Isa 25:8; Rev 21:21—Isa 65:17; Rev 21:4—Isa 25:8, 35:10, 51:11, 65:19; Rev 21:5—Isa 43:19; Rev 21:6—Isa 55:1; Rev 21:8—Isa 30:33; Rev 21:10—Isa 52:1; Rev 21:19—Isa 54:11-12; Rev 21:23—Isa 24:23, 60:1, 19; Rev 21:24—Isa 60:3, 5; 49:23; 60:16; Rev 21:25—Isa 60:11; Rev 21:27—Isa 52:1; Rev 22:5—Isa 60:19; Rev 22:12—Isa 40:10, 62:11; Rev 22:13—Isa 44:6, 48:12; Rev 22:16—Isa 11:1, 10; Rev 22:17—Isa 55:1.

90. Isa 41:2 and Rev 7:2.

91. Isa 66:6 and Rev 16:17.

92. Isa 65:17 and Rev 21:1.

93. It is followed by Rev 18 and 19. The same imageries in Isaiah inspired the renewal of Jerusalem, the fall of Babylon, and the Lamb's wedding with the bride in Revelation.

prophet's testimony is an indispensable read for those wishing to understand the evangelist's vision.[94] In fact, Isaiah has more connection with Revelation than with the prophetic texts of Ezekiel and Daniel.[95]

Other citations from Isaiah in the NT are about the end-time frequently addressed in Revelation.[96] When the apostle Paul, for instance, describes the resurrection as "death has been swallowed up in victory," this resembles Isaiah's words, "he [the LORD God] will swallow up death forever."[97] In the epistle to the Romans, there is that final pronouncement of "every knee shall bow to me, and every tongue shall give praise to God"; this, too, is in Isaiah, as "every knee will bow, every tongue will swear allegiance" to the LORD God.[98] Such imagery resonates with what the evangelist witnessed in heaven.[99]

The parallelism between Isaiah and Revelation hinges on the majestic plan for humanity. It does not pertain exclusively to the promised hope after the destruction of Solomon's temple and Herod's temple but, more importantly, refers to the period around the eschatological judgment. Jan Fekkes alludes to this conception: "His [John's] interpretation of Isaiah in particular was one of the more important previsionary influences which provided the substance and inspiration for the vision experience and for its final redaction."[100] These reinforce Isaiah's role in decoding the symbols in Revelation.[101] Even John's vision of hope cannot be divorced from Isaiah's testimony. David Matthewson reiterates that visionary language and experience of John are allusions to Isaianic prophecies.[102]

The future of Israel and the world coincide with the prophecies about the identity and work of the Messiah. The future is always with God (its holder), as the former find surety in the latter. Whenever Christ's

---

94. Ellis, *Christ and the Future*, 55–56.

95. Ezekiel contains around sixty-three cross-references with Revelation; likewise, Daniel has about fifty-five.

96. Of course, not all events in Revelation speak about the end of the world. See Sweeney, *Prophetic Literature*, 215–16.

97. 1 Cor 15:54 and Isa 25:8 NRSV.

98. Rom 14:11 and Isa 45:23 NASB.

99. Rev 20:13; 21:4; 7:9–12.

100. Fekkes, *Isaiah and Prophetic Traditions*, 290.

101. Stefanović, *Revelation of Jesus Christ*, 632–34. See also Musija, "Eschatological Hope," 2.

102. Mathewson, *New Heaven and New Earth*, 22; Matthewson, "Isaiah in Revelation," 189–90.

disciples (including the evangelist) meditate on the Messiah and his mission, they were not "simply thinking of Isaiah" but were shaped by the entire Torah.[103] From these allusions, we can deduce that only in the renewal of Zion can Israel perform his duty to the world.

In sum, the reasons for reading Isaiah through Revelation are as follows: (1) The evangelist directly quoted the prophet's words. (2) Several terms, symbols, and thought patterns used in Revelation are similar to those in Isaiah. (3) Both books specifically talk of the eschaton. (4) There are many analogous events in them. (5) They picture God as the ultimate Judge. These make the reading of Isaiah through Revelation plausible and necessary in conceiving an apocalyptic eschatology of hope.

SYNOPSIS OF THE STUDY

In speaking of a blissful future, chapter 1 concerns itself with whether or not God was behind the downfall of Israel. I will argue that the terms *permit* or *allow* do not do justice to the notion of divine sovereignty.[104] They suggest that God is neither highly active nor truly caring for Israel. The deity who had raised Babylon and Assyria to strike rebellious Israel is also the deity who heals him, as appointed.

The first section (Isa 1–12) deals with divine sovereignty paired with divine love. God as a parent is central in the discussion: God calls on Israel to repent and return to his father (or mother). God disciplines Israel, then restores this child to his rightful state. Israel's mortification, consecration, and mission are the fundamental components of the section. The section culminates with the announcement of the coming Messiah for Israel's exaltation.

Investigating the reason for God's utmost concern for Israel is crucial in the second chapter. I shall argue that God knows what is best for his people, as God is their creator. God in his might causes all things necessary for Israel and also for the neighbors. Here the powers of worldly kingdoms are subservient only to the power of God.

In the second section (Isa 13–27), God's right to direct the destiny of Israel (and other nations) will be investigated in connection with the

---

103. Wright, "Fifth Gospel," para. 10.

104. This concurs with John Calvin's take on divine providence (Calvin, *Institutes of Christian Religion*, 1.18.1).

concepts of divine authority, justice, righteousness, mercy, wisdom, and constancy.

Chapter 3 will consider in depth the recurrent striking-healing theme evident in Isaiah, with the accent on divine providence. I will argue that God is indeed highly active in the affairs of Israel, as well as in Assyria, Babylon, and Persia. In God the Sustainer, the divine grace is foundational in the diagnosis of God's ways and means, furthermore in the talk of theodicy.

The third section (Isa 28–39) treats the divine providence in conjunction with God as the Potter, Revealer, Upholder, Protector, Healer, and Restorer; all of these names are considered in view of the covenant. The section ends with a serious concern that resonates with the underlying thought in the introduction: it is implausible to attribute evil to God simply because of God using natural evil (and, to some degree, human evil) to accomplish his purpose.

The motif of divine discipline continues in chapter 4 with intensity. I shall argue that despite the concept of pretemporal determination of actions and events in time, God can also be real time in consummating what he has foreordained. The electing God in the elected Israel is key in critically analyzing what it means for God to be eternal.

The presentation in the fourth section (Isa 40–48) concentrates on the doctrine of election, emphasizing the eternality of the honor, reliability, and integrity of God. The promised better times ahead are sure on the grounds of the One who promised it.

The effectiveness of the system of striking-healing is tested in chapter 5; the subject in review is God's character. I shall argue that God does not shy away from being involved with the misery of Israel, and, more importantly, God can justify his actions. In so doing, God's rulership cannot be properly understood apart from the self-sacrifice of the Messiah. Here the doctrine of redemption will be examined in strict concurrence with the formulation of the Servant-King.

Such formulation is exemplified in the fifth section (Isa 49–55). The notion of divine suffering is rendered consolatory owing to the faithfulness, blessedness, purity, and selflessness of God. With these points, the issues of theodicy will be engaged substantially.

Congruent with previous considerations, the final chapter seeks to unpack some implications of divine sovereignty on eschatology. To that end, it will inspect God's equal treatment of all peoples. I shall argue that God is *universally inclusive* in exalting humankind. The glory ascribed to God is somehow applicable to the undeserving. As embedded in the prophet's messages, the will of God is for the benefit of all. Election, therefore, is viewed against the concept of particularism.

The ending section (Isa 56–66) handles the divine glory in consonance with divine inclusivity. The all-embracing restoration of humanity is considered in concert with God's outworking, namely, covenant with Israel, promised rest, call to the world, and favorable judgment. I will argue that the renewal of Zion and the service of Jerusalem signal the deliverance and exaltation of the human race. Such universal dispensation of charity and glory is feasible through the death and resurrection of the Messiah—Jesus Christ.

In my conclusion, I shall reflect on divine sovereignty unfolded within Isaianic eschatology: the end of the history of Israel reflects the end of the history of humanity—things that *shall* happen, not what may happen. Here, the hypothesis: that Jerusalem stands as the center of eschatological hope will be firmly established.

We will now discuss the doctrine of God in view of evil and suffering by probing who *is* the sovereign God.

CHAPTER I

UNSEEN COMPASSION

"Holy, holy, holy is the LORD of hosts;
the whole earth is full of his glory."[1]

THIS CHAPTER EXPLORES THE PREDICTIVE DECLARATIONS of the prophet Isaiah concerning the people of Israel. It will be argued that despite the confusions inherent in Isaiah about God's dealing with Israel, there is a way to conceive God as the One who foreordains in love. To support this, I will begin with pericopes in the first twelve chapters of Isaiah in which the concepts of foreordination and divine love appear.

Principally, the chapter is concerned with the following questions. Is God truly sovereign in the affairs of Israel? Also, to what extent can this sovereignty be applied to the fall of Zion? To what degree might this sovereignty represent God's love, notwithstanding the seemingly predetermined captivity and exile of the Jews? In response, the following will be examined: (1) the prophet's warning of invasion and destruction in view of foreordination; (2) the relation of divine judgment to divine compassion in light of the covenant with Israel; (3) judgment as contributory to God's healing; (4) Jerusalem as the locus of eschatological hope for humankind.

Let us now turn to the first section of Isaiah with the emphasis on God as sovereign.

---

1. Isa 6:3 CEV.

1. SUMMARY OF ISAIAH 1-12

This section focuses on the prophet's vision of judgment and hope for Jerusalem. It begins with the accusation of the leaders of Jerusalem for insurrection through idolatry and injustice. Here the sovereign God was about to judge the city by sending heathen nations to conquer Israel. According to Isaiah, the judgment would be like a purifying fire that burns away all dross in Israel to give way to the new Zion. The remnant would populate the new Zion. When all nations heard about the kingdom of God and learned justice and righteousness, they would come to the temple in Jerusalem. This ushered in the age of universal peace and harmony.

At the outset, the storyline of the transformation of old Zion into the new Zion is repetitive throughout Isaiah but rendered with increasing detail. In the middle of the section, the prophet sees God (through a vision) sitting on his glorious throne in the heavenly temple and strange creatures around the throne shouting, "Holy, holy, holy, is the LORD!"[2] While in awe, the prophet suddenly realized how corrupt he was and, by extension, Israel. He was sure that God's holiness would destroy him, yet, fortunately, such holiness (depicted by a burning coal) burned Isaiah's filth instead, not his body and soul. That demonstrated the purification of his sin, applicable to Israel, too. With this thought, the prophet was encouraged to keep announcing the coming judgment because of the purification that came with it.

Notably, Israel had reached a point of no return in which the prophet's warning was to have a paradoxical effect of hardening the people; nonetheless, such hardening is part of the Lord's master plan. Israel was about to be chopped down like a tree and left like a stump in the field. In due time that stump would be burned. But after burning, God declared that this smoldering stump would be a holy seed that would survive into the future. This was a beacon of hope. Who was the holy seed?

The holy seed, Isaiah predicted, was David's descendant—a king of Jerusalem. Yet the seed would arrive after the sack of Jerusalem. God would raise Assyria to chop down Israel by devastating the land, but that was not the end of it. In fulfillment of the promise to David, the beacon of hope would reign afterward as the king of the new Jerusalem. The king would also be called "Immanuel" (God with us), and his kingdom was to free Israel from the shackle of the imperial overlords; hence Israel was the small shoot coming out of the smoldering stump. Crucially, the shoot

---

2. Isa 6:3.

likewise represented the coming of the holy seed stemming from the old stump of David's family.[3] King Immanuel of the new Jerusalem would rule by the Spirit of God to bring justice and righteousness, not only for the abused Jews but also for all distressed peoples. An eschatological hope prefaced the dominion of the Messiah; his kingdom would transform all creation, bringing everlasting peace and harmony. The prophet finished the section with the message of judgment *and* hope.

After summarizing the first section of Isaiah, we will now investigate how and why invasion and destruction is what God had foreordained.

2. GOD AS SOVEREIGN

In Isaiah, there is only one Master of Israel—the LORD God.[4] The prophet writes,

> Therefore says the *Sovereign*, the LORD of hosts, the Mighty One of Israel: Ah, I will pour out my wrath on my enemies, and avenge myself on my foes! I will turn my hand against you . . . . Afterward you shall be called the city of righteousness, the faithful city.[5]

What does it mean for God to *be* sovereign? The being of God is in conjunction with adjectives belonging only to God. One of the approaches in conceiving God is in terms of God's self—that is, a category of its own (*sui generis*) in relation to time.

It is foundational in the doctrine of God to view God as unbound by time and noncontingent to time. God is sovereign before time, in time, and after time. God transcends time, but he chooses to associate it with himself. God therefore is a being outside, as well as inside, time—distinct from human beings. That means God can exist without time, impossible to any created being. Anything created has a beginning, so whatever is created has an end. In contrast, God has no starting point, since God has no endpoint; this captures the character of the Alpha and Omega.[6]

---

3. Jesus Christ represents (not replaces) Israel (Parry, "Wrestling with Lamentations," 186).

4. The word *sovereign* in Hebrew is *âdôn* (אָדוֹן), which means controller, master, or owner (*SECB*, ho113). For assertions on sovereignty in God's name, see Bulkeley, "Living in the Empire," 75.

5. Isa 1:24–26 NRSV; italics added.

6. Isa 9:6b; 44:6.

In being so, God is "the Mighty One." God reveals and implements what he has foreordained for Israel, unswayed by human decisions. In this foreordination, negative prophecy is unavoidable, hence the expression "I will turn my hand against you" (mortification). No doubt, God was behind the downfall of Israel. Nonetheless, in examining the prophecy, the ṇo serves the yes. The "I will" (negative) leads to the "you shall be" (positive). God, in his might, causes all things necessary for Israel and his neighbors, too. World powers are subservient only to the power of God. The recurrent striking-healing of God makes Zion "the city of righteousness" (consecration). The effectiveness of this system arises from God's selfless character. God does not shy away from involvement in the misery of Israel, and, more importantly, God justifies his actions. As divine sovereignty unfolds in eschatology, it is rational to presuppose that the end of the history of Israel reflects the end of the history of humanity. This is made possible in the reign of King Immanuel. This King rules by the Spirit of God with justice and righteousness, not only for the abused Jews but for all distressed peoples, too. Such eschatological hope signals the dominion of the Messiah. The messianic kingdom would one day transform all creation, bringing everlasting peace and harmony.

The Lord is not, in the Platonic sense, in which God (transcendent) cannot be amongst the non-God (immanent); that which is divine cannot be human. In Isaiah, however, the things in heaven can *also* be on earth.[7] This is somehow expressed in Isaiah, but as Robin Parry elucidates, "It is impossible to tell—the lines between the two are very blurry at times because the earthly temple functioned as a gateway to the heaven."[8] In this observation, God becomes Creator-creature as God becomes divine-human; the antecedent assumed the consequent, manifested in the prophesied Messiah—Jesus Christ.

Furthermore, the divine rules over the human; this is not reversible. How can something temporal (by necessity) be above time? There is a great irony in thinking that someone limited by time (by force) can genuinely control what is in time. God, in time though uncoerced by it, administers humans. If one supposes that humans, in some ways, have a hold on the divine, that is idolatry. Here the "divine" arguably, is as an imaginary god, a delusional god. We deal with the Creator God—One

7. Isa 6:5; 7:14; 8:14.

8. In the reading of Isa 6:1–4 (Parry, *Biblical Cosmos*, 147).

who wills to be in time. The Creator God is "in the beginning."[9] In self-existence, God made all things exist. Suffice it to say that there is none like him.[10] In other words, the Creator is sovereign in managing the creation: the non-God and the anti-God.

That is vital in understanding divine sovereignty. If one misses who God truly is and what he is capable of, then distortion of God is expected.[11] For instance, God is seen as aloof, distant from creation, and has nothing to do with the actual happenings in the world. Such a deistic view of the Creator God compares God to a watchmaker, for the earth runs like an automatic watch, as the cosmos functions with a very reliable operating system. God is understood to relegate the management of the world to human beings; hence the sovereign One becomes an observer. Nevertheless, the prophet confirmed that this is not the God of Israel.[12] God is busy mending Jerusalem; put into words, "I will." The rebellious city is meant to be "the faithful city"—the wellspring of eschatological hope (mission).

God is *highly active* in managing the world and all human affairs. Whatever God has begun, God will bring into completion.[13] So when God created heaven and earth, these were considered very good in the Bible, yet it does not mean that creation can sustain itself apart from God.[14] Creation was, is, and will be fully dependent upon its Creator for its continued existence and prosperity.

Since God is like a parent, he rules with warmth.[15] This is reflected in a mother's compassion for her child, motivated by pity and mercy.[16] Such compassion is the first and foremost character God associated with himself in passing before Moses on Mount Sinai.[17] The Creator God, however, is very unlike the mother in the animal world. When the mother eagle

---

9. Gen 1:1.

10. *The God*, in the beginning, is *'ĕlôhîym* (אֱלֹהִים)—singular in meaning yet plural in form; this is foundational in the doctrine of the Trinity (*SECB*, h0430).

11. Bulkeley, "Living in the Empire," 75.

12. God reveals himself in an intimate relationship with human beings (Isa 1:1–3).

13. Isa 1:2; Gen 1:31.

14. It states in Isa 2 that God can accomplish what he has planned for Israel.

15. In Isa 1, God is like a father who calls on his son Israel.

16. *Compassion* is from the Hebrew root *râcham* (רָחַם), which denotes pity or mercy "from the womb" (*SECB*, h7356). God, in this case, is not androcentrically envisioned.

17. Exod 34:6.

is assured that her fledglings can fly, she will then leave them. God will never, ever leave behind what he created. In reality, without God, creation stops existing.[18] God has not abandoned creation in time immemorial and will continue to keep it in eternity. The God of the eternal past, eternal now, and eternal future is the same caring and sustaining deity.

2.1 Sovereign over Israel

A few generations after creation, God chose the descendants of Abraham to be the people of God. We know that later on these people were called Israelites and lived in Canaan. It is clear in the Bible that daughter Zion is God's elect.[19] Here we can see that the One who does not need time comes into time and works *through* those in it. Israel is elect, and so the prophet Isaiah is to make God known to all peoples. Karl Barth says that Isaiah's calling is "on a much grander scale" compared to the calling of Moses because of the way God introduced himself. God revealed himself to the prophet in the heavenly temple; God revealed himself to the lawgiver in the burning bush.[20] But much more important, Barth continues, is that that which is shown to Isaiah constitutes "a historical declaration which goes beyond" what is previously made.[21] Barth is right that Isaiah seems to have been summoned more impressively than Moses. They, however, are somewhat equal in terms of eschatological significance, given Moses's presence at the transfiguration.[22] It means that his calling bears significant weight, as it is connected to the Messiah.[23] Moses was there talking about Jesus's departure from the world that was about to happen in Jerusalem, an act that would deliver the promised glory to Israel.[24]

The *šekīnah* (the settling of divine presence) is what the prophet referred to. Its implication for humankind is profound due to its universal coverage.[25] It is asserted that the doctrine of election ties in with that

18. Isa 10:23; Col 1:16.

19. Chapter 4 is focused on the doctrine of election.

20. Barth, excursus in *CD* IV/3, 579.

21. Barth, excursus in *CD* IV/3, 579.

22. Matt 17:2–4.

23. Luke 9:30–31.

24. Mark 9:4.

25. Isa 6:3. Although the word *šekīnah* (Romanized *shekinah*) is not in the Bible, it usually stands for God's glory or the dwelling of God's presence (LaHaye and Hindson, *Exploring Bible Prophecy*, 126–27).

of divine sovereignty. How God rules, how he demonstrates his power, how he cares for the people are the interests here. Israel is chosen to accomplish God's purpose on earth. This is why Israel is under God's sovereignty—authority, rulership, direction, sustenance, maintenance—and the entire experience of Israel is according to the eternal plan. The prophet made this notion apparent.[26]

When sin entered the world, it could not have total dominion. In and of itself, sin is also limited in time. This conception is evident in Isaiah, where the prophet affirms that "a great light" will shine over on "a land of deep darkness."[27] The former refers to the Messiah (the *šekīnah*); the latter refers to where sin is said to cast its potency—the shadow of death.[28] However, sin becomes impotent before God but not before the elect. Israel had been sinning despite God's guidance.[29] The following are the major Isaianic themes concerning divine sovereignty: first, God disciplines whom he loves; second, the disciplined are renewed. The prophet remarks,

> For the people do not turn to *Him who strikes them*, nor do they seek the LORD of hosts.[30]

> And it shall come to pass in that day that the remnant of Israel, and such as have escaped of the house of Jacob, will never again depend on him who defeated them, but will *depend on the LORD*, the Holy One of Israel, in truth.[31]

The first text undeniably ascribes the act of striking to the LORD God. That is why the prophetic warning of invasion and destruction is what God had foreordained for Israel. Now, this is not one step to say that God willed Israel to be rebellious, let alone to attribute some kind of evil to God's master plan—not at all. The divine consequent will (temporal) works with and against every resistance to the divine antecedent will (pretemporal). That is how God rules; that is how God sustains whom he had preserved. We know that Israel did not fulfill his mission but even

---

26. Isa 2:1–4; 11:1–5.

27. Isa 9:2 NRSV.

28. The "land of deep darkness" is a symbol for the Hebrew *tsalmâveth* (צַלְמָוֶת), which is the "shadow of death" (*SECB*, h6757).

29. In Isa 3, God judges Zion by removing her pride through painful means—decimation and captivity.

30. Isa 9:13 NKJV; italics added.

31. Isa 10:20 NKJV; italics added.

turned to other gods.[32] With that, discipline came to Israel in the form of smiting or striking.[33] Notice the word "strike" is harsh indeed.[34] When God struck his people, calamity, slavery, disease, death, destruction, and all the negativity one can think of that could happen to a nation or people happened to Israel.

The second text shows that a time will come when Israel will no longer rely on the wrong allies who, in the end, seek to destroy him. This shows the effect of a reformed heart, from straying away from God into deliberately staying with God, from worshipping false deities to worshipping the true deity. When Isaiah is read closely, the word "strike" cannot be taken apart from the word "heal."[35] We can see below the operation of such a paradigm:

> And He will strike the earth with the rod of His mouth. And with the breath of His lips, He will slay the wicked.[36]

> For the earth will be full of the knowledge of the LORD as the waters cover the sea.[37]

God will "strike the earth" so that it will be "full of the knowledge of the LORD." How did this happen when these passages talk of punishment? Notice that the means of striking is "the rod of His mouth," the source as well of God's breath causing the death of the wicked. From the same mouth, nonetheless, came the complete knowledge of God. Something bad (appearingly so) produces something good (definitely so). This features a diagnostic aspect for conceiving of divine sovereignty. In other words, when God chastises, God also mends. When God sustains his people, part of this is done by striking and healing.[38] Healing, in this framework, is also rendered as cleansing from moral evil, so the object of healing is to "seek justice, rescue the oppressed."[39] That is why the prophet

32. Isa 2:8, 18–20.

33. Isa 1:5; 5:25; 9:13; 10:20; 10:24; 11:4.

34. Hebrew *nâkâh* (נָכָה) means "to severely beat" (*SECB*, h5221).

35. Isa 6:10; cf. 19:22. Hebrew *râpâ* (רָפָא) or *râphâh* (רָפָה) (*SECB*, h7495). The latter is also attributed to God: "Jehovah Raphah" (Exod 15:26).

36. Isa 11:4b NASB.

37. Isa 11:9b NASB.

38. In Isa 4, God cleanses Zion and makes her holy.

39. Isa 1:17 NRSV.

foretold that Zion "will be called the city of righteousness" in the effect of divine punishment.[40]

Moreover, God disciplines Israel for failure to share the kingdom of God with all nations. Israel had failed miserably. He is guilty not only of neglect but also of insubordination. The people of God had turned instead to foreign gods—something they could control. This means that Israel did not want to be controlled but wanted to be *in control*. Consequently, the Jews had to face the inevitable desolation and serfdom by the people they were supposed to convert to the Jewish faith.

The sovereign One (God) will never be conditioned by the non-sovereign (humans). It is always the other way around; there is no way it can be interchanged. God controls humanity, and this is how God does it: in his way, by his own choice. There is no scarcity of contention about this matter, for example, between John Sanders and Thomas Jay Oord, albeit the divine control does not inevitably override the self-agency of humanity in terms of reaching its potential.[41] Regarding Israel, he had been under the Lord's control, not without orientation for his progress. Israel needed to stay grounded in his God before he could be a model to the world. Israel had to learn meekness—full submission to the LORD God. It will be so according to the Isaianic vision.[42] God disciplines according to his will and in his own time. As foreordained, the kingdom of God saturates the whole earth through the *šekīnah* from the new Jerusalem. In line with what God has foreordained, the wayward becomes compliant, typified by the remnant.

2.2 Sovereign over All

Our task now is to understand why God's will is always for the good of his people. We can never capture the way God disciplines if we take divine compassion out of the equation. This God is the same God who chooses the church in the NT.[43] Here the concept of divine choice is coincident with that of divine providence. Christians (the church of Jesus Christ)

---

40. Isa 1:26.

41. Sanders is quite sympathetic to this subject matter, whereas Oord is not. For a peek into their dialogue, see Sanders, "Why Oord's Essential Kenosis Model," 186–87; Oord, *Uncontrolling Love of God*, 88–89.

42. Isa 3:8; 4:2.

43. Barth, *CD* II/2, 202–5.

are chosen unto salvation and glorification, foreordained to triumph in the last days. This imagery fits the category of the smoldering "stump" eventually bearing fruit abundantly.[44]

God can make that happen by his omnipotence, omniscience, and omnipresence, all partnered with omnibenevolence.[45] Altogether goodness is intrinsic to God, and its core is in the incarnation. Let us take omniscience as a test case for the veracity of God's compassion in foreordination. How can God be good upon foreknowing, let alone *causing*, the destruction of Israel?

At least two camps of worldviews surfaced concerning divine omniscience: the first asserts that God is all-knowing, for God has seen what is to come; the second asserts that God is all-knowing, since God has determined what is to come.[46] I call the first view the "telescope model" in which God simply sees the horizon of time and human existence, as if looking through a telescope, and with it, God is said to have advanced knowledge (prescience). What is put forward here is the second view, which I call the "hands-on model"—that God knows the future simply because God has planned what happens and about to happen. In other words, the accent in the former is on God's knowledge *about* the future, whereas in the latter, the accent is on God's knowledge *of* the future. God is of the future, being in the eternal now (the presently future). In being so, God is highly active in managing things to come.

Notice in Isaiah that the repeated phrase "in that day the Lord" gives the exactness of God's action in that specific moment or situation.[47] It is far from having a high probability of occurring or from being the most likely scenario to happen, but rather, that *shall* happen as foretold. Foreordination, in this sense, funds the Isaianic prophecies. The deity of possibility or potentiality is not the sovereign One in the Bible, so this is not the God in Isaiah.

When God foreordains, God is the One who makes it happen in the first place. In the talk of omniscience, God is not passive. God is highly active, in which everything that takes place and will take place corresponds

---

44. Isa 6:13; 11:1.

45. See Mann, *God, Modality, and Morality*, 19.

46. Cf. "perceptualist model" and "conceptualist model" of divine foreknowledge (Moreland and Craig, *Philosophical Foundations*, 521).

47. Literally, "In the same day shall the Lord . . ." (בַּיּוֹם הַהוּא יָסִיר אֲדֹנָי). Isa 3:18; 4:2, 7:18, 20; 11:11; etc. NKJV (Leningrad Codex).

to the master plan.[48] There is nothing that slips through God's grasp or might sneak out of his attention. The God in control, who foreordains, is One who takes accountability and responsibility for actions and events concerning Israel, as well as for the whole of humankind.[49]

In the hands-on model, God is highly active in setting actions and events in time. Things will happen in the future not just because God has planned them to be, but cogently no one or nothing can hinder God's work in time. God, in this context, is not a passive observer; God is the active mover in living with humanity. God is the Prime Mover and the unmoved Mover, Lord in and of everything that exists. This is the foreground in explicating the eternality of God. It is also here where we can come to grips with God as the cause of earthly occurrences, as well as the guarantee of the good coming out of it.

God is eternally self-existent. God does not need time, space, matter, energy, or whatever element in whichever dimension non-eternal beings bank on. Whatever one can think about existence and what involves it, God can exist without it. God can cause such elements to work for his bidding, hence the name "LORD God."[50] God can be so and can do so, as God is the holder of omni-attributes; he alone exists as such. In this sense, whatever God foreordains, it shall be so. Now to what extent is foreordination? In dealing with this concern, we have to wrestle with the terms "full ordination" and "partial ordination."

Full ordination refers to God's work *ad extra* without merit to actions and events other than God's. Creation is a good example. Partial ordination refers to God's outworking *in partnership* with creatures. Procreation is a valid exhibit of such kind of appointment.[51] Whatever the case may be in the plight of Israel, God intends his people to be productive with what was entrusted them. Unproductivity is the handmaid of indolence, inevitably leading to deterioration. In line with the divine appointment, God comes into time to use it to work out his will for Israel.[52] He wills to happen everything that will happen to the Israelites and,

48. God "takes a hand in the game" when it comes to world affairs (Forsyth, *Christian Ethic of War*, 30–31).

49. Isa 7:7–17 (Reichenbach, *Divine Providence*, 29–31).

50. The name "LORD God" is used in Isaiah approximately thirty-two times; it signifies that the God in Isaiah is preeminent and commands all actions and events in and around Israel.

51. Full and partial ordination will be expounded in ch. 3.

52. Isaiah 5 shows God as a vinedresser tending Israel like a vineyard. Unfortunately,

whatever happens, develops it into something profitable. This is clear in Isaiah's narrative: God is the mover of Israel, Judah, and Jerusalem. God is also the mover of Assyria, Babylon, and Persia. In that regard, God is impartial in judging believers and unbelievers, Jews and non-Jews. Here divine sovereignty manifests itself through equitable compassion for all humankind.

In speaking of God as reliable in causing goodness in the end, it is crucial to view God against creaturely reality. The God in creation cannot be the God *of* creation since he can never be of creaturely reality *per se*. God, in other words, can exist with and in the created, but God remains in himself—sovereign.[53] The accurate picture of God is in the being of Jesus Christ.[54]

The transcendent God became the immanent God. That which exists before time is transformed into that which is *in* time. The invisible God assumed flesh and dwelt among people, hence the name Immanuel.[55] "For a child has been born for us, a son given to us."[56] But this being cannot be seen in pantheistic terms, for God cannot be imprisoned in human reality like the human-made deities of Babylon. The God outside the world is also in the world and after its renewal. The future is very promising, as the One who promised is also the God of the future world.

Concerning eschatology, David Bentley Hart posits that any posturing about the end-times should always be biblical and discard "any theological pronouncements in total abstraction from or contradiction of scripture." Thus Hart concedes "a certain presumptive authority" inherent in God's word that must be observed.[57] However, being attentive to such authority does not guarantee rigid scripturality of one's discourse, especially in formulating a dogma. Karl Barth argues that the task of dogmatics is what gives theological pronouncements—the Trinity, or, in this case, eschatology, its "own special character," distinct from the Bible but

---

God turns Israel into a wasteland because of unproductivity.

53. Isa 10:13–14; 11:3b.

54. Heb 1:3.

55. Hebrew 'immânû (עִמָּנוּ) means "with us," and êl (אֵל) is "God" (Isa 7:14; 8:10; SECB, h6005; h0410). Cf. Matt 1:23. Although there is no confirmed etymological connection between immanence and *immanu*, these words are related. They contrast the idea of transcendence, and crucially, the former comes from the Latin *manere*, meaning "to dwell in," a notion similar to God dwelling with us.

56. Isa 9:6a; cf. Luke 2:11.

57. Hart, *That All May Be Saved*, 92–93.

not necessarily in contrast to it.[58] But even in the attempt to be true biblically, the risk of error is unavoidable.[59] That is why despite the embedded
scriptural presumptive authority in the conception of foreordination,
foreordination is still peppered with objections. Concomitantly, it is safe
to say that the locus should be on the LORD God alone—the Master of the
eschatos—and should be maintained henceforth. If not, the theological
conundrum is unchecked.

Before time (God had humanity in mind in foreordination), in time
(in the incarnate God), and after time (God in the final judgment), the
sovereign God has always been with us. This prefigures Godness over
against evil. It also presupposes that even though the promise does not
seem to match the actual at present, the present will eventually mutate
into God's actuality; whatever is foreordained shall be so. The goodness
and certainty at hand emanate from God's transcendence, immanence,
and assumption of flesh. In other words, the Godness of the sovereign
One is the basis for interfacing divine actualities of God and humans.

En route to expounding divine actuality, the three facets of God's
omnipresence are to be understood inseparably. If one facet is detached
from the other two, God will no longer be seen as "always present" with
humanity. The solid signification of this formulation is evident in the being of Jesus Christ. Jesus Christ is the pretemporal God (*Logos incarnan-
dus*), Jesus Christ is the temporal God (incarnate God), and Jesus Christ
is the post-temporal God (the Judge in the final judgment). In navigating through the terrain of divine actuality, we can trace the unbreakable
hands-on activity of God. Likewise, the unstoppable foreordination in
place is paramount in speaking of eschatological benevolence. Things
will be so because of who God *is*.

In the doctrine of God, the apophatic side is equally substantial,
namely, God is immutable, impassible, and impeccable. Here God is
conceived in the negative—that is, what God is not. The "not" is more
apprehensible if paired with the term "capable" to denote that God is very
unlike us. God is so in which he is incapable of changing himself. God is
not capable of suffering, and he is not capable of mistakes. Perhaps one
might inquire: if nothing is impossible with God, what is the basis of such
incapability in God? Yes, everything is possible with God (divine sovereignty); however, when God is understood to be incapable of something,

58. Barth, *CD* I/1, 309.
59. Barth, *CD* I/1, 309.

this is not to say that there is something beyond God—that which God cannot do—but rather the emphasis is on being divine in contradistinction to being human. In other words, when it is said that God is incapable of change, it conveys that God cannot be other than God; he cannot be not God, for he is eternal in himself. This is basic in understanding why God's dealing with Israel can be altogether good and certainly good.

In being eternal, God is also perceived as incapable of suffering pain and misery or even showing human-like emotions. Now this might be a red flag to the reader. There are several scriptural evidences of God suffering and God experiencing emotions.[60] Again, divine impassibility is viewed against the changing of emotions or mood swings akin to a human person. Divine feelings are real but have no kinship with creaturely existence. They are completely non-reliant on creaturely reality. God's emotions are self-generated and self-nurtured. This does not mean that God lives in a bubble (although that can be true with God). Rather, it means that it is God's choice to manifest emotions *in* time. Being so, however, does not mean his Godhood has become contingent on the world. God shows emotions so we can see that he is truly a relational deity—able to sympathize with us in all things. In other words, the emotions of God are not humans', hence the term divine feelings.[61] The Greek bishop Irenaeus (c. CE 130–202) has a similar understanding of divine feelings when he says that God expresses emotions yet in a different ontological order from that of humans.[62]

2.3 Sovereignly Perfect

In the uniqueness in ontological order, incapability for mistake is ascribed to God. It is foundational to the doctrine of God that God is perfect and whatever he does is perfect, as the latter arises from the former. The divine outworking and the idea of a flaw, inaccuracy, or lack are incompatible. Imperfections apply to beings other than God. What God is not is seized with deficiencies. But what about Jesus Christ? Did God not subject himself to imperfections in Jesus of Nazareth? God did become human in this man but is unique. Christ's humanity is *always* with

60. God grieves (Gen 6:6), God loves (John 3:16), God hates (Ps 11:5), God rejoices (Isa 62:5), and God becomes jealous (Exod 34:14).

61. Matz and Thornhill, *Divine Impassibility*, 4.

62. Irenaeus, Haer, 2.1.1; 3.8.3; PG 7 (1857): 709–10, 867–68.

Christ's divinity. Furthermore, the susceptibility to defects and decline inherent in humanity has no efficacy to make Jesus Christ imperfect in the ontological sense.

It is true that Jesus suffered, bled, and died, but this fact does not, in any way, postulate that this man became imperfect in being. Jesus was subjected to world reality without being conditioned by it. For instance, Jesus Christ remained holy despite being in unholy surroundings. Jesus had been tempted to sin yet was without sin.[63] It is also true that Jesus became sin, but in being as such, he overcame sin instead of being overcome by it.[64] In Isaiah, we can speak intelligibly of the holiness of God despite Israel's exile and captivity. This holiness will eventually shine in Israel's situation as victory awaits him.[65] The sacrifice of Christ brings the renewal of Zion; here Zion has "more than one referent" employed as a theological symbol.[66]

The triumphant God is viewed in contrast to the sorry condition of Israel. In Isaiah, God initiated the regeneration of his people. On his own, he could not have a slight chance to actualize a change of heart without the work of the messianic King. The new King shall establish the new Jerusalem and will never be corrupted, hence exists forever. The transformation is the by-product of the Lord's full control of the circumstances in and around Israel. All actions and events work together in preparation for the coming messianic King—One who rules with empathy.[67] Here the idea of divine impeccability is articulated against being otherworldly. God's perfection shines forth amid sin and its effects.

In dealing with impeccability, God's independence is underlined because he is perfect *in se*. God does not need whatever is imperfect to highlight his perfection.[68] God is not the white in the yin-yang symbol, where the white is appreciated contra the black. The God-self is not evil and can stand without evil, yet he cannot stand evil. God had broken the

---

63. Luke 4:2–13; Heb 4:15.

64. 2 Cor 5:21.

65. It is undeniable in Isa 6 that God leads Israel into exile to accomplish God's purpose for his people.

66. Isa 9:7; 53:11 (Hooker, "Zion as Theological Symbol," 107).

67. Isaiah 7 presents God as the true Counselor who guides Judah by accompanying her (Immanuel).

68. Or the Godness of God, for example, transcendence, "is not something achieved by the negation of its 'opposite'" (Hart, "Providence and Causality," 35).

evil devices of the Jews, so God is not liable for their undoing.[69] As evident in Isaiah, God is unassociated with evil despite the evil that befalls the people.

Another example of divine independence is seen in the perichoretic being of God. The triunity in God is a stand-alone concept in theology. The Trinity is systematically expounded without contrasting it to the outside.[70] If the Trinity is explained by using matter, for example, the different forms of H2O—water, ice, vapor—it likely leads to misrepresentation, let alone perversion of the nature of God. Besides, if the Godhead is viewed with respect to humanhood, this perspective is doomed to fail due to the incompatibility inherent in the argumentation. It is better to apply the Kantian approach to God's perfection: in its own terms (divine ontology) and scope (divinity).

God has the final say according to his enduring will. The decree shall come true in the preeminence of the LORD God. Without seeing the perfection of God's nature, foreordination will be robbed of its true essence—for the welfare of its object. On this point, as we shall immediately recur to it, it is necessary to insist further on the tight connection between judgment and covenant.

We can now investigate the relation of divine judgment to divine compassion in light of God's covenant with Israel. This in turn will cover why divine sovereignty is partnered with divine love.

3. THE LOVING GOD

In considering all the horrific things Israel had to go through congruent with foreordination, divine sovereignty seems at odds with divine love. And in regards to the death of thousands in the sack of the Northern and Southern Kingdoms, the Epicurean trilemma that Scottish philosopher David Hume popularized comes to mind.[71] It is about the problem of evil in concert with the existence of God, called theodicy.

---

69. That is why in Isa 8, God is the mighty Instructor.

70. Allusions to the concept of the Trinity can be extracted from Isaiah, namely, God as a Father ("everlasting Father"), the promise of a son, the mention of the "Spirit of the LORD" (see Isa 1:2b; 9:6; 11:2).

71. Hume reinvigorated the Epicurean trilemma at the end of the eighteenth century. The theodicy trilemma still finds strong traction today (Sneed, *Social World of Sages*, 322–24; Lazar, *Talking about Evil*, 130–32).

If God is all-powerful, yet he could not stop the ravages of the heathens against Israel, this implies that God is not omnipotent. Or, if we say that God is all-good, but God did not want to stop the massive violence committed against Israel, this means that God is not truly omnibenevolent.[72] But what if God is both all-powerful and all-good; why then did ancient Jews, including the elderly and children, have to die or suffer in horror? This is the trilemma we all need to ponder in considering divine sovereignty with divine love. One cannot escape the challenge against God's essential attributes in contemplating the sad truth inscribed in Isaiah. In this context, a valid explanation is demanded without a doubt, especially in speaking of God as eternally loving.

The answer proposed here to that trilemma is to not directly engage how the issue is framed but to converse out of the framework. The answer is not reliant on our reasoning or rationalism but based on the accounts in Isaiah. The prophet himself had been struggling with the same question: how long will you, O God, not answer? Or, how long will the terrible situation last?[73] Interestingly, God was not *in absentia*. God's mighty hands were actually upon the situation, hence the phrase "I will."[74] It just so happened that the prophet could not figure out why the ways of God sometimes appear nonsensical; that is, God's response was nonresponse: "I will not listen." Or, God would use non-believers to punish believers.[75] This seems to point to a grim outcome. God is not sinister; hence the divine operation does not end in darkness.[76] The actions of God towards Israel will make sense if one is to follow closely Isaiah's narrative. The obscure thought is due to our inability to comprehend the divine. What is divine is brightly revealed in the prophesied Messiah:

> Authority rests upon his shoulders; and he is named *Wonderful Counselor, Mighty God, Everlasting Father, Prince of Peace.* His authority shall grow continually, and there shall be endless peace for the throne of David and his kingdom. He will establish and uphold it with justice and with righteousness from this time

---

72. Hume, *Dialogues Concerning Natural Religion*, 186.

73. Isa 6:11a. The prophet Habbakuk was similarly perplexed by his situation (Hab 1:2–3).

74. Isa 1:24–26; 3:4, 7; 5:5–6.

75. Isa 1:15; 9:11–12; 10:5–8.

76. Isaiah 9 stresses the surety of God's ways and intent; it is to bring hope to Zion by sending the light (the Messiah) to people groping in darkness.

onward and forevermore. The zeal of the LORD of hosts will do this.[77]

That which is transcendent became immanent by being that to which humanity can relate, such as a "counselor," "father," and "prince of peace." Yet as such, God remains in God's self because divine peculiarities predicate all these functions, namely "wonderful"[78] and "everlasting," consonant with being the "Mighty God." The Jews can relate to "the throne of David," but what is dissonant to them is that the messianic kingdom is said to last "forevermore." That is undoubtedly not the work of human ingenuity but divine appointment, thus the last sentence: "The zeal of the LORD of hosts will do this." What is construed here purports to build on the *innocence* of God in the face of evil, not the ignorance of God, as the term *counselor* means to determine or to plan.[79]

3.1 Love beyond Comprehension

It is only the latent reference of the opposed elements to a whole that embraces the concept of compassion *with* discipline. The transcendence of divine outworking is key in the argument of theodicy. There are remarks such as: a God worthy of our worship cannot be Someone who causes or allows pure evil. In my estimation, the statement is indiscreet and half-baked.[80] The ways of God are totally unlike ours. The thoughts of God are far beyond ours.[81] In other words, God was *in* Isaiah's situation, but Isaiah could hardly see God. The issue was not with God, but with the prophet, and with Israel, too. Like any other human being, the prophet could not get his head around why God used the heathens to teach the people a lesson on humility. Even so, he resorted to "waiting for the LORD" and not to thinking like his fellows.[82]

The humble were to trust in God, as opposed to the proud blinded by their arrogance. P. T. Forsyth alludes to this arrogance with King Hezekiah and King Sennacherib in mind as he writes, "We are learning to protect ourselves from disaster, and we fail to feel the presence or

---

77. Isa 9: 6–7 NRSV; italics added.

78. From the Hebrew *pele* (אֶלֶפ), which connotes a miracle (*SECB*, h6382).

79. Hebrew *ya`ats* (יָעַץ) (*SECB*, h3289). Cf. Isa 14:26–27.

80. Oord, *Uncontrolling Love of God*, 68.

81. Isa 6:9; 55:8, 9; 1 Cor 1:25.

82. Isa 8:11–12; 17.

need of another protector."[83] Yes, God indeed is the protector of all, but sometimes divine protection is not easily welcomed. Israel instead opted to seek human protection like that of Egypt and Babylon or imagined defenders like that of Bel and Nebo.[84] Forsyth's allusion is somewhat disconcerting given the Jews' reaction when faced with an insurmountable threat. Judah felt the need for protectors. Unfortunately, the one who offered was neither capable nor caring. The people could have reached out to the LORD God whose power never wavers and whose care never betrays.

With arrogance, people rely on their ability to reason and choose the best possible option available. Sadly, it was the same arrogance that brought shame and destitution to Israel.[85] Humility allows for real comfort in times of need. Condescension avoids the paralysis brought by psychological weight and rather brings an inspiring vision of the future. Although the prophet struggled to think differently about his immediate situation, still the disturbing fact remained: the divine judgment came in the form of Israel's adversaries. The LORD God was too complex for the prophet to apprehend. Conversely, the reader is challenged to make sense of how God is seen as the true Protector although the failure of Israel's so-called allies was also foreordained. The enigma at play here is: God was in control of his people; likewise, God was in control of the enemies.

God was not merely sovereign over peoples but also responsible for them. In this background, the concept of the unmoved mover is better appreciated. God was unmoved to revive Israel; also, God had moved Assyria and Babylon to smite Israel.[86] The intention of healing came after the striking. God had to discipline his people because he wanted to revive them. But the object of striking is brought into submission before the transformation begins. Unmistakably, God disciplines whom he loves,

83. Forsyth, *Descending on Humanity*, 198.

84. Egypt and Babylon were Israel's wrong allies; the former could not protect the Jews, while the latter treacherously ransacked Zion of her wealth (Isa 31.1, 3; 39:6–7). Bel and Nebo are father and son protector gods in contradiction to God the Father and God the Son, who never failed to protect their loyal subjects and kept the destiny of true worshippers (Franke, *Isaiah 46, 47, and 48*, 26–29).

85. Isa 2:12–17.

86. We can read in Isa 10 that God had raised Assyria to destroy Israel. Then, Assyria was also destroyed by the Babylonians. God is just with Israel, and so with Assyria and Babylon. Authentic justice is inherent in God and should not be stacked up against human justice.

and whoever God loves is under his discipline. The divine striking-healing is a recurrent theme in the first section of Isaiah.[87]

Of course, hundreds of thousands of people suffered terribly and
were killed mercilessly. Where was God in all of this? I ardently propose
that God was precisely right in the midst of it. The outcome of sin grieved
God; nonetheless, he has made the world with humans having a certain
amount of freedom.[88] It is easy to paint an ugly God whenever God is
conceived alongside natural evil. It is equally true in terms of having a
mere caricature of a beautiful God. The Godness of the sovereign One
should be seen in its complete and unadulterated picture. God can be
neither an absentee deity nor a calloused deity in dealing with the elect.
Etiologically speaking, the electing God is the One who foreordained the
humiliation of Israel. God did not have to prevent the downfall of Zion by
acting against Assyria and Babylon; it was preappointed for the heathens
to humble the people of God. God is their protector, yet also, God is their
nemesis. This is the heavy imperative Israel had to face.[89] In this sobering
thought, the charitable theodicy and the repulsive theodicy are in tension. This tension also confronts the mismatch between the promise and
the reality.

3.2 Sovereign Love

Why would God go against himself by nullifying his decree?[90] If God
is truly impeccable then everything he has foreordained is flawless and
definite. It is flawless as it arises from God's character, definite since it is
God's covenant. The foreordination of the destiny of Israel comes with
the Lord's stipulation for his people: he will be their God, and Israel will
be the people of God.[91] In this fashion, God determines himself to *be* the
God of Israel as Israel is predetermined to *be* God's people. God can never
be other than this God, so Israel can never be other than this people. It is
in such an analogy that earthly consummation of foreordination is properly understood. Without fail, the promise will soon match reality. God

87. Charlesworth, *Unperceived Continuity of Isaiah*, 4.

88. Allen, *Theological Approach*, 36. The balance between divine sovereignty and
human choice will be discussed in ch. 3.

89. Isa 1: 24; 5:25.

90. Isa 3:13; 10:24a.

91. Isa 10:20–23.

will hear the prayer of Zion. Parry attests, "And just as the enemies of Zion are punished for their cruelty to God's people so the humiliation of Jerusalem is reversed."[92] The humiliation set for Israel is also determined for his bullies. The reversed humiliation in Parry's attestation, however, alerts us to the equitable dealing of God with humanity. As the enemies of Israel are chastised, too, it implies that God loves them as well.[93] Isaiah foresees:

> For though your people Israel were like the sand of the sea, only a remnant of them will return. Destruction is decreed, overflowing with righteousness. For the LORD God of hosts will make a full end, as decreed, in all the earth.[94]

There are some significant points here given the decree: first, it is about *destruction*; secondly, it overflows with *righteousness*; and finally, it is applied to *all the earth*. The sovereign God has determined the destruction of Israel.[95] Such destruction bears the notion of completion, giving the reason for the punishment to accomplish its purpose.[96] The purpose cannot be simply annihilation due to the mention of the "remnant." Instead of destruction, the context dictates that the object completes its transition—from proud to humble.[97] This is the most logical interpretation of the destruction in conjunction with the idea of "overflowing righteousness."

The humbling of the proud is applicable not only to Israel but also to the regional empires. It is not confined to the ancient Near East region but worldwide. However, with a heavy heart, Herbert Gordon May remarks, "Biblical scholarship in general has tended to minimize the extent of theological universalism [belief in one God worshipped by all peoples] in the Old Testament and to exaggerate the particularistic elements of post exilic Judaism."[98] May instead qualifies that the special consideration to Israel does not mean that other nations are not special in the eyes of

---

92. Parry, "Prolegomena," 403.

93. Isa 10:24b–34.

94. Isa 10:22–23 NRSV.

95. See Isa 10.

96. The Hebrew for *destruction* is *kilâyôwn* (כִּלָּיוֹן), a derivative from the root "to accomplish" (*SECB*, h3631).

97. Isa 9: 2–3; 10:20; 11:16; 12:4–5.

98. May, "Theological Universalism in Old Testament," 100.

a cosmic God.[99] This strengthens the argument for unbiased sovereignty over the Jews and non-Jews. Now does this mean that the covenant is extended to all? Again, the answer lies in the nature of God.

The covenantal paradigm hinges on God alone. Even if Israel had been disloyal in this contract, the fact remains that it is forever binding. That is why despite the setbacks incurred by Israel's failure to remain true to the covenant, God remained true to his decree by facilitating the contract unto *completion*. What God has begun, it will be done, and will never be undone. Now if the LORD God is the One who executes and consummates the covenant then there is no reason why such covenant cannot be extended to all peoples. God is the God of all.[100] And besides, God elects, and he is unconstrained as the Elector.[101] Furthermore, the inclusive nature of the covenant dismisses any suggestion of favoritism from God. Being within the covenant implies unconditional submission—under divine terms, as God sees fit in the grand scheme of things. Unless the reader finds comfort in this thought, I think, true peace in facing life's uncertainties remains elusive.

In other words, during tragic events prophesied in this section of Isaiah, one can still confess that the sovereign God is the loving God. Even the destruction of cities and kingdoms is not to the demise of peoples; it is for the good of their posterity. "Tragedy," says Tenzin Gyatso, "should be utilized as a source of strength."[102] The prophetic anticipation of healing and rejuvenation outweighs any splenetic denunciation of foreordination.[103] This monarch is holy. Justice and righteousness return, symbolized by a small shoot coming out of the smoldering stump. Truly King Immanuel is a beacon of hope and an agent of everlasting peace and harmony. It is not an over-construal that God reigns in love, loving the unlovable—rebellious Israel and other nations. Yet the people of God will not remain rebellious; the prophet exclaims,

> Then you [Israel] will say on that day, "I will give thanks to You,
> O LORD; for although You were angry with me, Your anger is

99. May, "Theological Universalism in Old Testament," 100–101.

100. The following stress the universality of divine outworking, namely, "all the nations," "all kings of the nations," "all the people," and "all the earth" (Isa 2:2; 14:9; 9:9; 25:6–7).

101. Habets and Grow, *Evangelical Calvinism*, 174.

102. Words of wisdom from the fourteenth Dalai Lama.

103. King Immanuel in Isa 11 is Jesus Christ whom the Father glorifies; in turn, Christ glorifies Israel.

turned away, and You comfort me. Behold, God is my salvation,
I will trust and not be afraid; for the Lord God is my strength
and song, and He has become my salvation."[104]

Israel does not travel an endless road of perdition. God shall bring
an end to his people's confusion and hardship.[105] Those who cannot appreciate the method of discipline will eventually realize the rationale and
grandeur of the primordial plan. The line between respect and resentment about God will no longer be obscured. What will stand out is pure
gratitude and adoration. Thus we can have confidence amid skepticism
over God's consistent power and mercy. And if we go back to the trilemma, such consistency becomes apparent: the over-all-in-charge-God
and the absolutely-hands-on-God is *also* the all-loving-God.

In the twists and turns of Israel's experience, one thing stands out—
enacting the divine restoration of Zion and all cities.[106] That is crucial in
conceiving divine sovereignty in tandem with divine love. Without pairing the two, in philosophical terms, the dialectical pattern of the negation of negation can take the dominion of the Lord as domineering. The
divine lordship is demonstrated in self-giving, in being the long-suffering
God in and of the covenant. Given this consideration, the Godness of
God, in essence, *is* the goodness of God.[107]

3.3 Reading Isaiah through Revelation

So far, we have considered the reasons for divine punishment given foreordination and why God reigns in compassion. We are now in position
to directly engage these pressing concerns, namely, how divine judgment
activates renewal and why Jerusalem is the nexus of eschatological hope
for humankind. This is doable by critically analyzing the prophet's testimony alongside the evangelist's vision right before the touchdown of the
new Jerusalem upon the earth.[108] It is written:

---

104. Isa 12:1–2 NASB; italics added.

105. Goldingay, *Theology of Book of Isaiah*, 32.

106. In Isa 12, God is salvation as God saves Israel from destruction—a mirror of
what befalls humankind.

107. de Vera, *Suffering of God*, 98.

108. Cf. Rev 19:19–20; 20:7–10; also in Isa 66:18–20. This passage will be examined in ch. 6.

> Now it shall come to pass in the latter days that the mountain of the LORD's house shall be established on the top of the mountains, and shall be exalted above the hills; and all nations shall flow to it. Many people shall come and say, "Come, and let us go up to the mountain of the LORD, to the house of the God of Jacob; He will teach us His ways, and we shall walk in His paths." For out of Zion shall go forth the law, and the word of the LORD from Jerusalem. He shall judge between the nations, and rebuke many people; *they shall beat their swords into plowshares, and their spears into pruning hooks*; nation shall not lift up sword against nation, neither shall they learn war anymore.[109]

Jerusalem is the prototype of the church as it pertains to both the Jews and non-Jews, representing all peoples.[110] The passage attests to eschatological reality, hence the term "latter days." What is very interesting is the mention of the "mountain of the house of the LORD" mirroring "the beloved city" in the evangelist's vision.[111] In the time of the prophet, the Jerusalem temple was on a plateau in the Judean Mountains. Isaiah continues, "many nations shall flow to it," which John describes as an attack of the united nations upon Jerusalem.

Another remarkable insight is about the aftermath of God's rebuke of the nations. Instead of being devoured by fire, the nations learned about God and unlearned violence. Why? The turning of weapons into farming tools hints at the conversion of humankind and an era of universal peace and harmony.[112] The context implies that social justice is in place as the elites' instruments of subjugation (swords and spears) are gone, and the bourgeoisie's tools of the trade (plowshares and pruning hooks) are multiplied. This is not an overstretched claim, since there is an underlying structure here that conjures the idea of healing after the eschatological judgment. Rather, this is an outstanding outcome accounting for both Israel and the whole of humankind.[113]

There is a stark contrast, in this context, between Isaiah and Revelation, namely, the peoples' intent for heading to Jerusalem and the consuming fire from heaven. Isaiah accentuates the intention to learn from

---

109. Isa 2:1–4 NKJV; italics added.

110. Acts 1:4–8; 2:1–21 (Livingstone, *Studia Patristica XXII*, 215).

111. Rev 20:9 NKJV.

112. This concept inspired the statue in the garden of the United Nations Headquarters in New York City.

113. See Childs, *Isaiah*, 29–31.

God, whereas Revelation accentuates the intention to fight God. With this, one might argue that these scenarios are not talking about the same event. The gap here, I think, is bridged by the unequivocal reference to the upcoming battle. The depiction of an end to war is central in matching them to form a cohesive conclusion. Granting that in Revelation, the heaven-borne fire consumes the vast armies marching into Jerusalem, this does not negate the *purifying* motif in Isaiah. The fire (burning coal) that removed the guilt of the prophet will be the same (from heaven) to eliminate the guilt in humanity.[114] Such a fire can burn away all impurities in Zion because it is the Holy One—the Son of God.[115] That is why it comes from the altar of God, or more accurately, from God himself.[116] The holy fire cleans the unclean; the unholy become holy before entering the new Jerusalem.[117]

What is the compelling evidence that the fire here is a purifying fire, not a tormenting or annihilating fire? It is in the inclusion of *sulfur* with fire.[118] Fire alone is potent to torture or extinguish, but sulfur can purge the dross from the wicked, not obliterate them. Sulfur (archaic: brimstone) is used often as a refiner, disinfectant, ferment, and preservative and also has macronutrients essential for life. These properties are far from causing extinction. Yes, the concept of torment can still be correlated in this respect, but the fact remains, the trajectory is to complete the process—purification. That is to say, that sanction is not opposed to amelioration. The purification schema is also compatible with the striking-healing paradigm, more coherent to the Hebrew thought of refinement unto perfection.[119] The construal of the *refiner's fire* in Revelation gives room for divine discipline in the confines of divine love. The very words in the language of the evangelist hold to the idea of reinstitution, not extirpation. The assertions laid out, thus far, support the undergirding

114. Isa 6:7; cf. Rev 20:9.

115. Isa 30:33; 34:9; cf. Rev 9:17–18; 14:10; 19:20; 20:10; 21:8. See also Gen 19:24; Ps 11:6; Ezek 38:22.

116. Rev 20:9 NKJV. In Greek, it says, "fire came down from heaven out of God" (κατέβη πῦρ ἐκ τοῦ οὐρανοῦ ἀπὸ τοῦ θεοῦ) (Greek RP Byzantine Textform 2005; see https://biblehub.com/text/revelation/20-9.htm).

117. Isa 6:5, 8; cf. Rev. 21:27.

118. Isa 30:33; 34:9; cf. Rev. 9:17–18; 14:10; 19:20; 20:10; 21:8. See also Gen 19:24; Ps 11:6; Ezek 38:22.

119. Isa 48:10; Zech 13:9; Mal 3:3 (Yutzy, *God's Plan for Man*, 197).

hypothesis: Jerusalem is the hub of eschatology and the beacon of hope.[120] As divine sovereignty is central in Isaiah, so it is in Revelation.[121]

The conclusion drawn here, however, is cohesive, not absolute. It is cohesive in terms of the eschatological judgment, while it is not absolute in terms of the different demographics and social backgrounds at play between Isaiah and John. The reader is reminded that Isaianic eschatology is not a perfect fit in Revelation or even in the NT; as Soo Kim puts it, "Seeking the one-by-one fulfillment in the New Testament or in actual history is not a recommended goal," due to the potpourri of voices addressing composite concerns in the extended saga of the Jews.[122] Nevertheless, since I strongly suggest that the end of Israel's history reflects the end of humankind's history, the hermeneutical underpinnings of these prophetic texts point to none other than the triumph of the messianic kingdom. This is taken not in the Aristotelian sense that things to happen could potentially happen, but rather these things *shall* happen. The certainty is not in the prophecy itself, albeit in its Giver. The epistemological ramification is substantial to the actualization of the promised hope. More on this to come: the seemingly negative prophecies are positive (in eschatological reality).[123]

In revisiting the doctrine of God, the focus is not on the intent or outcome of humanity but on the impact of foreordination. Of course, our response is significant, yet not so relevant insofar as the covenant is concerned. The human response cannot and will not overshadow God's activity as decreed. The divine will to counter the nihilations fueled by created freedom is the *raison d'être* of foreordination. Even if the force of God's compassion does not appear glaring to the reader, I suppose, it is apparent to the prophet.[124]

No matter what the reader thinks of the two prophetic scenarios considered, the proclamation of sovereign love should be heard loud and clear in the eschaton. The steadfast God is rich in tenderness, manifested conspicuously in the renewed Zion:

> It will come about that he who is left in Zion and remains in Jerusalem will be called *holy*—everyone who is recorded for life

---

120. Cf. Mic 4:1–5.

121. Grabiner, *Revelation's Hymns*, 2n3.

122. Kim, "Eschatology in Isaiah," 352.

123. It will be discussed in ch. 4, "God as Elector," and ch. 5, "God as Redeemer."

124. Isa 1:2; 5:4; 10:25.

in Jerusalem. When the LORD has washed away the filth of the daughters of Zion and purged the bloodshed of Jerusalem from her midst, by the spirit of judgment and the spirit of burning, then the LORD will create over the whole area of Mount Zion and her assemblies a cloud by day, even smoke, and the brightness of a flaming fire by night; for over all the *glory* will be a canopy.[125]

The inhabitants of the renewed Zion are called holy by purging their disgusting "filth" with fire.[126] Truly the extremeness of sin is no match for the purifying power of God.[127] As a result, the glory of God is revealed in them as they share with it. The Messiah made it possible—the *šekīnah* of Israel in which the glory of God is overpowering.[128] As the pillar of cloud and fire foreshadowed the presence of God, so is King Immanuel the actual presence of God. The LORD God had to humble Zion for cleansing unto holiness to take effect. In so being holy, Jerusalem can fulfill her mission to the world; afterward, the Messiah will glorify all humankind. The Christian reading of Isaiah is indispensable; as Wilhelm Vischer affirms, Jesus Christ is the "hermeneutical key" in fully understanding the OT.[129]

There is one aspect needing further investigation: the employment of the heathens to execute the decree. In the next chapter, we will discuss this by delving into the meaning of God the almighty Creator as chronicled in the next section of Proto-Isaiah.

125. Isa 4:4–5 NASB; italics added.

126. The Hebrew for *filth* is *tsôʾâh* (צֹאָה), meaning "excrement" (*SECB*, h6675).

127. Isa 1:18. Scarlet and crimson correlate with spiritual fornication and blood, or the violence of bloodshed (Isa 1:21; cf. Rev 17:4), whereas snow and wool correlate with righteousness and justice (Isa 1:26–27; cf. Rev 1:14).

128. Isa 11:10; 6:3; Num 14:21; Ps 72:19.

129. Gignilliat, *Karl Barth and Fifth Gospel*, 17.

CHAPTER II

KEEPING IN TOUCH

"At that time the people will turn and trust their Creator, the holy God of Israel."[1]

IN THE PREVIOUS CHAPTER, WE STUDIED why love is indeed the telos of divine sovereignty. This chapter investigates the reason for God's utmost concern for Israel. I shall argue that God knows what is best for his people, as God is their Creator. The maxim "Look back over the past, with its changing empires that rose and fell, and you can foresee the future, too" is applicable here since to know the conclusion of humanity is to know first its commencement.[2] I will begin with a study of passages showing that the Creator God causes all things necessary for Israel and the neighboring nations. In the end, this is *beneficial* for them.

The chapter chiefly addresses this issue: how do we know that what happened to Israel was best for him? In what follows, we will analyze (1) God's jurisdiction to direct the destiny of Israel, (2) the connection between God's justice and righteousness, (3) divine wisdom as the handmaid of divine mercy, (4) the constancy of God's power over the powers of worldly kingdoms.

---

1. Isa 17:7 CEV.

2. Marcus Aurelius, *Meditations*, 7.49. In Mark Brett's observation, "The scroll of Isaiah was formed in the tides of successive empires—Assyrian, Babylonian, Persian, and Hellenistic" (Brett, "Postcolonial Readings of Isaiah," 621).

We now come to the second section of Isaiah with specific attention to God's authority and wisdom in Israel.

1. SUMMARY OF ISAIAH 13-27

This section focuses on the prophet's vision of judgment and hope for *all* nations. It begins with the judgment of Babylon. Isaiah had foreseen that the Babylonian Empire would be an imposing world power that would one day replace the Assyrian Empire. The Babylonians would be more destructive and arrogant than their predecessors, and worse, the Chaldean kings would claim superiority over all other gods, including the God of Israel. As a consequence, the Lord God vowed to bring Babylon to her ultimate ruin, with all kingdoms who were proud and abusive. But for the prophet, divine judgment was never the final word for Israel or his neighbors. This judgment led into elliptical poems which tell a tale of two cities: the lofty city that had exalted itself above God and became utterly corrupt and another haughty city that had been subdued and reinstituted. By God's authority, one city would be the recipient of divine indignation. By God's wisdom, the other city would be the recipient of divine mercy.

The first city (Babylon) was an archetype of rebellious humanity described with the language borrowed from the prophet's earlier descriptions of Jerusalem and Ashur (religious capital of Assyria). Babylon would end in a disaster where rehabilitation was impossible. The second city (Jerusalem) also characterized human recalcitration, but her end would be entirely different. Being attentive to Zion, the prophet's oracles revealed that Jerusalem would one day revive faithfulness through the messianic initiative, and in effect, God's reign would be manifested in the nations. There would be no more death or suffering according to Isaiah. The narrative climaxed into a universal execution of justice and righteousness. The storyline anticipates global healing and, more comfortingly, obliterates oppression and violence.

After recapitulating the second section of Isaiah, we will now examine *why* God knows what is best for Israel as the Creator.[3]

---

3. The discussion on *how* God does what is best for Israel will be in ch. 3.

2. GOD AS CREATOR

What is striking straightaway is that there is no biblical account of a pre-creation deity. We simply do not know God before revealing himself as Creator. The Bible begins with the Creator God, and this God is "in the beginning."[4] He is first in everything—in place, time, order, and rank.[5] What do we mean when we say that God is the Creator? The prophet writes,

> When its limbs are dry, they are broken off; women come and make a fire with them, for they are not a people of discernment, therefore their Maker will not have compassion on them. And their Creator will not be gracious to them.[6]

In the passage, the true God is contrasted to false gods. The true God is the Maker of Israel, whereas an idol, for example, Babylon's patron deity Marduk, is only carved by the Israelites.[7] God made his people realize that despite their worship of the Chaldean god, ironically, the Babylonians themselves turned against Israel. For idol worship, Israel's fate will be that of the false deities'—rot and burn. In figurative terms, Israel is likened to a dead branch good only for fuel. He is "broken off," which means that Israel is detached from the source of life (the Creator God).[8] The stupidity and folly underline the incomprehension of God's ways and the unrecognition of evil ways.[9] Seeking what is created, not the Creator, shall bring condemnation and desolation. To avoid such a downhill fate, Israel needed to turn back to the Creator God.

Being the Creator, God governs the creation, for the whole creation—heaven, earth, and beneath the earth—is under his jurisdiction.[10]

4. Gen 1:1a. At the outset, the Bible's main concern is not to prove the providential existence of the things around us but rather fairly to explain the origin of the natural world based on the human capacity to comprehend. Although nobody can neither prove nor disprove the probability or the improbability of the Genesis account on creation, this fact only shows the need for faith to grasp extremely difficult concepts. This chapter focuses on God's identity and purpose in creation and how he illuminates the reason for human existence.

5. This is the literal meaning of the Hebrew *bêrêšîṯ* (בְּרֵאשִׁית), "in the beginning" (*SECB*, h7225).

6. Isa 27:11b NASB.

7. Isa 27:9b.

8. Isa 27:9b.

9. See Jer 5:21; Hos 4:6.

10. Isa 24:21; Phil 2:10–11.

There is no being above God, namely, rulers, authorities, powers, and principalities—all are under the administration of the Creator.[11] In other words, all entities in the spiritual and physical realms are at the command of the LORD God. Under the controlling rubric of divine supremacy, the hand of God is felt in the twists and turns of Israel's circumstances. Isaiah claims that God has "commanded" his warriors (the Medes) to pulverize Babylon beyond recovery.[12]

Whoever God summons shall obey, and whatever God summons shall be carried out as foreordained.[13] The divine appointment shall never be disappointed in creaturely reality; foreordination is unstoppable and irreversible. Creaturely reality only follows the path set by divine actuality. The Creator is the author of all reality, including the creature's freedom in the created world. Even so, God remains its Lord. Adhering to God's bidding satisfies the creation, as it exists *by* the word of God.[14] This explains that by the Creator's voice, the creature obtains its validity and meaning.[15] This concept provides us with the basics of divine operation and human agency in creation.

In the beginning, God *is*, and, in the beginning, God *does*. In time immemorial, God created corresponding to his character. The Creator remains a God of utmost concern to will what is good for those who treat him as Lord. Israel, in due time, unfortunately, decided to forsake their Lord. Still, within the divine will, it was shown to the prophet that treachery and turmoil would be prevalent in his period and would continue until his purpose was accomplished.[16] God had set Isaiah as a "watchman" to declare to the people what he saw; and being a genuine Israelite, the prophet had been faithful to his duty.[17] What the prophet witnessed was deplorable to Babylon yet comforting to Israel. The positive prophecy

---

11. In Isa 13, God is the great Commander by deploying Babylon to destroy Judah. The deployed also is punished at the order of the Commander.

12. Isa 13:3. The word *commanded* in Hebrew is *tsâvâh* (צוה), which means "to appoint" (*SECB*, h6680). In this case, the Median (and Persian) soldiers were deemed "sanctified" because they had been set apart for God's purpose. See Isa 21:2; Jer 51:27–28. Notably, the Persians had no temples or altars for idols; they destroyed the images of Bel-Merodach or Marduk—patron deity of the city of Babylon (Herodotus 1.131; see Jer 50:1–3).

13. Isa 13:17–22.

14. Isa 17:7; 19:18–20; Heb 1:2.

15. Isa 14:24; Ps 148:1–5.

16. Isa 21:2.

17. Isa 21:6, 10.

overtakes the negative prophecy. The agent of treachery and turmoil will fall; it will never pull itself out of the rubble.[18]

The negative prophecy, however dismal it is, is instrumental to the rise of the new Jerusalem—the positive prophecy. Babylon, the tormentor of the old Zion, will be a thing of the past, whereas the new Zion, born out of mischief and misery, will not be forgotten because of her enduring King. The Creator God, once again, still "chooses" Israel for himself—meaning that Israel's restoration arises from his election.[19] God always rescues his people and turns their fate. The captives shall soon overrun their captors. This communicates the reinstatement of Israel.[20] That is how the Creator God is seen to "have worked wonders" based on planned things "long ago."[21] God is truly faithful to his chosen people as he is faithful to himself.[22]

When we speak of God as Creator, a corollary is that God has no creator; he is self-existent as discussed in the previous chapter. The God of Israel is neither the philosophical deity nor the humanist deity.[23] Skeptics push the agenda of a created god. They ask: if God created everything, then who created God?[24] In the Cartesian method of inquiry, the *cogito* is fundamental in rationalistic discourse. It is, however, inimical to the doctrine of God. God's view of humanity is prime in informing knowledge, whereas the "rational self" maneuvers the conversation towards our view of God.[25] The calculative conception of God inevitably ends in anthropocentricism, not in a theocentric worldview. The search for the epistemological *a priori* is a non-question here since the *ergo sum* is the Creator. God, in my postulation, transcends such a question. He alone is the *a priori*; there is none like him.

God, Isaiah illustrates, has "made the earth tremble, who shook kingdoms" without end. Other forces can send shockwaves, too, yet temporarily.[26] On one side, there is a created god, an idol—a sort belonging

18. Isa 21:9. The repetition "fallen, fallen is Babylon" aids in ensuring that Babylon's devastation is sure and permanent. See Jer 51:8; Rev 18:2.

19. Isa 14:1. The election of Israel is expounded in ch. 4.

20. Isa 14:2.

21. Isa 25:1.

22. Isa 25:1b.

23. Isa 14:26–27; 19:12, 21.

24. Dawkins, *God Delusion*, 109.

25. See Descartes, *Meditations on First Philosophy*, 10–11.

26. Isa 14:16b NKJV.

to the figment of the imagination, hence a counterfeit deity. On the other side, there is a self-exuding god—aspiring to be *like* the true God, but merely *a posteriori*. The prophet himself alludes to the fact that that which is created tends to make itself what it is not.[27] The seismic shift in formulation from the human-made deity to the God-made human upholds the Kierkegaardian concept of discontinuity between the divine (Creator) and the human (created).[28] That which is divine, in the Isaianic narratives, is disconnected from that which is human. The divine connects with the human, yet the latter is dependent on the former to apprehend what is beyond.[29]

Only the Creator can properly exalt a creature in stature and knowledge. What is exalted in this case is the meek, not the conceited. Whoever wants to be like the Most High, on one's own accord, will be brought to the "lowest depths," like what happened to King Sennacherib of Assyria and King Nebuchadnezzar II of Babylon.[30] The simulated reality, against the determination of the Creator, remains unreal. By contrast, God is real, far from being psychologically imagined or philosophically constructed. Of course, creatures cannot manipulate the Creator. In righteousness, God is; whereas, in unrighteousness, humans fashion their god.[31] In wisdom, God acts; whereas in folly, humans are acted upon. We can see a manifestation of this in how God exposes the imprudence of people and how he influences the aftermath of such stupidity.[32] Here, it is not difficult to conceive of God in his constancy—who affects *in se* instead of being affected *ad extra*.

---

27. Isa 14:12–15. The language "the fallen morning star" is primarily framed to apply to the Babylonian king; secondarily, it could pertain to his shadow entity: Satan—the enemy of God and humanity—because of the Hebrew *hêylêl* (הֵילֵל), a derivative of the name Lucifer (*SECB*, h1966). Jesus Christ is also referred to as "the bright and morning star" (Rev 22:16); accordingly, the king of Babylon and Satan are looked upon as usurpers of what is the Son of God and Son of Man—hence, antichrist (see Fekkes, *Isaiah and Prophetic Traditions*, 186). The literal King of Babylon and the symbolic representation of him (Satan) have limited power and jurisdiction as set by the Creator God.

28. Søren Kierkegaard's notion of the "infinite qualitative distinction" clearly separates God (infinite) from humans (finite) (Hannay, *Kierkegaard*, 437).

29. Isa 14:26; 18:3–4.

30. Isa 14:15, 25; Dan 4:30–33.

31. We can read in Isa 14 that God is righteous, and God *is* righteousness. Whatever is not righteous aspires to be on an equal level with the Most High.

32. Isa15:1–5; 17:1–2.

2.1 The Uncaused Cause

God *is* in God's self. God is, as always, replete and complete. He is God with or without human expressions of emotions and intellect. In being so, God is the uncaused Cause. If God is the efficient Cause of every being, by extrapolation (with caution), he brings about the expediently necessary things, such as the entrance of sin in this world. I will unpack this later; for now, let us concentrate on God as the Cause. As corroborated in the Bible, nothing has brought God into existence.[33] In the beginning, there is only God. The all-causing God, however, is self-caused by becoming human. God empathizes with Israel so much that he determines himself to be *of* Israel. The Messiah (a descendant of Jacob) is a devotee of Jerusalem, a beholder of its temple.[34]

Critical to this formulation are two natures in the self-caused deity: divine and human. In the beginning, God is divine, yet God determined himself to be human. This is not out of necessity, not because he needed to; rather God becomes divine-human out of his own choice. God, with respect to his nature, is absolutely free. It is only God who is free in this way, no one else. It is in such freedom that God becomes Immanuel. In theological terms, the Son of God *becomes* the Son of Man. Albeit when God becomes man, the divine remains, obviously in union with the human. This explains how Jesus Christ is truly God and truly human. He will always be God inseparable from us. We cannot think of God apart from the being of Jesus Christ. He is the "exact imprint" of the everlasting God.[35] Concomitantly, we cannot discuss the creation, or understand who the Creator is, if we look outside Christ, since he is the Creator.

So, when one thinks of the Creator, that is Jesus Christ. The Son of God is the One who creates, and the Son of Man is the One within creation. Creation is not only made through Christ but crucially, creation is made *for* him. Creation, in other words, cannot be properly understood without approaching it Christocentrically. Christ cannot be detached from the discussion about creation; the LORD God is Jesus, therefore Christ is the God of Israel.[36] Israel will never have its existential identity and purpose without him.

33. Isa 26:4; 40:21; Ps 102:25.
34. Isa 16:5; Mark 11:11.
35. Heb 1:3; Ps 110:1–2.
36. Isa 25:6–9.

Besides, the Creator God is also the One who upholds creation.[37] Since all creation is by and for Jesus Christ, all creation can be sustained only *by* him. In the tight connection between Christ and Israel, the Genesis chronicle serves as a platform for salutary vision. As Jesus Christ is inseparable from creation, the history of creation cannot be divorced from the history of Jesus Christ. Creation history is united with Christ's history. The former is the six days of creation in Genesis account, and the latter is the incarnation, life, death, and resurrection of Jesus. When God created all things in six days, God revealed himself *with* the created things.[38]

It raises concern in Isaiah that the Creator God who commands the heavenly bodies to shine also commands them to do the opposite. In effect, the sun darkens, and the moon becomes but a shadow.[39] This displays a gloomy picture for Israel. Isaiah, as well as Jeremiah, had predicted something unthinkable and very unlikely to happen—that is, massive paranoia and cannibalism, in consequence of a detestable act. More so, rampant idolatry and human sacrifice are very unexpected in Jerusalem.[40] This strikes at the heart of theodicy and directly challenges the argument for the persistent mercy and righteousness of God. One might suspect the inconsistency in God's mercy and righteousness if the notion of Immanuel were isolated. The God of Israel is the God of intimacy and action—a relational being. God dwells among his people, and God does it out of his own decision. He does not need Israel, and it can never be otherwise. If God (in and through Jesus Christ) determines himself to be with creation, so creation is also determined to be *with* God. I call the account of the self-determined Creator and the determined creature *tadhana* history or, in short, *tadhana*.[41]

Now, what is *tadhana*? This is the total account of God with humanity. In other words, the *tadhana* is the Creator's story shared with creatures. It is rendered here, so there is no God's history without us; we are always included in the story of God. Of course, this does not mean that God's account is contingent on human existence, not at all. We have cemented this point in the first chapter. When it is said that there is no

---

37. This topic will be discussed in the next chapter under "God as Sustainer."

38. I hold to the literal day (twenty-four hours) as I hold to the literal incarnation.

39. Isa 13:10.

40. Isa 22:1–8; 24:5; Jer 19:5, 9.

41. *Tadhana* is a Filipino word that literally means "destiny."

story about God without us, this amplifies our perception of God. Again, he is perfect in God's self, and this notion is non-negotiable in the doctrine of God. In this sense, the doctrine of creation is under the doctrine of God; the former is the fruit, while the latter is the root. Thus the divine subsistence is not subordinate to any human substance: God is the Subject and human is the object.[42]

God is the Subject in *tadhana*, since there would be no story to share without God, whereas we are the object in it, since we are the beneficiaries of what is shared. The role of humankind is not essential in theological conversation in this context. What is essential is the divine will to make humankind participate in God's story. God is the logical proposition that denotes the entity of humankind. God is the logical imperative that affirms humans in *tadhana*. God, in other words, remains God absent of *tadhana*, but there is no humanity in absence of it. He *is* God in eternity, but humanity is *not* without God. No human *being* is disassociated from the being of God, simply because the caused is not without the Cause. *Tadhana* has a twofold injunction: first, one can apprehend the being of God only with human beings; second, to understand the being of humanity is to first understand the being of God.

Apprehending the being of God is entirely dependent on how God reveals himself, and as his self-revelation manifests in creation, our apprehension of God is tightly woven with his relationship with us. Having that in mind, when God decides to *be* with us, this makes God's being conjoin our being. Being human, in this sense, can never be detached from God's being. Our identity and purpose are dependent on divine identity and purpose.

Accordingly, God's decision to attach himself to humans is the foreground in understanding the being of God. Also, human attachment to God is the background in understanding the being of humanity. That is why the concept of *tadhana* is a prerequisite in anthropology as well as in theology. When seeing through the spectacles of *tadhana*, we will better grasp the christological ramification of the being of the Creator God—Jesus Christ.

We can properly apprehend God by looking at Jesus of Nazareth. Nevertheless, since this human is altogether divine, the being of Jesus also remains beyond our intellect. It is in Christ's humanity where human beings are represented. However, Christ's humanity is also unique

---

42. Isa 25:1; 26:13.

as it is the humanity of God. This is what Karl Barth calls God's "veiling in unveiling."[43] If Barth is right, then *tadhana* can only be dialectically understood. In such shared history, moreover, there is no equal footing. God remains superior over us even in Jesus Christ. God shares his story with us, yet, in the strict sense, we have no say in this story. In other words, even if we are part of *tadhana*, God alone drives the story, for it is within his jurisdiction to do so.[44] In cinematic terms, Jesus Christ is both the director and main actor of this movie; we are mere background characters.

With that perspective, there can be divine history without human history, but in speaking of the Creator God (Jesus Christ), the creature's history is indispensable in considering the doctrine of God. Rightly so, there is no human history without divine history, yet the latter is comprehensible in the former. If the story of Jesus Christ is also ours, then the creature's story is written by the Creator. In this respect, when we talk of human history, it is not only with God but, poignantly, *by* God. God, in *tadhana*, is once more the Companion and Commander of humankind—King Immanuel.

That brings us to Jesus Christ. Christ's story *is* Israel's story, not the reverse. What the prophet had observed in real life was not the whole story of Israel; the complete story was in his vision.[45] The inclusion of the coming Messiah is fundamental in the trajectory of hope in the eschatological history of Israel. This is surely not the Confucian hope, which hinges on self-confidence, but rather, the prophet's hope is based on having confidence in no one except in the Messiah.[46] Sennacherib, Nebuchadnezzar II, even Cyrus the Great falter in comparison with the *Rex Iudaeorum* (King of the Jews), Jesus Christ. The reign of these emperors ends, whereas Christ's kingdom is everlasting.[47] By interjecting the negative and positive prophecies in Isaiah, we can deduce that the messianic reign is contemptible for those who do not accept Christ as King but comforting for those who respond otherwise. The former reaction is the ultimate human ignorance and folly; the latter response is the ultimate human comprehension of God's ways and recognition of evil ways.

43. Barth, *CD* II/1, 257, 262.

44. Isaiah 15 makes the reader understand that God can pursue his will into completion.

45. Isa 14:1–2; cf. 22:4–5. For contrasting scenarios, see Isa 24:16.

46. Isa 26:4, 13. "Confidence breeds hope" (Brewer, *Quotes of Confucius*, 126).

47. Isa 15:5; Ps 145:13; John 19:19–20; 2 Pet 1:11.

In the messianic initiative, people "will turn and trust their Creator, the holy God of Israel."[48] Through the messianic reign, humankind eventually finds meaning in life by having satisfaction in accomplishing God's purpose.

This purpose, vis-à-vis Israel, is also better appreciated in christological terms. The resurrection and glorification of Jesus Christ is the path where the people of God shall tread. There is no elbow room here for minor diversion, let alone deviation. The path to glory, nevertheless, is through pain and suffering. Christ's resurrection is the result of his death through crucifixion. In light of *tadhana*, Israel's path to restoration and glory is also through pain and suffering—hence defeat and captivity. These were the events the prophet had witnessed. Restoration and glory were the events the prophet had hoped for. In that case, the plight of Jesus of Nazareth informs the plight of the people of Israel, and more importantly, the prophesied messianic reign completes the history of Israel.

2.2 The Fountain of Rest

Further in the discussion of *tadhana*, the creation story is paralleled with the redemption story. As I hold to the literal days of creation, I also uphold the literal seventh-day Sabbath. Time and again, the concept of rest is cited in Isaiah with different emphases, namely, first, relief from suffering and turmoil;[49] second, the land in peace;[50] third, alleviation of distress;[51] fourth, finding refuge;[52] and last, worship of the LORD God.[53] These facets are inseparable from the Creator—the fountainhead of rest. And since Israel did not enjoy the Sabbath during the prophet's lifetime, it is mandatory to include the redemption rest in the equation. In this line of thinking, the Creator is synonymously rendered with the Redeemer.[54] The emancipation of Israel experienced with Cyrus was but a reflection of what is to come, effected by the Messiah.

---

48. Isa 17:7.
49. Isa 14:3.
50. Isa 14:7.
51. Isa 26:16.
52. Isa 27:5.
53. Isa 27:13.
54. This facet will be unpacked in ch. 5 under the section "God as Redeemer."

The mental image of God as a "freedom fighter" is shared more or less across the Christian traditions (in various hues). God does not only relieve suffering, but he also removes the trauma of suffering.[55] God is the only One who can pacify the land, and consequently, its inhabitants rejoice in the stillness of their situation.[56] Nonetheless, more often than not, the discipline of God (as evidenced in Israel) is the *bona fide* way to alleviate the distress of the people. Under divine chastisement, people learn to call upon God.[57] God is the true refuge. People who seek help from him will have protection.[58] Above all, the real spirit of Sabbath is in recognition and service of the Creator God.[59] Unless the fractured covenant is fixed, creatures will never enjoy the blessings of the Sabbath. It is intrinsic to the Isaianic prophecy that the Lord's invitation of rest is not exclusive to Israel, but crucially, it is also for Israel's enemies.[60] On the same note, its touch of phenomenal relevance is still felt today.[61]

Israel enjoyed peace when God halted the Babylonian cruelty, especially when the indignation was over.[62] God will not prolong his anger. In *tadhana*, he desires to be God *pro nobis*. Showing no compassion is but momentary, since God is morally committed to Israel.[63] The God who gives rest to creation is the same God whose rest abounds. True and lasting Sabbath can be drawn only from its Creator; creatures will neither rest nor find peace apart from the author of Sabbath. Where will humanity be rest-full and peace-full in this world? It is only in, through, and with Jesus Christ. When we say that Jesus Christ is King Immanuel, this implies that in the divine companionship, rest abides; and in the divine fiat, peace prevails.

Moreover, as God has chosen us, we have to choose God. In the divine choosing, we are summoned to choose Jesus Christ. Although God has the final say in *tadhana*, he also desires us to decide to be with God. It does not mean that without our cooperation, the offer of rest

55. Isa 14:3.

56. Isa 14:7.

57. Isa 26:16.

58. Isa 27:5.

59. Isa 27:13.

60. Isa 27:13.

61. Hays, *Origins of Isaiah 24–27*, 8.

62. Isa 14:4; 26:20b. God's universal invitation will be discussed in the section "The Almighty God."

63. Isa 26:20.

is wasted. The Creator initiates the Sabbath by "blessing" and "sanctifying" it without any human contribution.[64] The Sabbath is beneficial to the partaker, for the one who partakes is blessed and sanctified. As the Son of Man is the essence of the Sabbath, God thus offers the Son of God.[65] In the suffering of the Son, we do not need to suffer any longer. This is the reason for Jesus's invitation to come to him.[66] Accordingly, in the shared rest, *tadhana* becomes a Sabbath history.

When we conceive that God shares the Sabbath with humanity, this means that humanity does not have its own story of rest divorced from God's story. Surely, the flip side pictures a different scenario. The Lord God is the eternal rest, yet he chooses to be God *with* us (Jesus Christ), so the rest in God is disturbed, not unnecessarily. God wills it in the first place. In short, the Giver of rest is, at the same time, in need of rest. How? It can be understood only christologically: the Son of God is *always* the Son of Man. The former is the Benefactor, and the latter is the Beneficiary. This does not suggest incoherence in God. In being fully God, Jesus Christ is the abiding rest; and in being fully human, Jesus Christ fitly foreshadows humanity's need for rest. Remember, it is Jesus of Nazareth who invites the helpless and the hopeless to come to him to rest.

So when we consider the Sabbath history (creation and redemption), it is the divine and human accounts combined. God, being the rest over human restlessness, is central in the discussion. The six-day creation is about the Creator God preparing for a lasting relationship with creatures. After six days, God ceased his creative work to establish his relation with humanity. It is on the seventh day when he celebrated that relationship, making the Sabbath special.[67] When God ceased work on the Sabbath, he never ceased working in and through creation. In other words, creation itself is completed, but this does not mean that God's outworking with creatures is complete. The same is said for the story of God with creation; it thrives and finds its epitome in the identity and purpose of Jesus Christ.[68]

On the seventh day of the creation week, the Sabbath is ordained. The One who ordains the Sabbath is its Lord. How is it so? The One who

64. Gen 2:3.

65. Mark 2:27–28; Isa 53:6b.

66. Isa 26:20; Matt 11:28.

67. Gen 2:2.

68. God continues his story with creation, being the Sustainer, Elector, Redeemer, and Glorifier—topics in the succeeding chapters.

establishes the relationship with humankind is also the One who pre-serves it. The reason behind the Sabbath being part of a weekly cycle is for God to offer himself continuously within the covenant. Isaiah reveals that Israel had forgotten God.[69] God sent the prophet to tell Israel that it is only God who prospers and protects him, which, in a sense, means that it is God who solely preserves the covenantal relationship.[70] Here, the messianic initiative is intertwined with the ordination of the Sabbath.

That provides the reason to look at the Sabbath vis-à-vis Jesus Christ (not elsewhere). He alone is the source of true and lasting rest—the sort of rest humanity needs. "You will find rest" is the assurance for the seek-ers of Christ.[71] This is the Creator speaking with a commanding voice for humankind to rest. Israel had been restless, for he had been missing the One who initiates and implements rest. Israel failed to enter the rest since he had sought respite from his neighbors, not *from* God.[72] Conse-quently, God had been the source of Israel's enduring distress and unrest. Although the Sabbath was primarily for Israel, spiritual and physical rest became elusive as a result.[73]

The perpetuation of the Sabbath day signals that the Creator God has not given up on his people.[74] Rest is for Israel, and Israel is meant to rest; this is the epistemology behind the birthplace of the Messiah. The promised Messiah is the core, as well as the periphery, of the Sabbath. The Jewish Shabbat observance is the letter of the Sabbath, while Jesus Christ is the spirit of it. The observance is meaningless without Christ. Christ gives vitality and dynamism to the Jewish custom.[75] In the christological treatment of the Sabbath, the Son of God is the Lord *in* it as the Son of Man is the Lord *of* it. The former accentuates Christ as the Initiator of rest while the latter accentuates Christ as the Implementor of rest.

Jesus Christ is the Initiator of rest, for he is the Creator on the sev-enth-day Sabbath. The Son of God ordained the Sabbath to exemplify rest in the Godhead, and the Son of Man observed the Sabbath to constitute humankind. There can be no other projection unless one reformulates

69. Isa 17:10.

70. Isa 17:11–12; Deut 32:18.

71. Matt 11:29b.

72. Isa 20:5–6; cf. Ps 95:11; Heb 4:3.

73. Isaiah 24 shows that God is no respecter of persons, including the Jews. God exposes guilt and treachery to achieve his ultimate purpose.

74. Isa 26:12; 27:5; Heb 4:9.

75. We will continue our discussion on the Sabbath in the next chapter.

the implication of the Son of God as the Son of Man. If the Creator is the God of all, the purpose in assuming flesh is to represent all. Particularism will not work in this paradigm. The humanity Jesus Christ takes to himself blankets the entire humankind. The universalist conception of the Creator God does not end in creation. God's work continues and finds its epitome in the identity and purpose of Jesus Christ, thus the divine outworking should be viewed in a universalist fashion. If God was universal in his outworking during creation, why would God change his ways at the end of creation history by being selective in dealing with creatures? That is why the conception of *tadhana* is pivotal in considering the represented rest for humankind.

As the Creator rested on the Sabbath, the implication is that rest is determined for creatures. When the Creator decides to *be* in human flesh, the Creator decides to self-sacrifice for humanity. In this respect, God not only wills to be disturbed sequential to being Jesus of Nazareth, but God also wills to lose rest and be distressed for our sake. The Creator is the sacrificing God, and the sacrificing God is the Creator.[76]

Given the established relationship with creatures, when humanity sinned, the Creator sacrificed himself to uphold the continuity of that relationship. God is constant in the relationship even if humans are not. The distress in God should not be taken as self-inflicting, yet it could be thought of, to some extent, as self-incriminating. God chooses to be distressed by being vulnerable in the covenantal relationship. We can see here the constancy of God in terms of the covenant. God is constantly in himself as God is constantly the Lord of the covenant. In such lordship, God selflessly commits to us; also, God overcomes our efforts to fracture the covenantal relationship. This is the God of Israel: self-determined to suffer to maintain the covenant with the people.[77]

The over and above God is at the same time the condescending and serving God in the covenant. Being a covenantal being, he is indeed a loving God, as he made himself vulnerable to pain and suffering to show the seriousness of his commitment. When we consider creation, this consideration must be Christocentric. This is not an easy integration because of these reasons, namely, the time gap between creation and incarnation, and the character gap between the Creator and the Redeemer. Given the shared purpose of creation and incarnation, the time gap is bridged.

76. This subject matter will be expounded in ch. 5 under "The Suffering God."

77. Isa 25:1; 27:3; cf. 24:5.

Given the shared identity between the Creator and the Redeemer, the character gap is also bridged.

The shared purpose of creation and incarnation is to bring about the fulfillment of the positive prophecies out of the negative prophecies. In view of the doctrine of God, the latter somehow implies an ambiguous deity, while the former conveys a compassionate God. Since there is no deity behind and beneath Jesus Christ, the ambiguous God is dismissed here. The God who foreordained the destruction of Zion and the exile of her people is none other than Jesus Christ. The God who had raised Babylon to an empire and the God who also brought Babylon to her knees is Jesus Christ. The deity who called Isaiah to be a prophet and the deity who called Cyrus to be Israel's deliverer is Jesus Christ. The formidable God on Mount Sinai and the crucified God on Calvary is Jesus Christ. In other words, God is not only sovereign and loving, God is also strong and gentle. The One in the OT is the same being in the NT who is compassionate, merciful, and sorrowful.[78]

It cannot be smoothly argued that God has foreordained only the rise of Israel, not his downfall. Whatever happens to the people, God willed it; and, relatively speaking, it is for the good of the people. The spoken word is also the living Word. It is the same word of judgment against Israel and the word of restoration of Israel. In this purview, the downfall of Israel is part of the rise of Israel. That, without a doubt, greatly worried the prophet, even caused him to weep.[79] Isaiah's lamentation reflects the mourning of the entire creation: "The earth dries up and withers, the world languishes and withers; the heavens languish together with the earth."[80] When God created the earth, it was wholly pure and pleasant, but when humanity sinned, it was marred, as the prophet affirms:

> The earth is polluted by its inhabitants, for they have transgressed laws, violated statutes, broken the everlasting covenant.[81]

It is emphatically expressed here that when humans breached their part within the covenant, they broke their bond with God. This resulted in the alienation of creatures from the Creator. In spite of the destruction

---

78. God is depicted in Isa 16 as full of compassion; God laments for the destruction of Moab.

79. Isa 21:4.

80. Isa 21:4 NRSV. The prophet Isaiah weeps for Moab, too (Isa 15:5).

81. Isa 24:5 NASB.

of the Jerusalem temple, the Jews kept their confidence in God.[82] They praised God amid anguish and affliction. The burden of their songs reflects the dialectical operation of God axiomatic in the talk of theodicy.[83] With God, the singing of the oppressed is relentless, whereas the singing of the oppressor will cease completely.[84] Within the covenant, creatures can maintain their purpose.

Creatures, especially humans, are designed to "fill the earth and subdue it."[85] Humanity is designed to be fruitful in all its endeavors, having dominion over other creatures.[86] The term *dominion* in this context is crucial in understanding Israel's role since it presupposes the concept of growth and satisfaction.[87] It interjects with the idea of prevailing against something.[88] Adam and Eve are appointed to multiply their kind, likewise, to oversee the multiplication of other kinds. In that manner, what is created is meant to be abundant and continue to be so. Moreover, the first couple is commanded to overcome what is before them, anything that would hinder the Creator's appointment. Unfortunately, the first couple neglected their duty, and so did Israel. Instead of enriching the earth, the people, says the prophet, plundered the earth and left her desolate.[89] The people of God added corruption to the world, rather than stopping it. As a result, that which is created inevitably heads toward that which was before creation—unspeakable pandemonium and inanition.

With the help of the concept of *tadhana*, it becomes manageable to see that Israel's way to success runs through the tides of successive destruction and construction. Truly, it is in times of helplessness that help comes. Similarly, it is in times of hopelessness that hope is riveted. When the prophet predicts the captivity of Israel, it is in captivity wherein the promised Deliverer will come. It is in the time of Israel's disappointment that the appointment for Israel will occur. The horrible events that happened to the people cannot be used against God. Israel will always be

82. Isa 24:16.

83. Isa 12:2; 26:2.

84. Isa 25:5b.

85. Gen 1:28a.

86. Gen 1:28b.

87. The Hebrew *mâlê'* (מָלֵא) for the word *fill* means "to accomplish" or "to satisfy" (SECB, h4390).

88. The Hebrew *râdâh* (רָדָה) for the word *dominion* also means "to prevail against" (SECB, h7287).

89. Isa 24:5.

God's. The people of God will always be dear. God never lost his identity and purpose as the Creator; it is humanity who lost its identity and purpose according to the Creator's design—humans failed as stewards of nature, and worse, humans dominate other humans. It was not intended for Adam to dominate Eve or other humans; God made it clear that human domination is applicable only to lower life forms.[90] The sheer fact that God created humans in his resemblance and manner declares out loud that humans are destined to resemble God—to use power and authority to make life dynamic and delightful.

We can better appreciate the above notion by viewing the triadic act of God. It is by the will of the Father for creation to exist and for it to exist dependent on the Father. It is through the Son speaking out "Let there be . . ." that creatures come into being. And it is through the Father's and Son's Spirit whereby creatures continue to exist. Before things such as stars, animals, trees, etc., exist, we can read the phrase: "And God said." This means that by the power of the Word of God, things exist; and it is the same Word, the Logos, manifesting power in the NT. When the Creator says "Let there be light," such light is not merely useful in showing the physical path, but likewise, it is useful, too, in showing the spiritual path, for the Creator himself is the Light.[91]

2.3 The Prime Mover

Light is always associated with God; it is God who created light. But the flip side is equally true and valid. It is God who created darkness, too.[92] If it is insisted that God is not the source of darkness, then this interjects that darkness has another creator or it is self-existent. Biblically speaking, there is just one Creator, as there is just one self-existent being. If this is indeed the case, then one cannot separate darkness from God, as light cannot be separated from him. When God commands the light to appear, he is not countering darkness. It does not make sense for God to go against something he has created. By analogy, the creation of light does not oppose darkness but rather complements it. This view is useful in examining the determined fall of Babylon and the other enemies of Israel.

90. Gen 1:26, 28; 2:23.

91. Gen 1:3; cf. John 1:4–5.

92. Isa 45:7. For more discussion on God creating the darkness, see de Vera, "God of the Covenant," § 6.1.

Devastation, depicted as the coming of the night, awaits the antagonists through war among themselves.[93] In the revealed things to come, the notion of darkness is outstanding in the prophet's vision.[94] As the key to the future lies in the beginning, we have to consider first what darkness is in the context of creation.

Darkness is not the default background of whatever is created. The default is God, hence, in the beginning—God. Although we can read that such darkness before creation is proportional, to some degree, to the formless and voidness of the earth, darkness is indeed an arresting term.[95] Yet it can be properly appreciated if it is stacked up against the action of the Spirit of God.[96] For now, we will focus on the role of the Spirit in creation before we consider the role of darkness in the grand scheme of things. The opening of the "windows of heaven" and the trembling of the "foundations of the earth" remind us of creation.[97] The Spirit of God moves over the face of the waters.[98] The text reveals that the absence or withdrawal of God naturally results in darkness and death.[99] The earth was "formless and void" before divine intervention. However, the text also confirms that if the Spirit hovers over something barren, then life begins as a result.

Interestingly, a plain investigation of the context unfolds that *râchaph* is used only once in the entire Bible, and I think scholars used the translation "moved" only for lack of a better term. It is reasonable to recognize that we do not do justice to its uniqueness if we limit it to

93. Isa 21:11–12; 17:14a.

94. Gen 1:26.

95. Gen 1:2. *Darkness* in Hebrew *chôshek* (חֹשֶׁךְ) also means "obscurity," figuratively denoting misery, sorrow, wickedness, and death (*SECB*, h2822). The concept of the Hebrew *tôhû-bôhû* expresses the idea of emptiness or a place of chaos and indistinguishable ruin (*SECB*, h8414; h0922).

96. In the treatment of the Trinity, it seems that it is somehow deprived of understanding of the third person of the Godhead, perhaps because the Spirit is thought of as a magnificent force or unequaled influence; for example, the wind *rûach*. There is nothing wrong with that common notion as long the Spirit is seen as a self-existent rational being who has concern and compassion.

97. Gen 1:2b, 6–8; Isa 24:18b NRSV.

98. The term *move* in Hebrew *râchaph* (רָחַף) means to spread over as in brooding, shake; while the term waters *mah'yim* means spring water, juice (of the earth) (*SECB*, h7363; h4325).

99. Isa 20:5–6; Gen 6:3; Jer 4:23.

only a mere movement.[100] The Spirit's *rāchaph* was so compelling and overwhelming that the earth tremendously shook and the waters in the abyss could not help but gush out with might and purpose in response to the divine activity.[101] Life without God is not only empty but is also literally desolate like a desert. People who want to live apart from God do not fully realize the implication of their aspirations. The downhill experience is not sudden but gradual according to Israel's experience.[102] Life without God will naturally lead to ignorance, then wickedness, misery, sorrow, and finally death. Darkness indeed symbolized all these awful conditions, which is why God had provisioned the light into the universe and human lives as well.[103]

The Bible attests to the complex Entity that has inherent power to marvelously disrupt the order of things for the best. The divine prime Mover can use scrap, cultivate the barren, and bring to life the dead. He gives warmth and life to something deceased and protects his beloved ones like a mother eagle brooding over her chicks. The Spirit who miraculously transformed an unimaginable and undistinguishable ruined and wasted massive land into a habitable land (with paradise) is also the same Spirit willing and waiting to transform even an empty life.

Darkness is the ground zero of existence. It is something present before the Creator willed the agencies of nature to have their manifestation temporally, hence physically. In this sense, darkness constituted what creation is not—chaos, wickedness, and death; it was an old thing God rejected. It is in the darkness, therefore, where God demonstrates what he is—order, righteousness, and life. In short, we could say that darkness is the divine workstation wherein God expresses his creativity. This is not corrosive hypothetical speculation calling into question the divine essentialities, because God's being, as Barth posits, is *in* God's act.[104] What is utilized in the creation and how it is performed reveal the Creator's operation and character. This is why the Thomasian Mover is at variance with the Barthian Mover; the former is the "unmoved mover" whereas the latter is the "self-moved mover."[105] For Aquinas, God cannot

---

100. An act exclusive to the Creator.

101. Gen 1:2b. Here the deep, Hebrew *tᵉhôm* (תְּהוֹם) is construed in such a way to express that from the abyss surges out the massive amount of water (*SECB*, h8415).

102. Isa 17:4–6.

103. Isa 17:7; Ps 107:14; Mic 7:8.

104. Barth, *CD* II/1, §28.

105. Aquinas, *Summa Theologica*, 1.2.1; Barth, *CD* II/2, 78.

be affected by anything external of God; for Barth, however, God can be affected *ad extra*, for God wills it to be in the Son. The self-moved Son is the Creator who chooses to coexist with creatures.

As the Creator makes something wrecked into something beautiful, obscurity and emptiness become comprehensible and abundant. This is the kind of scenery of creation—filled with brilliance and activity. In the talk of the misery and sorrow that Israel experienced, it does not seem odd to view it through the window of God's creativity. The seeming *tôhû-bôhû* (emptiness) in and of Israel is determined to be a paradise. What is empty and lifeless, framed eschatologically, shall be filled with meaning and vitality. Israel will not be forever neglected and rejected; this is not what God has preordained. Israel is ordained to be a light in the darkness by being the distinguishable instrument to "recreate" humanity from indistinguishable ruin.

Dust is the simplest form of what is burned or decayed. Nonetheless, it is from dust that humankind is created. The insignificant and valueless has not merely attained a sort of significance and value but become of great worth! As we bear the image and likeness of the Creator God, whatever tragedy befalls us will be resolved, according to Rabbi Akiva.[106] That which is intrinsically impossible has become possible. That which is intrinsically incapable is enabled to do its task. The simplicity of the creature reflects the magnanimity of the Creator. It is fundamental to the supposition that there is nothing too difficult for God. Before the outstretched hand of the Lord, the prophet affirms, the contemptible will be honorable.[107]

On the contrary, God is also capable of bringing the wicked and arrogant to the ground, "to the very dust."[108] The Creator God will trample the ruthless and the schemers.[109] In that respect, we should confess "everything we have done was by your power."[110] In this power, we will see the almightiness of the Creator God, which we now investigate.[111]

106. See ben Yosef, "Pirkei Avot," 3:14.

107. Isa 23:9, 11.

108. Isa 25:12.

109. Isa 25:4, 11.

110. Isa 26:12 CEV

111. This will be unpacked in "The Almighty God."

3. THE ALMIGHTY GOD

Isaiah exclaims, "The LORD All-Powerful will rule on Mount Zion in Jerusalem, where he will show its rulers his wonderful glory."[112] What does
the Bible mean by God the Almighty? In Isaiah's thought, the "Almighty"
means the One who oversees any earthly jurisdiction. The powers of the
world are bound to the power of that One beyond the world.[113] People will
marvel at the abundance of justice and righteousness of the One revered
as the Almighty.[114] As there is no account in the Bible of a precreation
deity, likewise, there is no account of God who is not Almighty. In other
words, God is all-powerful before, during, and after the captivity of Israel.

Yes indeed, God Almighty (*'el šaddai*) was at work even in the fulfillment of the negative prophecies, God can be said to be working out his
tremendous power when the unthinkable and unbelievable happened to
God's people under the hands of the ungodly. We have discussed earlier
that King Immanuel is key in theodicy. The argument for divine mercy
and righteousness amid cruelty and crime is sustainable if it takes the
validity of the covenant and what God had risked to preserve it. Given
in ineffable terms, the unthinkable and unbelievable negative events in
Israel, in the end, will be turned into something unthinkable and unbelievable, too, yet in a positive way. It will be so since King Immanuel is not
only all-powerful, he is also all-wonderful.

The Almighty is all-powerful. What has been foreordained will
be all-consummated. Being all-powerful, God is supremely assertive in
pushing his interest for the benefit of humanity. Thus God is the 'āmen,
the covenant-keeping deity in the ever-changing thoughts and actions of
the people of the covenant.[115] It is clear in Isaiah that the whole world is
the seat of power of the Almighty, and everyone will be glad.[116] Zion will
be converted first, and all cities will follow suit.[117] "On this mountain,"
testifies the prophet, God removes the cloud of sorrow over nations.[118]

112. Isa 24:23 NASB; italics in original.

113. Isa 24:21–22.

114. Isa 24:23.

115. Isa 25:1b; Ps 106:48b; Rev 3:14. The Hebrew *'āmen* (אָמֵן), when used as a
noun, means "truly faithful," where the Greek *amén* (ἀμήν) translates as "trustworthy"
(*SECB*, h0543; g021).

116. Isa 25:6.

117. Isa 25:7.

118. The phrase "on this mountain" indicates that revival begins in Jerusalem (Isa

The time of favor has come to Israel, and it will spill over to the ends of the earth.[119] Once overthrown, Jerusalem is strengthened; and so are her neighbors.[120]

The Almighty is all-wonderful. In the astounding wisdom of God as the chief Architect of creaturely reality, all actions and events work together in accomplishing his purpose. This framework is supported in Isaiah but is expressed metaphorically. "Sea dragons," says Robin Parry, "personify the chaos that must be defeated and put in its place so that order and life can flourish."[121] In the majestic design, there is nothing out of place, for the Alpha is simultaneously the Omega.

When we think of God as the Alpha and the Omega, it bears in mind that creation begins with him and creation ends with him. It points to the formulation of *exitus-reditus*, which states that whatever is from God will return to God.[122] Given the formula, since humanity is through Christ and for Christ, humanity will end up alongside Christ. As God the Son is faithful to God the Father, by correlation, the faithfulness of the Son will be communicated to humanity in light of the *tadhana*. No human exists and has its being apart from Jesus Christ, thus such existence and being have its merit *in* him. Nothing that comes from Christ (the source) in the end will find itself elsewhere (away from the source). We can see here how the doctrine of God informs the doctrine of creation. Everything that happens to creation cumulatively contributes to the desire of the all-wonderful God.

What is rather surprising is that idol worshippers, like the Canaanites and Israelites, will eventually abandon their abominable practice and shift their allegiance to the real God. This presupposes that the final destination of humanity is with Jesus Christ—the Creator. The prophet alludes to this:

> At that time the people *will turn* and trust their Creator, the holy God of Israel. They have built altars and places for burning incense to their goddess Asherah, and they have set up sacred poles for her. But they will stop worshiping at these places.[123]

25:6–7, 10; Ezek 43:12).

119. Isa 26:15; Ps 102:13–16.

120. Isa 26:1; Zech 2:4–5.

121. Interpreting Isa 27:1 (Parry, *Biblical Cosmos*, 35).

122. Rom 11:36; Isa 27:6, 13.

123. Isa 17:7 CEV; italics added.

The Phoenician goddess Asherah is the alternative deity for *Yahweh Elohim* in the ancient Near East in terms of life and productivity.[124] The "sacred poles" represent the deities and hosts of heaven—a stark contrast to the God of creation who made the heaven and its hosts.[125] These explain why Israel turned to foreign deities when the LORD God had been silent. The more desperate the people were, the more they worshipped idols. God also rebukes Damascus (capital of Syria, north of Jerusalem) for abandoning him, as in the case of other regional nations.[126] Fortunately, the positive prophecy outweighs the negative prophecy: we can see here that despite Israel's apostasy, the people eventually return to their Creator.

The concept of *exitus-reditus* coheres with that of *tadhana*. The realization of the former is in the actualization of the latter: whatever is misaligned (human activity) and disaligned (being human) shall be aligned (the efficacy of Jesus Christ's humanity). Since creation is from Christ, through Christ, and *to* Christ, all things, in the end, cannot have a separate identity and destiny from the Son of God and Son of Man. This is exactly what it means to be created by the Creator God: we come from him, we return to him.[127] Humanity exists because of the existence of Jesus Christ. What is the purpose of humanity? It is to live *for* God and stay *with* God. In doing so and being so, humanity aligns itself with the design of the Chief Architect.

Human alignment with the divine will be so, for Jesus Christ has willed it so. In the foreordination of human beings, humans find their meaning in the One who foreordains. Christ takes the form of humanity to give substance to it. Because Jesus Christ exists, therefore, humanity exists; and if Jesus Christ exists forever, then by analogy, humanity's existence coincides with that of Christ. With this respect, we have our *being* in Jesus Christ. The being is the summation and progression of why we are created in the first place. The summation of our being is to live *in* Christ, and the progression of our being is to be Christ-like. In P. T. Forsyth's assertion, to be Christ-like, a person should love, forgive, and release an enemy from blame and rather take the blame and suffer from it.[128] In hu-

124. See Deut 12.

125. See 2 Kgs 21:7; 23:5 (Jamieson et al., *Commentary on Whole Bible* 2, https://biblehub.com/commentaries/jfb/2_kings/21.htm).

126. Isa 17:1–2.

127. Isa 17:7; 26:13; 1 Cor 8:6.

128. Forsyth writes, "But it is that He should love, forgive, and redeem His

man terms, this is self-contradicting, but with God, this is self-attesting. What is required of humanity is already accomplished in the humanity of Christ. Under such circumstances, what is not self-contradicting for humans but self-affirming is to choose to be *in* the eternal covenant. To be Christ-like means to cherish the eternal relationship God has offered to everyone. As the Son of God is always the Son of Man, humankind will always be with its Creator. Since the Creator wins over all threats to the covenant, so the creatures (humans) will overcome them as well.

More generally, in the eternal past, eternal present, and eternal future, God wills to be the God of humanity. This means that the eternal now of humankind, by inference, parallels with the eternality of God, and it will be so in eternity. It may sound repetitive, but it is not inexpressive since it is reiterative and indicative. It reiterates the oversight of the All-Powerful and it indicates the foresight of the All-Wonderful. This is a recipe for salutary consummation. Only that which is determined is that which is transformed. As there is only one chief Architect, there is also one eschatological end for one design.

The All-Powerful is truly All-Wonderful in terms of scope, as his jurisdiction is universal.[129] Drawing on the prophet, the "whole earth" is subject to the counsel of God, and "all nations" are under God's hand.[130] This attests that God's purpose embraces all peoples at all times. As described in Isaiah, all nations partake of the Lord's feast. This showcases the universality of divine mercy. In effect, *all* tears of sorrow shall vanish.[131] The prophet saw that the "whole world" will be filled with fruit; it is the outcome of Israel's global mission.[132] The Almighty is absolutely the God of all.[133]

The almighty God is very unlike the Akkadian deities, whose influence is only regional and whose power is only a pretense. The Almighty

---

enemies; that His heart should atone for them to His own holy nature; that He should consecrate, [by means of] a suffering greater even than they devised, all the suffering they might have to endure, and by their central sin and its judgment destroy sin at its centre" (*God the Holy Father*, 7).

129. Isa 25:6.
130. Isa 14:26.
131. Isa 25:6–8.
132. Isa 27:6.
133. Isa 25:8a CEV.

is the true "I am," and there is no one besides God who generates global transformation.[134]

3.1 No Other Almighty

As just explained, what the Almighty opens, no one can shut, and what the Almighty shuts, no one can open.[135] This means that there is no one mightier than the God of Israel, not even human decision and action.[136] Human decision and action are subservient to divine decision and action. Why? Because the telos ascribed to humans conforms to the judicial decision and executive action of the divine. God (*a priori*) indeed gives humanity (*a posteriori*) its validity and meaning.[137] David Bentley Hart argues, "As God's act of creation is free . . . all contingent ends are intentionally enfolded within his decision."[138] This conception flies in the face of some philosophers of religion. For them, human free will is not only real, but it is a force to reckon with. Concerning the ongoing debates on the tension between divine sovereignty and human choice, Parry asks, "How is it that if people have free will—understood in terms of the ability to do something or not do it—how is it that God can ensure that you do the thing that he wants you to do, without forcing you? If he can't force you, how does he ensure that the end of the cosmos will ever be what he wants? Does it mean we can thwart God's purposes?"[139] To answer these questions, I suggest that the best way forward is to focus on the gravity of the term *free*, not on the weight of the term *force*.

In agreement with the freedom of Hart's God, I stand by the position that no one is absolutely free except the Creator. In such freedom, God is exemplified as the absolute prime Mover. Therefore in the eschatological perspective, God's decision and action shall prevail over human's decision. If the free agency of the human is to be insisted, it should be done so within the doctrine of God; otherwise, it would somehow

---

134. Blenkinsopp, "Second Isaiah," in *Essays*, 52. See Enuma Elish VII 14, 88.

135. Isa 22:22b.

136. Isa 19:14, 21, 25.

137. Isa 22:25; 26:12.

138. Hart adds that "all causes are logically reducible to their first cause. This is no more than a logical truism" (Hart, *That All Shall Be Saved*, 69–70).

139. Parry, "Debate over Universalism," para. 3.

end in quasi-Arminianism at best[140] and anthropocentrism at worst—worldviews I intentionally avoid for their lack of acuity for the *already* accomplished in Jesus Christ. By the Christocentric handling of human choice, the worry about "being forced" will gradually fade. Everyone is eternally covered in the death and, more importantly, in the resurrection of Christ. By God's grace, no one is coerced; everyone abides well.

The Almighty is constant in strength and dependability; hence God is "Israel's mighty rock."[141] He is the fortress of his people against alien invaders, and God is the stronghold in times of calamities and diseases.[142] He is the Rock—strong and unshakable, truly dependable and trustworthy.[143] The poor and the oppressed find strength and comfort in God, for he provides them justice.[144] God alone can provide solid satisfaction from an immensely proportional indemnity made possible by his self-sacrifice. God indeed is the mighty Rock. No one or nothing can stand in his way.[145] The God of Israel is the *'ēl šaddai* who sets the judgment for Babylon, and he approaches like a devastating storm.[146]

In the thick of the negative prophecies, we can see the highest degree of immovable force, the Rock of ages.[147] The Rock is the "hammer of the whole earth." Whatever attempts to frustrate the primordial direction is hammered down; whatever is so succumbs to the Lord's oversight and adjusts to it. This is not an overstatement of the almightiness of God. The often overstated is the capacity of humanity to thwart the primordial direction set by the dependable and trustworthy God. What needs to be muted is the potentiality of the rejection of the covenant. No matter how persistent the rejection is, the divine constant (Jesus Christ) has already prevailed over human weakness and dubiousness. Anyhow, I would rather overrate God's determination for us than undermine God's capability

---

140. Jakob Hermanszoon, better known as Arminius, was a student of Theodore Beza, Calvin's successor at the University of Geneva. Arminius insisted on human participation in achieving salvation, a position that was later branded as Socinian and viewed as a serious departure from the Reformed tradition (Bettenson and Maunder, *Documents of the Christian Church*, 268; De Witt, "Arminian Conflict," 8).

141. Gen 49:24 CEV.

142. Isa 17:10.

143. Isa 26:4–5.

144. Isa 26:6.

145. Isa 14:27.

146. Isa 13:6; Gen 17:1; 35:11.

147. Isa 26:4; 45:17; Deut 32:15.

to make things happen in our interest. What I would not underrate is the representation of Jesus Christ. In his humanness, we are freed from being overcome, for we are decreed to overcome. The determined humanity is as stable as the Rock—the divine determination.[148]

The determining God is the almighty Rock that shatters every empire and pounds every emperor. God had crushed the towering pride of the Babylonians through the Persians, and fortunately for the Jews, Cyrus was on their side, of course, by God's will.[149] The ways of the Almighty are sure and the means of the Almighty never fails. He is almighty in the land and the sea, as God is in control in and of everything.[150] This denotes that the power of God is not only irreversible and unstoppable but also unbounded and versatile.

God's power is unbounded as it caught up with the routes of the "ships of Tarshish."[151] Busyness indicates the accumulation of material wealth; yet in riches, the people of Tyre strayed away from God.[152] As a result, they had consecutive calamities that made them bankrupt.[153] Even so, the divine power is versatile. Tyre will be restored (like Israel) and enjoy the splendor she never had before. This is consequent of the divine rigor. One day, the Messiah will visit Tyre, and his influence will abound there.[154] That is why in the eschatological construct of Isaiah, the wealth of Tyre will profit the Lord's cause.[155] Things last and things end by the will of God—nothing else. Having in mind the roller-coaster experience of Jerusalem and other cities, the reader is reminded who is truly the almighty Rock—Jesus Christ. In Christ, whoever stumbles will not quite fall but will soon recover to be reunited with God.[156]

---

148. Isa 14:12; Jer 50:23.

149. In Isa 26, God is the Rock that smashes the proud and flattens every lofty disposition.

150. Isaiah 23 says that "the LORD's hand has reached across the sea," invoking the unrestricted power of God to enforce his will. See also Isa 25:11a.

151. Isa 23:1a.

152. Isa 23:1; 1 Kgs 10:22.

153. Isa 23:12.

154. Isa 23:17–18. See Matt 15:21; Acts 21:3–6.

155. Isa 23:18.

156. Isa 26:8–9; 27:9; cf. 1 Cor 10:4. Jesus is the cause of stumbling, to be lifted afterward (1 Pet 2:8, 10).

3.2 Impressively Proficient

Speaking of the reunion between God and humanity, the Sabbath comes to mind. The All-Powerful is truly All-Wonderful in terms of rendering rest. Jesus Christ, the Initiator of rest, is synchronously the Implementor of rest.[157] Christ is the Implementor of rest. Whatever the Rock shattered—that is, arrogance and injustice—shall never recover. What will recover are the victims and perpetrators. The former are reinstated; the latter are regenerated. The aggravated and the aggravator both find settlement before the Rest himself.[158] As the Rock *is* the Rest, the implementation of rest is solid, and the effect of such implementation is soothing. The Rock of ages brings Rest for ages; whoever is disciplined is blessed with healing. Whatever setback besets us, humanity always bounces back because of the implementation of rest. In having that rest, we are empowered to stay within the covenant. With it, the broken bond with God is mended, and more substantially, helplessness and hopelessness become impotent. Only the potency of God remains.

The potency of God's rest nullifies what darkness symbolizes. Being the Creator of darkness, God is the Ruler of and in darkness.[159] To give us a window of comprehension, let us consider the prophet's oracle about Cush (present-day Ethiopia):

> In that time a present will be brought to the LORD of hosts from a people tall and smooth *of skin*, and from a people terrible from their beginning onward, a nation powerful and treading down, whose land the rivers divide—to the place of the name of the LORD of hosts, to Mount Zion.[160]

God humbles the ancient Ethiopians and bids them to acknowledge the true God. Consequently, they will be converted, too, and will worship the LORD God in new Jerusalem.[161] It was in the darkness where God called out the Ethiopians to repent and serve him. They were once brutal in conquering other nations, which explicates the far-reaching fear they cast upon their enemies. These once "terrible" people will bring gifts to Mount Zion and worship the almighty God.

---

157. Isaiah 27 emphasizes that God is rest; Israel will find genuine rest only in God.

158. Isa 19:23–24.

159. As is evident in Isa 18, God rules amid conquests and destruction.

160. Isa 18:7 NKJV; italics in original.

161. See also Ps 68:31; 72:10.

Why do we usually associate darkness with evil if God created darkness? If the Light (Jesus Christ) is the bringer of darkness, then darkness is not altogether bad, let alone evil en masse. Granting that evil can be located within the quantum sphere of Godness, it still does not promote a sinister being cloaked in majesty. There is nothing evil in God, so darkness should not be confined solely to the idea of evil. Moreover, God uses darkness to contrast it to light. Jesus Christ is life, and by being so, light came to us; the light overcomes darkness by shining in it.[162] Remarkably, nothing is too dark or sinister for God, Isaiah declares:

> On that day Israel will be the third *party* with Egypt and Assyria, a blessing in the earth, whom the LORD of hosts has blessed, saying, "Blessed is Egypt My people, and Assyria the work of My hands, and Israel My inheritance."[163]

God's outworking is impressively proficient; by disciplining Israel, as well as Egypt and Assyria, these nations will indeed return to the Creator. It is undeniable here that the former enemies of Israel shall be counted among the people of God. The blessing usually understood as reserved for Israel is actually for Egypt and Assyria as well. The Egyptians and Assyrians are also the recipients of divine wisdom and divine mercy. This is not a distortion of the Isaianic message. It certainly is a move in the universalist direction.[164] The only theodicy that makes sense is the reacceptance and revitalization of the seemingly damned.

Darkness, in other words, is the location of the triumph of light. It is in the darkest place and moment that the light shines at its brightest.[165] With that in mind, the existence of darkness is essential for us to better appreciate the light.[166] Darkness is contrasted to righteousness; darkness is contrasted to consistency. It is in righteousness that Israel's affliction

---

162. Isaiah 19 demonstrates that God's ways and means are wise and effective. Cf. John 1:4–5.

163. Isa 19:24–25 NASB; italics in original.

164. See Kaminsky, "Election Theology," 37.

165. In Isa 20, God is the dependable deliverer. God destroys Egypt and Assyria to shame Israel for turning to wrong allies for deliverance.

166. God does not need anything other than himself to *be* God or to reveal the Godself.

will end and restore God's justice.[167] Accordingly, songs and laughter replace weeping and wailing, and contentment replaces resentment.[168]

Without resentment, the prophet went out naked and barefooted. With contentment, the prophet enacted the Lord's judgment against the enemies of Israel. Being naked and barefooted is a warning of stripping the confidence in things temporary, shaming the insolent against the One permanent.[169] Here, the realization of the plan for Israel is dependent on divine constancy. In God, being true to himself, the damned are reaccepted and revitalized; however, it is not a given in Isaiah's proclamations. We can only get a hint of the salutary end of the damned in the critical assessment of something good coming out of something bad. God's providence, to which the prophet alludes, is fashioned "long ago."[170] Nevertheless, because of foreordination, human privilege is accompanied by divine restriction to dishonor the honored in the world.[171]

The divine restriction is understood dialectically: God's correction is through God's permission. In the grand scheme of things, what appears intolerable is permissible to accentuate the divine imperative against human privation. The One who commands "If you eat any fruit from that tree, you will die" is the One who says "Your sins are forgiven."[172] The One who chides "You will have to struggle to grow enough food" is also the One who invites "Come to me and I will give you rest."[173] Dialectically speaking, the constant God of the Bible is where fear originates and terminates.[174] In other words, the Creator God (divine imperative) in the OT is the same compassionate God in the NT who addressed the fundamental problem in creaturely reality (human privation).

Peace became elusive for Zion; rather, paranoia became resident in her. Fear had overcome Zion simply because she resisted being overcome by God. Zion longed for fleeting power instead of longing for everlasting power. Depression reigns over Israel since he ignored God's impression

---

167. Isa 27:6. Righteousness, Hebrew *tsaddîyq* (צַדִּיק), means "just" or "lawful" (*SECB*, h6662).

168. Isa 24:11; cf. 24:14–15.

169. Isa 20:1–6.

170. Isa 22:11.

171. Isa 23:9.

172. Gen 2:17; Luke 5:20 CEV.

173. Gen 3:17b; Matt 11:28 CEV.

174. Prov 9:10; Ps 34:4.

through the prophet. It shows that there is nothing steady in this world except God and his will.

Stability of confidence comes from constantly believing that everything from God will eventually return to God. Everything that exists continues to be, so that what exists is for God. The formulation is christologically construed: human privation can be addressed only by the divine imperative. As far as God is concerned, the great chasm between the divine imperative and human privation is already bridged in the being of Jesus Christ. That imperative is given form in Christ's divinity, and human privation is given form in Christ's humanity. How is the great chasm bridged? As Christ's divinity is in union with Christ's humanity, it follows logically that the imperative incorporates human privation. It does not mean that the divine imperative agrees with human privation, but rather, the former strongly disagrees with the latter by assuming its weakness and dubiousness. The form has gained its substance in the triumph of Godhood in humanhood. God's perfection has accounted for imperfect humans; what is usually accepted as a liability has been turned into an asset. Humanity has no contribution to this; all is done through the messianic initiative. We can see this at work in Israel.

Because of the Messiah, Israel's guilt will be expiated. God does this by *cleansing* the iniquity of his people.[175] The people should not be intimidated by constant fear; what is constant is the divine plan for Israel. Israel had recognized in his downhill experience the lesson of God and that his fate belongs to God.[176] It is presumed here that the human system is disrupted to make way for the divine system. Based on Isaiah, God used the misfortunes of Israel as an invitation to return to his true Master. God's ways will never be wasted, and God's means will never be depleted.[177] Simply put, God uses darkness to save, not to harm *per se*. Whatever humanity can offer—brilliance, wealth, competency—can never and will never change what is foreordained. It is God's statement across generations: in the end, God triumphs!

---

175. Isa 27:9. To *expiate* in Hebrew is *kâphar* (כָּפַר), meaning "to atone" or "to purge away" (*SECB*, h3722).

176. Isa 26:13.

177. As affirmed in Isa 25, God is verily worthy of praise, because God humiliates the rich and enriches the poor. See also Isa 55:11.

3.3 Reading Isaiah through Revelation

After discussing why worldly power and influence are subservient to the Almighty, we are in position to test theodicy against reality or, in this case, expected reality—that foreordination concurs with the salutary outcome of humankind. We can do this by critically reexamining the Isaianic prophecy with Johannine prophecy to tease out the final status of humanity vis-à-vis the eschatological judgment.[178] The prophet writes,

> It will come about also in that day that a great trumpet will be blown, and those who were perishing in the land of Assyria and who were scattered in the land of Egypt will *come and worship* the LORD in the holy mountain at Jerusalem.[179]

The "great trumpet" signifies the calling of people to a holy convocation.[180] The *shofar* call is principally for the ten tribes of Israel dispersed in the Assyrian territory and the two tribes that fled to Egypt during the Babylonian captivity.[181] The LORD God discloses to the prophet the regrouping of Israel, with no tribe missing. Far more important than the physical restoration of Israel is the spiritual revival. God will summon Israel to worship in the renewed Zion. The positive prophecy is indeed a cause for jubilation, yet there is a higher reason to celebrate owing to the magnificence of the prophet's vision. The call to worship is also for the non-Israelites. Therefore by interpolation, it is a call for solidarity between God and humanity.[182] This is compatible with the inclusion of Egypt and Assyria in eschatological worship.[183] It presupposes that the Egyptians and Assyrians themselves are peripheral to the spiritual assemblage. It has become apparent that foreign nations will be counted worthy of holy convocation together with Israel. This adds weight to the universality of the divine summons.[184] Remarkably, the trumpet imagery serves as an overture for an international invocation.

---

178. Isa 27:13, 19:23–25; cf. Rev 11:15.

179. Isa 27:13 NASB; italics added.

180. Lev 23:24.

181. See Judg 3:27; Num 10:3; Jer 41:17–18.

182. The trumpet is a signal for all "inhabitants of the world," "who live on the earth" (Isa 18:3 NRSV).

183. Isa 19:19–25.

184. Isa 24:14–16a.

The context of the passage above provides us with a picture of a worldwide mingling of multiracial communities with a single purpose— to worship God in the new Jerusalem. This specific vision, somehow, is advocated in the writing of Revelation because, as Parry observes, Johannine visions "are overflowing with allusions to earlier prophetic texts" and, in this case, to Isaiah.[185] I claim that Isaiah 27 interconnects with Revelation 11 for the following resemblances: (1) the use of the trumpet as a symbol,[186] (2) the greatness of its sound,[187] (3) the call to worship,[188] (4) the global scope of the call,[189] (5) the mention of Israel in worship,[190] (6) the worship of the almighty God,[191] (7) the punishment for iniquities,[192] (8) the dead are left exposed,[193] (9) the mention of Assyria and Egypt,[194] and (10) Jerusalem as the location of worship.[195] With these in mind, we can better appreciate what the apostle John had seen in a vision regarding the ultimate human state.

According to the evangelist, upon the blowing of the seventh trumpet, there is a great shout in heaven exclaiming, "The kingdom of the world *has become* the kingdom of our Lord and of his Messiah, and he will reign forever and ever."[196] The vision has three emphases: the divine kingdom has conquered human kingdoms, the King in the divine kingdom is the LORD God and the Messiah, and this kingdom has no end. God has proclaimed the "everlasting gospel" to "every nation, tribe, tongue, and people."[197] No one is omitted in this great call, hence "who

---

185. Parry and Ramelli, *Larger Hope*, 272.

186. Isa 27:13a; cf. Rev 11:15a.

187. Isa 27:13a; cf. Rev 11:15. "Loud voices" is synonymous with an "exceedingly great sound."

188. Isa 27:13b; cf. Rev 11:16.

189. Isa 27:6b; cf. Rev 11:9–10.

190. Isa 27:13; cf. Rev 11:1. The inner court is exclusive to the Jews.

191. Isa 27:13b; 28:2a; cf. Rev 11:17.

192. Isa 27:1; 26:21a; cf. Rev 11:18.

193. Isa 27:10; 26:22b; cf. Rev 11:9b.

194. Isa 27:13; cf. Rev 11:8b. The city of Sodom is thematically identical with the city of Nineveh (Assyria); both are considered evil cities ripe for divine judgment. Gen 18:20; 19:13; Jonah 1:2; 3:10 (Bolin, "Nineveh as Sin City," para. 5).

195. Isa 27:13b; cf. Rev 11:2.

196. Rev 11:15 NRSV; italics added.

197. Rev 11:7a CEV; 14:6 NKJV.

dwell on the earth."[198] The seventh trumpet is the final invitation the Jews will heed, as well as the non-Jews.[199]

Notably, the background of the trumpet sound is the Jewish Passover, pointing to Christ's crucifixion.[200] This is the Day of Atonement for both Jews and gentiles. It means that the Isaianic vision is congruent with the Johannine vision in this respect: Jews coming to worship with the gentiles. The spiritual restoration of Israel, in other words, encompasses the revival of all peoples.[201] With that, the world has become God's. God conquers *all* human setbacks to consummate the universal revival.

It is arresting to notice that Sodom, like Nineveh, will be restored, too.[202] Here, Sodom is associated with Jesus (the Lord nailed to a cross), while Nineveh is associated with Jonah (the preacher of Nineveh).[203] Jesus cited the repentance of the people of Nineveh and, crucially, that he is greater than Jonah.[204] How is that so? The mission of Jesus is more extensive in breadth, and his achievement is more impressive in depth compared to Jonah's. The messianic mission covers the entire world and the messianic achievement applies to humanity in general. If God forgave Nineveh through Jonah, how much more through Jesus? Christologically speaking, the Godness of Christ embraces something wicked and converts it into something righteous. Also, the humanness of Christ arrests what is debased and makes it honorable. Only God can regenerate what appears condemned, hence the restoration of the defunct Sodom. This is a biblical fact, not an inadequate conjunction or a manipulative injunction.

God is the Lord of all kings and will so remain, for his kingship shall never be overthrown. What is overthrown are the kings who either challenge God's authority or mimic God himself. The kingdom is great, as the King is great![205] In the doctrine of God, there is no one great except God—great is the God who calls, and great is the effect of his call.

198. Rev 14:6 NKJV.

199. Zech 12:10; 13:1.

200. Jamieson et al., *Commentary on Whole Bible* 2, https://biblehub.com/commentaries/jfb/revelation/14.htm.

201. Isa 13:11; 25:9; 60:4–5; Mic 5:7; Zech 14:16; Rom 11:12.

202. Ezek 16:53.

203. Rev 11:8; Jonah 3:2.

204. Matt 12:41.

205. This is true as well in the worldly sphere. For example, Britain is considered great because of its monarch.

Nothing can stand against it.[206] The great trumpet sound awakens the
slumbers and excites the awake. When God summons the heathens to
acknowledge him as the one and only God, they will indeed come and
worship him.[207] It will certainly happen in the effect of divine discipline
combined with divine alleviation. Since God's ways will never be wasted,
and God's means will never be depleted, hence, no kingdom can hide its
decadence and no kingdom can deny its defeat. "Fallen, fallen is Babylon"
signifies that she is a failure to those who relied on her, as the gods failed
her.[208] In *tadhana*, the messianic reign is not only real, but significantly, it
is indeed a force no one can reckon with. In the reign of King Immanuel,
the *seventh*-day Sabbath is reestablished, signaled by the blowing of the
seventh trumpet.

Consonant with the seventh trumpet is the everlasting gospel—justice and righteousness for all. One of the reasons, I think, Jerusalem is
located on a mountain is to underpin she is indeed a beacon of hope;
people use her as a reference point (like the North Star) on their way
to God. In God's foreknowledge, no one is lost. This is the eternal good
news, and its realization is eternal as well. God is constant in his willingness to see all peoples worshipping him in the end; this is the realization
of Jesus Christ's initiation and implementation of rest. Despite the shift-
ing patterns in the course of nations, the garden temple in Eden does not
shift its course towards reemerging in the heavenly temple in the new
Jerusalem.[209] From the root of Israel (Messiah) comes the bearing of fruit
(restoration) layering over the earth (consolidated nations).[210] That is the
meaning of the unrelenting reign of King Immanuel in an unrestricted
kingdom. The final status of humanity, definitely so, coincides with the
eschatological convocation of all.[211]

Therefore, the end of the two cities (mentioned at the onset of this
chapter) is unlike the disparate culmination of Augustine's two cities,
because both cities will be rehabilitated. The only difference between the

206. Before God, people tremble (Isa 19:1; Rev 19:11). Before God, people are
converted (Isa 19:18; Rev 15:4b).

207. People will abhor idolatry and be loyal to the Creator God (Isa 17:7–8; Rev
14:7).

208. Isa 21:9b; Rev 14:8a NRSV.

209. Gen 2:8–9; Rev 22:1–2.

210. Isa 27:6.

211. For more information on what "eschatological" means in this section of Isaiah, see Hays, *Origins of Isaiah* 24–27, 29.

two is that the first city foreshadows the gentile community gaining tremendously from God's initiative of reconciliation. The second city foreshadows the Jewish community, which serves as a predecessor to such reconciliation. The reason behind the adjustment in the outcome of the first city, I maintain, is the eternal covenant with the *whole* of humanity. God has fixed the fractured covenant in the sacrifice of Jesus Christ, and it can never be undone—what comes from Christ (through the commencing remark "Let there be") returns to Christ (through the concluding remark "It is finished").[212] As God is truly faithful to his foreordination, God is truly faithful to self-determination to and for us. With this acumen, one would not think that the Spirit departs from the damned in the end. After all, in the eschatological landscape, the recipient of divine mercy received divine indignation and is reinstated. The recipient of the latter will then receive the former and be restored. This highlights that divine power is truly unbounded and versatile. Both cities are beneficiaries of God's consistent authority and wisdom.

One facet that demands further explication regarding theodicy is the fact that only a remnant is preserved after the Babylonian sack of Judah. Is this the best for Israel, and does it reflect God's utmost concern for his people? In the next chapter, we will discuss this by expounding the sustaining grace evident in the closing section of First Isaiah.

---

212. Gen 1:3a, 6a, 14a; John 19:30a. "The whole creation was restored through the Lord's resurrection" (Origen, *Comm. Rom.*, 4.7.3).

CHAPTER III

HIGHLY ACTIVE INDEED

"Although the LORD has given you bread of privation and water of oppression, *He*, your Teacher, will no longer hide Himself, but your eyes will behold your Teacher."[1]

IN CHAPTER 2, WE STUDIED why the Creator has the utmost concern for Israel despite the foreordained sack of Jerusalem and the exile of the Jews. Here, it will be argued that given the sustaining grace, the people of God are not completely doomed, for a remnant will be preserved.[2] God is indeed highly active in the affairs of Israel, as well as in Assyria and other nations. To support this, I shall unpack the recurrent "striking-healing" theme as evidenced in Isaiah 28–39 in light of divine providence.

The chapter critically analyzes God's ways and means with God's being parsed as follows: God as the Potter, Revealer, Upholder, Protector, Healer, and Restorer. We will do a myopic inspection of how God deals with Hezekiah in finding out if it is implausible to attribute evil to God because he uses natural evil (and to some degree human evil) to accomplish his purpose.[3] The aim is to replenish the lacuna in theodicy.

We shall now proceed to the third section of Isaiah with attention to God's sustaining grace to Israel.

---

1. Isa 30:20 NASB; italics in original.
2. The remnant is a constitutive factor throughout Isaiah (Hasel, *Remnant*, 250–53).
3. Hezekiah, son of Ahaz, the thirteenth king of Judah.

1. SUMMARY OF ISAIAH 28-39

This section returns the concentration to the rise and fall of Jerusalem expressed as poems where the prophet accuses the leaders of Jerusalem of turning to Egypt for military protection against Assyria. Isaiah knew this would backfire on Israel, and the impact would be devastating. In his mind, only repentance and trust in the LORD God could save Israel in this dilemma.

When the Assyrian armies attacked Jerusalem, King Hezekiah humbled himself before God asking for deliverance. God heard Hezekiah's petition and saved the city. However, the celebration was short-lived because of Hezekiah's careless move. To gain Babylon's political support, Hezekiah tried to impress the Babylonian ambassadors by showing the city's treasury, including the extravagant furnishings of the temple and palaces. He ran the risk of losing what he aimed to secure. Isaiah heard about the political movement, and he confronted the king for his foolish act. In effect, the prophet warned that this new ally would one day betray them by conquering Jerusalem.

Babylon would return to sack Jerusalem, not only to take her material wealth but also to carry her noblemen (and women) to exile in Babylon. The prophet foretold that the purpose of such judgment was to purify Jerusalem. It would happen in the reign of the holy seed—the Messiah. By the sustaining grace of the LORD God, the messianic kingdom would expand globally.

After reviewing the final section of First Isaiah, we will now examine why God is said to be highly active in and around Israel as the Sustainer.

2. GOD AS SUSTAINER

On its own, humanity can neither have life nor sustain life, even to dictate the course of life itself without the LORD God, as he is the foundation of life.[4] This is evident in the lives of creatures, especially in King Hezekiah, that have been sustained and developed.[5] That is the other meaning of God as the Alpha and the Omega: what he nurses, he flourishes; God does it following his master plan.

---

4. Isa 28:16, 18a.

5. Isa 28:24-26; 34:16-17; Isa 36-38.

God is sovereign as the Sustainer because humans are not self-existent and self-moved. These apophatic descriptions of humanity are viewed against the essentialities of God. The prophet says,

> You [Jews] are in for trouble if you go to Egypt for help . . . .
> Instead you should depend on and trust the holy LORD God of
> Israel. The LORD is not stupid! He does what he promises . . . .
> The Egyptians are mere humans. They are not God.[6]

The Egyptians in the passage represent humanity. Humans are incapable of fulfilling their promises. They are bound to the limitation of their existence. People are contingent on the actions and events surrounding them; many factors stand in the way of their intention and anticipation. The LORD God is different from that which is human. God is very capable of pushing his agenda (for Israel); it is considered not stupid, for the One who promises is "wise."[7] God is wise: he is skillful in foreordination and artful in making it real in the world. There is no escaping the fact that humans hold no say in inevitable circumstances, but God does; and God does this through the Messiah. The Messiah is the provider of stability and prosperity for Israel. It is through him and by him that the eternal covenant is deemed potent and enriching.[8] Isaiah writes,

> Behold, I [God] am laying in Zion a stone, a tested stone, a precious cornerstone *for* the foundation, firmly placed. The one who believes *in it* will not be disturbed.[9]

The Messiah is the firm foundation of Jerusalem. Whoever relies on him will never be stricken with panic or paranoia but will rather have unshakable hope in God.[10] The Messiah is the "glorious crown."[11] The crown is not only a Who but is also a what, since it can be interpreted as a kingdom.[12] It is *within* the messianic kingdom that people are sustained and developed; and as such, people become stable and prosperous. That

---

6. Isa 31:1–3a CEV.

7. *Wise,* Hebrew *châkâm* (חָכָם), means "skillful" or "artful" (*SECB*, h2450).

8. Isa 28:2a.

9. Isa 28:16 NASB; italics in original.

10. Isaiah 28 depicts God as the unshakable foundation of Israel. The Messiah is the *mûsâd* (מוּסָד), the "firm foundation" (*SECB*, h4143).

11. Isa 28:5a.

12. Mackie, *Expanding Ezekiel,* 202.

is why it is nonsensical that, on the verge of falling into desperation, it is assumed that God had abandoned his people.[13]

2.1 Sustenance within the Covenant

Why would God leave Israel when the people needed him the most? Even when Israel became unfaithful to the One who sustains him by entering another covenant, described in Isaiah as the "covenant with death," God remained true to his function as the Lord of Israel.[14] The covenant with death is seeking human help instead of seeking divine help. It is indeed foolish to neglect God, for it will bring only death, nothing more.

God will always be covenanted with Israel. In his initiative, God nullified Israel's alliance with death.[15] God did it by expiating their guilt and cleansing their iniquity through the Messiah, as discussed in chapter 2.[16] God overturned the alliance against the divine covenant, and in this way, the threat of death is dissolved, no longer binding. Through the "strange" deed and "alien" work of God, the divine covenant remained in application between God and Israel.[17] The deed and work here are God's, hence we cannot replicate them nor comprehend them. We cannot replicate them insofar as competence is concerned, and we cannot comprehend them insofar as intelligence is concerned. The strange deed is something terribly awesome, and the alien work is something surprisingly unimaginable.

The terribly awesome is the impact of a very alien sort of thing on finite understanding. The divine operation is done in such a manner that is unanticipated, totally unforeseen, which humans do not expect—in this case, what God had done *with* and *for* Israel. The divine operation is so ethereal that humans are completely astounded in witnessing such an act. The strange deed and alien work is the divine utilization of evil, not to proliferate evil but rather to destroy it. God sends calamity, disaster, and misfortune to bring about his will.[18] We seem to have little patience for

13. Isa 36:18–20.

14. Isa 28:15a.

15. Isa 28:18a.

16. *Annuled* in Hebrew is also *kâphar*.

17. Isa 28:21b.

18. The Hebrew for *strange* is *zûwr* (זוּר), meaning "to turn aside"; by extension it denotes the idea "to be estranged." The word for *alien* is *nokrîy* (נָכְרִי), meaning "unknown" or "unfamiliar," taken from the root *neh'ker* (נֶכֶר), having the connotation of

this assertion. Surely it arouses indifference or even hostility to God as its consummation is horrific, and its effect is enraging.

Concerning the covenant, I presume, no one among the people anticipated calamity, foresaw disaster, and expected misfortune from God, on such a massive scale, right before the Assyrian invasion of Jerusalem. Of course, some Jews might have expected God to use a "rod" to correct his people, but not an "axe."[19] In this case, it seemed that the descendants of Jacob were about to be chopped off; Jerusalem would end. The Davidic line would cease. God did send the Assyrians to Jerusalem. Why? To answer this, we need to discuss how God develops what he sustains.

God sustains Israel continuously. God develops his people until they become stable and be productive. The providence is within the covenant, where God is committed to prosper them. Bearing this thought, the potency of the covenant is without restriction. God shall enrich the covenanted people. As God is free within the covenant, he is unrestricted in developing the people he is committed to. In developing them, however, the Lord's method is indeed *strange* and *alien*.

2.2 The Intricacy of Providence

The Lord's strange and alien method is loathsome initially, yet astonishing in the end. The act appears unacceptable at the outset, but the effect is enriching. Let us take Hezekiah as an exhibit. The king became gravely ill to the point where the prophet instructed him to set his affairs in order for his imminent death.[20] What is striking here was, from Hezekiah's mouth, that God "Himself has done it."[21] In other words, God is responsible for his terminal illness. Maybe the reader would be taken aback by the remark, yet Hezekiah had uttered the truth. It was truly the LORD God who sent the call of death upon the king's doorstep. As the backdrop reveals, things that happened during this time had been "ordained" a long time ago, to be exact, pretemporally.[22] The plan of God was not only about Sennacherib but also about Hezekiah.

"calamity, disaster, misfortune" (*SECB*, h2114, h5237, h5235).

19. Ps 74:5; Matt 3:10.

20. Isa 38:1.

21. Isa 38:15a NKJV.

22. Isa 37:26a.

I am convinced of Hezekiah's correct interpretation of his condition. God did not rebuke him for what he said. The whole experience even enlightened the king. God did not shy away from causing or, more accurately, introducing death to him. This is evident when Isaiah instructs healing, not enforces censure.[23] At the heart of his introspection, Hezekiah confesses, "Surely it was for my welfare that I had great bitterness"—undeniably for him, affirming God's active hand at work. And for the reader, confirming the irrevocability of predetermination for the king.[24] Untimely death was not decreed for Hezekiah but a timely realization of his foolishness. In the strangeness of the divine deed, he is being developed. Furthermore, in the alienness of the divine work, he is being prospered.

God's strange deed and alien work caused Hezekiah's uncontrollable skin eruption (probably leprosy) to be fatal.[25] Here we can see that no mortal can send leprosy to agitate another, only God. To begin with, no one can fully apprehend why would God send leprosy, let alone to a righteous king. People are incompetent to replicate the act, and they lack the intelligence to make sense of such an act. Sending a gruesome and shameful blow to Hezekiah is indeed strange to behold and alien to contemplate upon. Leprosy was, no doubt, terribly awesome. In becoming a leper, Hezekiah experienced God's cleansing, hence the confession "You [God] have cast all my sins behind your back."[26] Also, it is in this condition where Hezekiah became aware of the surprisingly unimaginable divine rescue. And so he exclaimed, "You [God] have held back my life from the pit of destruction."[27] The misfortune (not just appears to be) had been turned into a fortunate event (definitely is). Instead of being turned aside and harboring enmity with God, or at least indifference to him, Hezekiah was aroused by pure consolation and joy. He was not only healed but also given fifteen years of peaceful and abundant life. It is exactly how God provides. It is precisely how God sustains.

23. Isa 38:21.

24. Isa 38:17a NRSV.

25. Isa 38:21. Leprosy was the likely reason why Hezekiah could not go to the temple. Being a leper denotes physical and spiritual defilement, hence being banned from the temple premises.

26. Isa 38:17c NRSV.

27. Isa 38:17b NRSV.

Another exhibit of divine utilization of evil to its detriment is chronicled in Sennacherib's premeditated devastation of Jerusalem.[28] Rabshakeh (Sennacherib's chief of staff) led the Assyrian attack of Jerusalem to force the surrender of Hezekiah; otherwise, Jerusalem would be obliterated.[29] What is noteworthy, in this scenario, was when Rabshakeh said, "Do not forget that it was the LORD who sent me here with orders to destroy your nation!"[30] Two options confront the reader, namely, either the remark was from God, or Rabshakeh was merely bluffing.

The remark at hand, I contend, was indeed from God. Why? Because the textual and contextual pieces of evidence support that claim, and it gives weight to the whole talk of foreordination:

> Sennacherib, now listen to me, the LORD. I planned all of this long ago. And you do not even know that I alone am the one who decided that you would do these things.[31]

The text shows that God foreordained what had been happening in and around Jerusalem during this period, thus concerning Hezekiah and the Jews. No doubt, the LORD God dispatched the Assyrians to Jerusalem, absolutely not to act out their plan but, rather, so "everyone will see the wonderful splendor of the LORD our God," says the prophet.[32] Isaiah adds, "Then everyone in every kingdom on earth will know that you are the only LORD."[33] Consequently, the Assyrians were right before Jerusalem not to enforce their will on their enemy, instead to enforce God's will on his enemy. Everything that had transpired was according to the master plan. Sennacherib and Hezekiah were blindsided by the divine preparation in the background and the divine effectuation in the foreground, simply because God's outworking is precisely strange and alien.

The two kings, as well as their armies, were bewildered with how things came to pass. It took only one angel to terminate (just overnight) 185,000 strong Assyrian soldiers (terribly awesome).[34] Hezekiah's army

---

28. Sennacherib, son of Sargon II, king of the Neo-Assyrian Empire from 705 BCE to 681 BCE.

29. Isa 36:1–2.

30. 2 Kgs 18:25 CEV; cf. Isa 36:10.

31. Isa 37:26a CEV.

32. Isa 35:2c CEV.

33. Isa 37:20b CEV.

34. Isa 37:36.

did not fight (not even one Jewish soldier) to win the battle (surprisingly unimaginable). God alone decided. God alone acted.

In keeping with the idea that God sent the Assyrians to Jerusalem, a review of the divine ways and means is a requisite. The account avers that, at this juncture, God used Sennacherib's arrogance (evil) to check the arrogance of Israel's enemies (evil). God mustered the Assyrian army (calamity) to bring about the divine will (redemption). There is no denying, of course, the tremendous agitation Rabshakeh brought against the inhabitants of Jerusalem and the angel brought in the execution of the Assyrian army, albeit, when we stack up what *appears so* against the *definitely so*, the outcome accentuates the strangeness and the alienness of God's ways and means. The panic and violence demonstrated in this particular event are unmistakably loathsome at first, yet astonishing in the end. At least for Israel, God spared them from imminent destruction. God preserved the remnant of Israel.[35] Isaiah puts it,

> And the *remnant* who have escaped of the house of Judah shall again take root downward, and bear fruit upward. For out of Jerusalem shall go a *remnant*, and those who escape from Mount Zion. The zeal of the LORD of hosts will do this.[36]

God had sustained Israel's survivors from the invasion of the Assyrian army under Tiglath-Pileser III.[37] The survivors in Judah are destined to expand in number and influence, hence the phrase "bear fruit upward."[38] It is the promise to the people grounded in the Root of Jesse—King Immanuel. In other words, the remnant has a national impact as well as international.[39] It shall happen in the sustaining power of the One who gave the message to the prophet.

From the ravages of turmoil and despair comes very welcoming news of impending recovery and prosperity. That is the persistent commitment of the LORD God—truly something that cannot be ignored or broken. Remember that such commitment is self-driven and self-renewed, with or without Israel's repentance or reformation.

35. Isa 37:4.

36. Isa 37:31–32 NKJV.

37. See 2 Kgs 15:19; Isa 10:20–22 (Kaufman, "Phoenician Inscription," 20).

38. The word *remnant* in Hebrew is *shâ'ar* (שָׁאַר), meaning "to remain" or "be left alive," from the root meaning "to swell up" (*SECB*, h7604).

39. Tiemeyer, *Oxford Handbook*, 7; Moyise, "Isaiah in New Testament," 536.

Providing an impetus for the veracity of God as the Sustainer, we can now view, with confidence, the divine ways and means in conjunction with the being of God—the being of the Messiah. We have seen that God embodied the Potter when he broke Hezekiah's pride with the impending invasion. God was the Revealer when he sent Isaiah to predict that the invasion would stop. God was the Upholder when he secured Hezekiah's kingship and lineage. God was the Protector when he decimated the entire Assyrian army. God was the Healer when he struck Hezekiah with leprosy yet eventually healed him. God was the Restorer when he prolonged Hezekiah's life and set his reign in peace and prosperity. The inhabitants of Jerusalem had benefited, too, from the bountiful blessings their king enjoyed.[40] What is not apparent is more important in this study—that God simultaneously sustained and developed the Assyrians.

Given that God treats all nations and peoples equally, the next question is: what good (for the Assyrians) came out of this? The fall of Sennacherib and the death of 185,000 men must have been a terrible blow, but I insist, the outcome is somehow illuminating, at least for Sennacherib, for he was forced to acknowledge the God of Israel after his empire was in dire straits.[41] As for the thousands upon thousands who died, I can infer that their death was very extraordinary, the sort beyond human comprehension—within the realm of the strangeness and alienness of divine operation.

In Isaiah, the telos of divine operation is always promising, if not unquestionably affirming. The prophet depicted Assyria as "the vegetation of the field" which, unfortunately, "scorched before it is grown up."[42] It is the effect when God shames the proud—a divine discipline exercised often in the Isaianic narratives. Having this thought, however, puts into perspective the divine healing which comes with it. We can read that the prophet speaks of the refreshing time, a welcoming event provided for all, wilderness (non-Israelites) and orchard (Israel).[43] By the Spirit of God, typified as rain or dew, the wilderness is transformed into fertile land, and the orchard is transformed into a forest.[44] Isaiah continues that that is how God's justice "dwells" in the wilderness, also, how God's

40. Isa 32:1–5.

41. Isa 37:23.

42. Isa 37:27 NASB.

43. There are instances in Isaiah where Israel is pictured as "wilderness" or "desert," yet those do not negate that Assyria is also pictured as such, as is the case here.

44. Isa 32:15.

righteousness "abides" in the orchard.[45] This proves the effectiveness of the divine ways and means. Further, it stresses the universal dispensation of grace.

The terribly awesome is the eventual repentance and reconciliation of Israel. The surprisingly unimaginable is the eschatological acceptance and holy convocation of Assyria (with Israel).[46] Could it be that Assyria's acknowledgment of the true God (explained in chapter 2) was the result of what had miraculously transpired? The signs in the circumstances point in the affirmative. The divine operation was done and is about to be done—a manner unforeseen by those to whom God was communicating his method of providence. And so the prophet proclaims, "*His* counsel [is] wonderful and *His* wisdom great."[47]

2.3 Striking-Healing as Providential

In further fleshing out the Isaianic theme of striking-healing, we have to deal with this in connection with God's being seen in the Messiah—the "Holy One of Israel." His counsel is wonderful, for it strikes bewilderment into the mind of the beholder. His wisdom is great, as it heals the recipient.[48] The Messiah will not stop confronting the people; he will not tell illusions instead.[49] The prophet sketches the Messiah as a Potter who is neither a respecter of persons nor a sparer of nations; he shall smash the pot (Israel), breaking it into pieces.[50] Yet the Messiah will do such a mind-boggling act to Israel in order to "nourish," as stated: "In returning and rest you shall be saved; in quietness and confidence shall be your strength."[51] Nonetheless, the fact remains: as the potter does not esteem the pot, so the Messiah does not esteem Israel.[52] The Messiah does so within his ways and means, within his freedom as the Lord of the covenant. Yet, in the firmness of the messianic initiative, the people flourish.

45. Isa 32:16.

46. See Isa 19:23–25.

47. Isa 28:29b NASB; italics in original.

48. The Hebrew for *wonderful* is *pâlâ'* (פָּלָא), denoting "something extraordinary and difficult to understand"; the Hebrew for *great* is *gâdal* (גָּדַל), meaning "to magnify" or "to nourish up" (*SECB*, h6381, h1431).

49. Isa 30:10–11.

50. Isa 30:14.

51. Isa 30:15 NKJV.

52. Isa 29:16.

Accordingly, it is futile for Israel to question that initiative, as the pot cannot question the potter. The rationale behind the analogy is the disconnect between God and people vis-à-vis the ability to understand complex situations. The prophet is aware of it because of the potter and pot imagery. The potter knows well what he is doing with the pot (or clay), whereas the pot does not know of it at all. It is simply incapable of apprehending the potter. Such a metaphor underlines the outright foolishness of humanity in facing the wonderful counsel and great wisdom of the divine.

The Potter knows well what he is doing since he knows the pot.[53] It is not ambitious to say that the pot, in this context, principally refers to Israel, then Assyria, because the Messiah operates universally.[54] Jesus Christ, being the Messiah, is undoubtedly for all humankind at all times. Christ molds everyone into the wonderful and great design he envisioned in creation. Human enterprise is dependent on the artisan of life—the Potter. Whatever is necessary for human stability and enrichment, like faith or belief, comes from God.[55] People will never have faith. They will never believe what is in the Bible without the help of the Spirit. Here, divine providence is the key thought, and dependency is the keyword.[56] When humanity is the subject, one has to consider the implication of the term *dependency*. The two are the Siamese twins in the talk of providence. By contrast, when divinity is the subject, one has to consider the implication of the term *independence*. Godness is always in partnership with independence.[57]

Like Sennacherib, no one is self-moved; humans are dependent on things outside of themselves.[58] They have no say against outside actions and events and are unable to affect them. Humanity is contingent on what makes it exists and what sustains its existence. Humanity, in other words, is restricted in the world. In this fact, humans are very unlike God. God, however, makes himself like humans in the person of the Messiah. Despite being self-existent, God wills to be moved, for instance,

53. Isa 29:15; cf. 37:28.

54. Isa 34:1.

55. Isa 30:23a; 33:6.

56. Isa 30:18; cf. 31:1.

57. Isa 37:16, 22b.

58. Isa 36:16–17; cf. 37:38.

in response to Hezekiah's petition and Sennacherib's insults.[59] What is outside of God, nonetheless, has no bearing or potentiality in him.[60] God, in his choosing, becomes very human. Such humanness is the undeniable evidence of divine movement. The very human in God is in union with the very divine in God. It is from this standpoint where we have to see God as One who sustains humankind. The Sustainer can fully relate with the sustained. The prophet confirms:

> Although the LORD has given you bread of privation and water of oppression, *He*, your Teacher, will no longer hide Himself, but your eyes will behold your Teacher.[61]

God, as a Teacher, fully knows how to develop his people. God is with them—the Immanuel. God knows how to be in need, how to suffer as a human. This makes God a reliable and sincere Teacher. God does not need to suffer to gain knowledge; he suffers because people need to know. Given the covenant, such knowledge is irresistible. God *knows* their need as the people know it. As covenant members, we are drawn to value God's empathy with us as we suffer. We are drawn to see that God knows what it is like to be in need as we experience it, hence the phrase "behold your Teacher." God truly experienced it all in Jesus Christ. In him, we are assured that God altogether understands us and, significantly, supplies our needs.

In Jesus Christ, we have witnessed in the NT that people were healed, fed, cared for, and protected. In Jesus, we have seen that the most vulnerable—the downtrodden socially and the destitute materially—are cared for. In Christ, we have been convinced of God's assistance in the struggle for acceptance and survival. We are the object of God's provision. Whenever we are in need, there will always be divine providence. Divine providence is earnest and enduring, for the Son of God is the Son of Man.

When humanity is moved, such movement is constant, as humanity is always dependent on God for its existence. No human should be self-flattered, like Sennacherib, for God is constantly active to strike the proud.[62] No human should be self-appeased, like Hezekiah. God is

---

59. Isa 37:5–7, 21.

60. Isa 37:26.

61. Isa 30:20 NASB; italics in original.

62. Isa 37:29.

constantly active to correct the wrong.[63] There is no escaping the fact that God consistently and positively affects humanity.[64] He moves people in the direction he has foreordained. It is clear in the prophet's mind: God constantly moves Israel—that is, Israel is continuously shaped according to the grand design.[65] God, in unrelenting and astonishing comportment, fashions the people for stability and prosperity.

If God moves the constellations, asteroids, comets, planets in the solar system, especially the things in the world, then how much more with us! If he is behind the wonders of the universe, it does not make sense to say that he has little, let alone nothing, to do with human affairs. If God is moving everything that exists, logically speaking, God is also moving people. Why do some revolt against the idea that God is moving their lives? What is proposed here is not akin to Voltaire's deistic conception of a supreme being, but rather, it is very similar to David Bentley Hart's stance. Hart accepts that there are "innumerable forms of 'secondary causality,'" nevertheless, "none of these can exceed or escape the one end toward which the first cause directs all things"—the personal God.[66] In other words, God administers the actions and events in the world precisely because he directs, in a way, every human thought and deed. To nail this point, Hart adds that "all causes are logically reducible to their first cause. It is no more than a logical truism."[67]

It is refreshing to learn that Hart and other philosophical theologians can see the logical truism of the constant movement of the mighty Sustainer, and such movement is positive in the grand scheme of things.[68] On the flip side, it is sad to see others, in the other camp of the argument, ignore or simply take it as ridiculous—for example, Augustine's insistence on the undirected choice of human beings. For him, although predestination rests on foreknowledge, still, it does not allow determinism.[69] Of course, this should be viewed in the critique of Cicero's readiness to deny divine omnipotence for the sake of human freedom. Yet I doubt if Augustine anticipated very well the repercussion of his theological

63. Isa 39:5–7.

64. Isa 39:8a.

65. In Isa 29, God is pictured as a diligent Potter.

66. Hart, *That All Shall Be Saved*, 69.

67. Hart, *That All Shall Be Saved*, 70.

68. For example, Sergius Bulgakov (*The Comforter*, xv, 2) and Hans Urs von Balthasar (*Dramatis Personae*, 41).

69. See Augustine, *De Libero Arbitrio*, III, ii–iv.

position. I refute any effort to undermine the essentiality of God. However-er, I do not set the tone for determinism but *supervision*. In determinism, we are looked upon mechanically; albeit, in supervision, we are regarded as covenant members. We are deprived of freedom of choice in the for-mer, whereas, in the latter, we indulge in it. In the covenant, we exercise genuine freedom in choosing the Partner.[70]

In the covenant paradigm, any mechanistic expression is shunned, denying the conundrum Augustine avoided; nonetheless, what is ad-vanced here is dissimilar to Augustine's God. The covenantal deity does not shy away from taking the *liability* of and so the *responsibility* for human decisions and actions. The covenant Partner rejoices in the free choice of humanity; however, he is not merely a co-signer in the agree-ment. The Partner is the Composer and Executor of the covenant. In be-ing so, he disallows the covenant to be broken by giving *naked freedom* to humanity; with it, covenant members will inevitably become covenant breakers. This explains why God supervises people to ensure the eternali-ty of the covenant. Such supervision coheres with the Anselmian concept of freedom. It is human and divine, and between them as the covenant Partner is Jesus Christ.[71]

The covenantal theme is vital in acknowledging and accepting God's unrelenting direction of human affairs. The cooperation of willing indi-viduals is essential. Humanity, however, has an innate distaste for any suggestion of being directed by another entity. The skeptics' revolt, pre-sumably, stems from self-centeredness. It is not a rail against the notion of control *per se*. It is because I presume, of what humans aspire or are absorbed with, as follows: first, humanity wants control; second, human-ity enjoys the idea that it is the master of life; and last, humanity gives so much potency to what it can do.[72]

We want to be in control of our affairs. We desire to have absolute control—an attitude that misdirects people. In seeking self-control, people end up self-destroyed, like Sennacherib. Humanity wants control of life. People are afraid of things they cannot control, as seen in Heze-kiah's political alliance with Egypt and Babylon.[73] The implication here is that people desire independence from God. People want to themselves,

70. Barth, *CD* II/2, 525.

71. See Anselm, *De Libertate Arbitrii*, III, iii–v.

72. Isa 36:4–20.

73. Isa 36:6; 39:2.

not God, to be in full control. That is why it is crucial to emphasize full reliance on God. Israel can rely only on God, no one else. God exposes Egypt, restraints Assyria, and shames Israel.[74]

If God is the One who sets the parameters concerning a person's birth (the date, place, parents, etc.) and, to a greater extent, death (the date, place, cause, etc.), then why not have God set all the circumstances in between? Humanity shies away from the idea that God controls everything that engages human beings. But when it comes to catastrophic events wrought by nature such as earthquakes, hurricanes, pandemics, or future events such as the possible extinction of the human race, we have little resistance in accepting that it is most likely God's act.

Furthermore, we toy with the idea that we are the sole managers of our lives, and we completely direct our lives. This discloses our wish to be master in life and of it. Doing so indirectly suggests that God is made after our image and likeness, as Sennacherib had thought.[75] This made-up god is undeniably an idol, a counterfeit deity—unable to provide, incapable to protect.[76] What humans envisioned does not make up the true reality of humanity. The deity of the Bible is the fully hands-on deity who makes things happen to accomplish his purpose and, likewise, who does not make things happen for humans—to frustrate their purpose, most likely, in eschatological perspective, to be detrimental to them.[77] Whatever God had revealed through Isaiah, it shall come to pass. God neither forgets nor abandons his promise to Israel. God is committed to the covenant.[78] True enough, God eventually shielded Jerusalem as he declared war against Assyria.[79] God is the only Master in this world, hence the master Planner.

Humans, regrettably, put a premium on what they can do, to the point of undermining, in the process, what God can do. Humanity renders its potency, usually, at the expense of the almightiness of God. We render so much potency to humanity, even to the enemy (Satan), especially in the end-time. Eventually, however, the destroyer is destroyed, and the betrayer is betrayed.[80] The potency not subject to any kind of

---

74. God is the Revealer of things to come, as is evident in Isa 30.

75. Isa 36:18, 20b.

76. Isa 36:19.

77. Isa 37:33–35.

78. Isaiah 31 shows that God is the Upholder of the covenant with Israel.

79. Isa 37:6–7.

80. Isa 33:1.

interruption or disruption is the providing hand of the Sustainer. Case in point: about a century after Hezekiah's death, Babylon returned to ransack Jerusalem of her riches—exactly what Isaiah predicted.[81]

This study is adamant in highlighting the unrelenting hand of the Sustaining God. Human dexterity proves nothing except self-attrition. Unless humankind acknowledges its nescience and impotence, it has no future. God holds the future. God directs what contributes to it—the *hic et nunc* of reality. God is in full control of the affairs of nations,[82] individual successes and failures,[83] protection of the righteous,[84] punishment of the wicked,[85] and intervention in nature.[86] Bringing the variables together purports that God is a refuge for the dependent but a threat to the self-sufficient.[87]

Our ups and downs are in the hand of God. There is no such thing as coincidence. Yes you heard me right! A perceived coincidence, in light of the doctrine of God, is actually providence. Nothing happens by coincidence; everything that happens is *providential*. I suggest that Hezekiah's terminal disease is not by accident, but rather, God planned it. That is why God can also heal Hezekiah, and God did.[88]

The safeguard of the righteous, and their human rights, are in the hand of God. It is God alone who sincerely, thus continuously, defends the innocent. But, when it is said that God protects the righteous, it does not convey that the dead are unrighteous. Our perspective is very limited compared to God's. God is altogether just and righteous in everything he does. In the divine act, God remains the all-interested, all-concerned Sustainer. Our daily affairs are very important to the Sustainer. God takes care of every human need, and he takes away every human worry.

The retribution against the wicked is in the hand of God; God will put an end to the arrogant who think to have mastered life. No one masters life except the Sustaining God. If we are really in control of this world, then why is it that we cannot control the forces of nature? Or even

---

81. King Hezekiah died c. 687 BCE; Babylon destroyed Jerusalem c. 587 BCE.

82. Isa 34:1–2; Job 12:23; Rom 13:1.

83. Isa 32:5; 35:3; Ps 33:13–15; Rom 9:10–12.

84. Isa 34:17; Ps 121:7–8; Rom 8:28.

85. Isa 35:4; Ps 12:3–4; 2 Pet 2:9.

86. In Isaiah 32, God is portrayed as the Protector of the unprotected.

87. Isa 33:2, 7; Ps 12:3–4; 2 Pet 2:9.

88. In Isa 38, God is the Healer.

microscopic menaces like the coronavirus? To assume otherwise is to give credence to human indiscretion.

More specifically, intervention in nature is exclusive to the divine department. What is not apparent in the treatment of miracles is that God does not distort the law of nature but "inserts a new category" into it—to enhance it, not diminish it.[89] In so doing, God is not only Immanuel, but he is King Immanuel. God works wonders amid chaos; he continues his story with us, having insight on a blessed end. What is out of our hands is in the hand of God. What we can control is under the discretion of the Sustainer.

It is nonsensical to presuppose that because of free will, humanity is exempt from divine supervision. I do not think that the free will argument is sustainable: God fully directs everything in the universe except human beings. The argument puts a lot of premium on the *being* of humanity, something very dependent and fluctuating. This is evidenced in Hezekiah. In witnessing how the LORD God miraculously defended Jerusalem, Hezekiah still relied on the imperial overlord for security. But such instability in conviction was exemplified about more than three millennia earlier—in the garden of Eden. To adequately revisit the first exhibit of human moral fluctuation, we have to review the dialectical function of darkness, discussed in the previous chapter, because it will amplify the position: God uses evil for his purpose. However, at this juncture, this will be argued in view of God's consistent grace.

3. THE GRACIOUS GOD

In accomplishing the good, God works with the evils of humanity. He does this neither indiscriminately nor capriciously. It is no easy feat to articulate, yet, it is doable as long as one is ready to uphold that there is no self-existent, self-determined being except the One who sustains Israel—the LORD God. We can see further that divine grace is manifest in unusual forms.

To believe that the darkness (at the start of Genesis) is part of creation is one step to understanding temporal reality. In effect, it would not be problematic to suppose that God created the tree of knowledge. When the Bible states that everything God had created was very good, it

89. Here I stand with John Lennox. See Dawkins and Lennox, "God Delusion Debate," video 1:35:28.

includes this tree. The Creator of light and darkness is also the Creator of the knowledge of good and evil.[90] If it is contended that God is *not* the source of evil-and-good, then it suggests that the tree's entity is independent of God's entity; but it is not. The sort of knowledge a human can have from the tree is not two, but one, one but in diastasis: good *and* evil, hence I call it the *twin knowledge*. Such knowledge is not to be confused with merism (the totality of knowledge) or practical knowledge because of its determined purpose.[91]

The twin knowledge, theologically speaking, cannot exist outside of God's will.[92] What is not apparent is whether God wills for humanity to have that knowledge. There must be a further step to exposit what appears contradictory: the creation of the twin knowledge and the prohibition to eat the fruit of knowledge. Here, the creation narratives are taken as revelation history and not merely as "stories" as Eleonore Stump presupposes.[93] The objective here is to highlight the gracious sustenance.

The advancement of consistency of the goodness in and of God is fundamental in rendering the twin knowledge. As the knowledge emerging from the tree is in tandem, thus the good comes *with* the evil.[94] It is of great interest to note that, in the beginning, Adam and Eve did not possess that good (with evil) knowledge. If they are "very good" irrespective of the good from the forbidden tree, this implies that the tree's goodness is excluded from the original state of human beings—maybe because of the evil conjoined with it. Nonetheless, it has to be qualified that the fruit is not intrinsically bad, since God created the tree.[95] It does not also mean that evil exists *in se*; its reality is not without the good.

The compassion and benevolence of God is righteousness.[96] God is conceived to be the bedrock of what is right, therefore, altogether good. It poses a challenge to speak ethics into society in ways that are truly believable and comforting, although much of Western society has moved far from an awareness of God. The idea of what is right, in a rigid sense,

---

90. Isa 45:7. For discussion on God creating the darkness, see de Vera, "God of the Covenant," §6.1.

91. Cf. Allen, *Thinking about Good and Evil*, 9.

92. Gen 2:9c.

93. Stump, *Wandering in Darkness*, 37.

94. Gen 2:17a.

95. Matt 7:17–18.

96. Exod 34:6.

is not quite clear due to the disconnect between the Creator and the crea-ture.[97] This conception has to be interjected in the talk of the evil-with-the-good in the fruit.

Adam and Eve were created very good (viz. in beauty) but *not* per-fect (viz. in character).[98] There is no scriptural proof that they were cre-ated perfect. This announces God's intent for them: to be "on the way" to greater and deeper humanity. This formulation is not alien in church history, as Irenaeus's idea of progression from a starting point called an "infantile" stage "ascending towards the perfect" is akin to the Eastern Orthodox view of "undeveloped simplicity" towards growth or maturity.[99] Although such references take the eating as a fall, these, however, postu-late an *upward falling*. Yes, the disobedience in Eden is a serious offense; however, the created world still "possesses continuity" given foreordina-tion. God continually upholds things that exist through reformation and regeneration.[100]

What the above reveals is the "unbreakable unity" of the divine operation in creation and redemption.[101] Creation is for Christ, through Christ, and unto Christ. The anthropogonic instinct is in play in the twin knowledge if it is approached Christocentrically.[102] In Jesus, the tendency is to see things from the future backwards rather than just past forwards. Thus, this study proposes that God foreordained the eating of the forbid-den fruit. Although the demise of the first couple was the outcome of disobedience (in aspiring to be *like* God), the twin knowledge was per-tinent to death.[103] Death was necessary for eternal life via Jesus Christ to take effect. Irenaeus is right in saying that the prohibition in Eden is "not the exertion of God's authority, but his dedication to the perfection of his handiwork."[104] In this case, the disobedience of the first couple became the catalyst to what they ought to experience—death—and to what they ought to be—perfect.[105]

97. See Kierkegaard, *Training in Christianity*, 139–40.

98. Gen 1:31. The Hebrew *ṭôwḇ meʾōḏ* (טוֹב מְאֹד) means "greatly pleasant" or "ex-ceedingly agreeable to the sight" (*SECB*, h2896, h3966).

99. Irenaeus of Lyons, *Adversus haereses* 4.38.1–3; Ware, *Orthodox Church*, 223.

100. Berkouwer, *Studies in Dogmatics*, 63.

101. Berkouwer, *Studies in Dogmatics*, 57.

102. Rom 11:36.

103. Sherlock, *Doctrine of Humanity*, 233–34.

104. Irenaeus, *Ad Autolycum* 5.20.2; *Epideixis* 15.

105. Cf. Wingren, *Man and the Incarnation*, 20.

I am convinced of the pre-human provision of essential things before God created human beings.[106] What is not convincing is that though humans bear God's image and likeness, they still would voluntarily, somewhat instinctively, go against God—the source of their humanhood.[107] It betrays the suspicion that there was a "glitch" in the creation itself or the created order.[108] To believe this would distort the entire theological landscape beautifully set on divine precision and majesty. I will explain it later; for now, let us attend to what the first couple had lacked in Eden.

If it is true that Adam and Eve were imperfect, then what would it take to make them perfect, for example, like Abraham and Job?[109] Here the answer lies in what the two patriarchs had, which the first couple did not have, before eating the fruit: *suffering*.[110] The patriarchs were made perfect through suffering—something the couple was unaware of. Adam and Eve had to possess good knowledge (perfection), yet it is tied to evil knowledge (suffering). It is contended here that perfection was foreordained for them; nevertheless, there was no other way to accomplish it without suffering.

How can Adam and Eve suffer if they remain in paradise? It is logical to presume that only by eating the fruit that suffering entered the created reality; however, suffering would be the path to perfection.[111] Something good comes out of the fatal act in Eden. Indeed, death came through the first Adam, for humans to be alive in the last Adam.[112] The last Adam (Jesus Christ) is the "quickening spirit" because through him human beings are reinvigorated physically and spiritually.[113] The paradoxical realities between Adam and Jesus are forthright.[114] Sin became the default reality by Adam's act, whereas righteousness reigns over sin by Jesus's act.

---

106. Gen 1:1–25.

107. Sherlock, *Doctrine of Humanity*, 234–38.

108. Wright, *Surprised by Scripture*, 20.

109. Gen 17:1; Job 1:1. Noah is also "blameless" or "perfect." See Gen 6:9.

110. In Jewish interpretation, this knowledge is not moral (in its absolute sense) but rather the ability to judge between good and bad (Friedman, *Commentary on the Torah*, 7). In contrast, according to David Kimhi, this is a piece of esoteric knowledge (Kimhi, as cited in Friedman, *Commentary on the Torah*, Gen 2:17, n.p.).

111. 1 Cor 15:21–22.

112. 1 Cor 15:45.

113. The quickening spirit or life-giving spirit is derived from the Greek *zōopoieō* (ζωοποιέω), literally "to empower with divine life" (*SECB*, g2227).

114. Rom 5:19.

Being made righteous means being set/appointed upright or faultless.[115] The apostle Paul continues, "[So] also grace would reign through righteousness to eternal life through Jesus Christ our Lord."[116] The optimistic reality of human beings, therefore, is beyond the Western-traditional concept of the fall. The above shows the interplay of being made alive and righteous vis-à-vis perfection. That is why perfection springs up *only* through Christ's intervention.

The evil knowledge is not the *privatio boni* (the corruption of good) as taught in Christendom.[117] In suffering, Adam and Eve will *know* that perfection is something God accredits to a believer (like Abraham). Moreover, in suffering, they will *know* reverence in God—it is amid suffering where commitment to God is demonstrated (like Job). In the treatment of providence, perfection is God's way, and suffering is God's means. The introduction of suffering to the equation does not contradict the character of God, as the act reflects the being. On the contrary, it is through suffering that the righteousness of God is elucidated.

In other words, the seeming glitch in creation is that which is bad brings about good. Correspondingly, there was no glitch insofar as divine appropriation of human causality is taken into perspective. If the human free choice is insisted in the talk of evil in a non-defective creation, I urge that its potency is *the* glitch, not in the created system but in the theodical conversation.

3.1 The Gracious yet Abstruse Sustenance

It is within the doctrine of God where we can better grasp why Adam and Eve were deemed *imperfect*. This study emphasized God's non-contingency to time, self-existence, self-determination, immutability, and impassibility. All these attributes speak of aseity. Aseity is exclusive to the LORD God; only the LORD God is aseitic *tous et tout*. In contrast, the created is non-aseitic. By default, Adam and Eve are contingent on their surroundings, which includes the tree of knowledge. For them, it is therefore very likely that they would be moved by the captivating pleasantness

---

115. The Greek *díkaios* (δίκαιος) means "correct" or "just in the eyes of God" (*SECB*, g1342).

116. Rom 5:21 NASB.

117. See Methodius, *De resurrectione*, part 3, and Ep. Diognetus, ch. 12.

of the fruit and the cunning enticement of the serpent because they are *not* God. As a result, the human will becomes in bondage to sin.[118]

As highlighted at the start of this chapter, God is the foundation of life: God sustains, develops, stabilizes, and prospers life, not otherwise. This explains God's command for Adam and Eve to not eat the fruit of knowledge. On the one hand, God created the tree of knowledge even though he knew that the two would *surely* eat its fruit vis-à-vis their non-aseity, and in effect, death is inevitable. On the other hand, God also knew that that was the only way for them to suffer and *be perfect*. This does not suggest a limit in the ways and means of God. The recourse to suffering is not merely to achieve perfection but also to point to the prototype of perfection—Jesus Christ. Concomitantly, suffering does not perfect Christ, not at all. That which is eternally perfect lacks nothing. By suffering, Christ can be properly understood as the covenant Partner. Armed with these dynamics, one can infer that the only way is the best.

God's compassion is exhibited in the order of things. It has to be pronounced that death is something not willed by God. God is not evil; hence, his ways and means are not evil as well. Why would God put something altogether evil before his presence in the garden *temple*? True, the demise of Adam and Eve is undeniable; but we cannot read explicitly in the Bible any rage or disappointment in God in reaction to the eating of the fruit.[119] What we can read instead is God's unwavering goodness exercised after the eating.[120] It is in this framework where we can critique the concept of the fall. God forbids the death of Adam and Eve, yet he does not hinder their perfection—through death. It is in this framework where the notion of the gracious yet abstruse providence is properly articulated.

Notice that the terminology "the fall" is bypassed in light of the gracious yet abstruse providence. I wish to problematize the thoroughly entrenched Augustinian classification of this particular account. Even if the usual pathway to communicate the Christian truth is followed, namely, from creation to redemption, the suggested framework breaks with the Western tradition. The restructuring of the fall, in a way, is Hegelian in spirit but not in letter. G. W. F. Hegel sees the fall as a condition of

118. Luther, *Bondage of the Will*, 70–73, 236–37.

119. God had cursed the serpent and the ground, not Adam and Eve. See Gen 3:14, 17.

120. Gen 3:21.

humanity in relation to God, thus he calls it "disunion."[121] This gives the idea of freedom renewed traction by exemplifying the responsibility of Adam and Eve as moral agents. In this case, Hegel employs the "philosophical mind" by focusing on the underlying concept of disobedience in Eden in order to give this religious truth its conceptual form. Such an approach is a reflexive turn from extrapolating the truth from the imagery or representation of eating conceived by the "religious mind."[122] The problematizing at hand is a by-product of the philosophical mind; nonetheless, the said alienation is not accidental but providential. Moreover, the moral agency of the first couple is not independent of foreordination. In other words, the formulation concerning the eating as disclosing the dialectical quality of divine operation is a Hegelian feature; however, the force of the language of disunion is inapplicable to the progression of thought promoted here. In disobedience, the first couple was not withdrawn from God but rather drawn to where God plans them to be.

Although Barth and I share that it is within the master plan for the first couple to eat the forbidden fruit, Barth however maintains "the fall of man."[123] Augustine of Hippo, with all good intentions, injected into the scenario a creaturely choice less than the good; such a choice needs liberation.[124] However, the Enlightenment sense of neutral options is the version that is funneled through dogmatic statements, resulting in the catastrophic elevation of human choice at the expense of divine sovereignty. It is a fault in the revisionist etiology of evil that initiates massive tremors in the doctrines of God and humanity. We should review Augustine's thoughts on the matter. It was out of his hindsight to reduce divine sovereignty. His exposition of human freedom is not absent of the overwhelming weight of foreordination and, critically, of original sin (the universal human bias towards doing what is wrong).[125] How can people have *freedom of choice* when marred by original sin, and the exercise of such choice is under the function of foreordination? We have to traverse carefully between divine will and human accountability; if not, the distinction between them is either blurred or neglected.

121. Hegel, *Logic of Hegel*, 50.

122. King, "Task of Systematic Theology," 16.

123. Barth, excursus in *CD* II/2, 165–66.

124. See Augustine, *De Libero Arbitrio*, III, ii–iv.

125. Augustine, *Contra Julianum*, V, 4.18.

The challenge is not visceral but highly logical, which hopefully opens new theological trajectories or offers salient areas of convergence vis-à-vis human will and divine will, also regarding the impeccability of the creation and the inherent "evil" in the forbidden fruit. All the said variables are encapsulated (as testified in Scripture) in the twin knowledge. Dialectically speaking, far from being an oxymoron, the evil is the no that serves the yes. In a way, God uses the good-and-evil to perfect the first couple and their offspring. This rendition is at variance with John Hick's "soul-making defense."[126] I say with Hick that suffering enables moral and spiritual development.[127] However, I digress as he goes deep. What we disagree about is the human incapability of virtue *sans* suffering—somewhat compatible with Stoicism. The first couple's "very good" status is synonymous with virtuousness; however, it is imperfect *with* Jesus of Nazareth. This facet is missing in Hick's defense because of his mythological approach to the creation story. Hicks looks at the eating of the fruit through the Origenean lens, while I look at it through the Irenaean lens.[128] The eating is not a "relatively minor lapse" but a strange yet copious act deserving critical appropriation.[129] Despite correlating the perfection process with suffering, our seminal postulations are in two pots, so our philo-theological yields are different.

Concerning the Irenaean corpus, I do not overplay the non-aseity proposition or the creation theorem for evil. However, I underline the imperfect status of the primordial humans upon creation and the exquisiteness of creation itself.[130] There is an argument to be made here from P. T. Forsyth: "The true end is the completion of that schooling of the soul, will, and person which earthly life divinely means, and for which God's side is constant new creation and its joy. It is perfect and active union with God's active Will, the barter of its love, and its secure intercommunion."[131] The premise in Forsyth's assertion is what has been reiterated all along—that is, perfection is *at the end*, not at the beginning. Nonetheless, in balancing this point, I likewise have to stress often the *reality* of suffering.

126. The phrase "the vale of Soul-making" was coined by the poet John Keats (Rollins, *Letters of John Keats*, 102–3).

127. Hick, *Evil and God of Love*, 253–61.

128. See Scott, "Suffering and Soul-Making," 314.

129. Hick, "Irenaean Theodicy," xviii.

130. See Irenaeus, *On the Apostolic Teaching*, ch. 17.

131. Forsyth, *Justification of God*, 74.

Suffering has binary effects: it brings out the best in some people and the worst in others. Critics, however, opine that suffering destroys more than it builds. This is especially true in the case of the victims of social injustice, such as the Nazi extermination of the Jews.[132] This animates the Rothian theodicy (or more accurately antitheodicy), as the myopic focus is on the horror of suffering. That is distinct but not entirely at odds with the Irenaean theodicy hinging on the ontology of suffering.[133] No doubt, the extent and magnitude of human suffering are horrific. However, they would stay horrific if not viewed against God's self-determined passibility.[134] God suffered first, and God suffered much by devoting himself to humanity. The primordial and unparalleled suffering is not applicable celestially, but it is applied *here and now*. The Son of God suffered by simultaneously becoming the Son of Man for us not to suffer forever. In Jesus Christ, humanity is assured of the divine real-time action; thus, misery does not have the final say at the eschaton but felicity.

But one might contend: is it not true that the "evil" knowledge is the critical mass exploded into disproportional malevolence in the world? It is true, but not without meaning and purpose. The theological oscillation of suffering set up between destroying and building must be in light of the one-fruit-dual-knowledge analogy: evil knowledge is *inseparable* from good knowledge. The disproportional evil is not, in actuality, as such, if it is viewed against good. As the evil explodes, it goes with the bursting of goodness across the globe. Logically speaking, it cannot be presupposed, too, that such bursting overshadows evil due to the one-fruit-dual-knowledge. What can be presumed is the abundant grace of the Messiah over the "horrendous evils" in world reality:[135]

> Therefore the LORD longs to be gracious to you, and therefore He waits on high to have compassion on you. For the LORD is a God of *justice*; how blessed are all those who long for Him.[136]

---

132. Davis, *Encountering Evil*, 62.

133. See Roth, "Theodicy of Protest," 4; cf. Irenaeus, *Adversus omnes Haereses*, xxxi.2.4.

134. de Vera, *Suffering of God*, 82.

135. Adams, *Horrendous Evils and Goodness*, 26.

136. Isa 30:18 NASB; italics added.

God's benevolence is shown in his justice.[137] It is in humanity's disruptive change that the *disruptive grace* of God takes place.[138] In Jesus Christ, therefore, the life-ruining potential of suffering is turned into a life-restoring agent. The conventional take on the evil of suffering is reconfigured given the self-sacrifice of God. In this regard, I stand with Parry when he construes, "It is not enough to show the horrendous evils experienced by some can bring benefits to the world *as a whole* or certain other individuals in it . . . . It is hard to think how God could be said to love a person he allows to be *irreparably* harmed for the good of some third party."[139] It is nonsensical to claim that God wills the eating of the fruit of knowledge simply for humans to achieve perfection without the defeat of evil and the end of suffering. God supervises human affairs *by* managing individual lives. It is through this spectrum where God, argues Parry, is said to be loving all.[140]

As the reader will see, God indeed loves all by sustaining all like a teacher and a physician. In reforming humans, God acted as the Teacher, and in regenerating humans, God acted as the Physician. This articulation coheres with Origen's notion of *medicus animarum nostrarum* (the physician of our souls). When the Teacher aims to instill a lesson (gracious), he sometimes employs a rod (abstruse). Likewise, when the Physician aims to heal (gracious), he sometimes prescribes "very unpleasant and bitter medicine" (abstruse).[141] However, I still keep a safe distance from Origen due to his tendency for eccentric theology. He tends to allegorize biblical accounts, making them esoteric in substance and tacit in spirit.

I am not rejecting the high contemplativeness of the divine approach to things. I reject that only the *spiritually advanced* enjoy "the lesson" or "the medicine."[142] The universal and equal dispensation of grace is the logical corollary of the doctrine of God as rendered here. There is neither bias nor prejudice in foreordination. The One who had been antecedently foreordained is Jesus Christ. He, in a sense, foreshadows God's embrace of all peoples. It is also true that some of Origen's thoughts, especially the Teacher and Physician metaphor, anticipate the kind of theodicy

137. Deut 32:4; Ps 10:14–18.

138. Brueggemann, *Disruptive Grace*, 3.

139. Parry, *Evangelical Universalist*, 161. Robin Parry here reacts to Marilyn Adams's discourse on the horror of evil in the face of a God who upholds human value.

140. Parry, *Evangelical Universalist*, 161.

141. Origen, *De Principiis*, 2.10.6.

142. Origen, *De Principiis*, 2.10.8.

expounded in the study. What is untrue is that neither Origen nor Irenaeus shaped the arguments here, but rather Barth over the rigid employment of the covenantal motif to the discourse,[143] not so much with theodicy but in the divine outworking in and through human beings. However, I also admit that the Hickian, Irenaean, and the Origenean formulations on human perfection are inextricably linked with what has been advanced thus far. These ideas append to the discussion on the vitality and dynamism of the divine ways and means.

The soul-perfecting theodicy does not sit well with other prominent theologians and philosophers.[144] The argumentation is too close to making God the author of evil. What is put forward hitherto is divine supervision (not divine puppetry) in handling the problem of sin. If the doctrine of providence is situated *inside* the doctrine of God, the outcome is not problematic. When the subject (God) sustains, the object (humankind) is developed, stabilized, and prospered; it is quite implausible to think the contrary. While God is not the author of evil, he is the composer of the twin knowledge. The stereotyping of evil wholesale is a caveat in expositing the sovereignty of God; clarity and coherence are non-negotiable in the ethos and pathos of theodicy. In considering the divine will with human accountability, the distinction between them is clarified and harmonized. Uncompromising acumen is basic in navigating through the seeming dead end just cited; it is punctuated in the subsequent argumentation.

God knows exactly what occurs in human affairs because he is hands on in it from beginning to end. Foreordination tells us that God is in full control of world affairs, macro and micro. He macromanages world events; he micromanages individual events in his way and by his means. To solidify the logic behind the impeccability of creation itself (the absence of glitch in the created system), we have to treat it in conjunction with providence: God's way is the reservoir of good, and God's means are necessary and beneficial. The former accentuates divine supervision *in* human choice while the latter accentuates divine operation *in* nature.

As the wonderful Sustainer, God supervises our affairs with the employment of our choices. This is observable in stirring up national activity by way of stirring up individual activities. This type of supervision validates that there is no supreme authority alongside God or besides

143. Barth, *CD* II/2, §33.
144. Sanders, "Freewill Theist's Response," 185–86; Oord, *God Can't*, 183–84.

God. But how does foreordination work given our participation? We can hold this tension in logical terms with the principle of compatibility.

The principle of compatibility is the idea that whatever is humanly decided or acted coheres with God's intent. Without awareness, people decide in line with God's will; people act in fulfillment of God's purpose. For example, we vote on a candidate for a specific leadership position, as if it is within our choice that that leader is in power. Yet, insofar as the Bible is concerned, God installs a prime minister or a president.[145] God governs the vital circumstances, things that matter, within the non-static master plan in God's willing. Human freedom, amazingly, is included in this paradigm; humans *freely decide*, humans *freely act*; regardless, the outcome is still within the real-time willing of God. How? Scripture shows that it is God who fashions the "heart."[146] He moves every person from his heavenly throne; he directs each individual's trajectory. This has nothing to do with the Schopenhaurian conception of "the will," an irrational force taking hold of people, since the overarching will is God's.[147] We are to reconfigure our understanding of the master plan: foreordination includes human agency. To do this, we have to stop giving privilege to human choice. There is no such thing as *naked freedom* in and with humanity, so libertarian free will is philo-theologically unviable.[148] To reappraise human freedom is to orientate oneself more towards favoring God's willing—a position, to a great extent, Hart shares. He posits: "Insofar as we are able freely to will anything at all, therefore, it is because he [i.e., God] is *making* us to do so."[149] This resonates with the ethical reflection engaged with the being-in-act of God.

I acknowledge the impasse in the debate on God's will and human will, yet I suppose I can contribute to the ongoing conversation in light of Isaiah. For instance, Sennacherib meant to devastate Jerusalem, but God meant to correct this city. Sennacherib employed his army, position, and coercion to achieve his plan. Conversely, God applied his power, disposition, and patience to accomplish his will. The two are unique paths with distinct teloses, but they are not separated. The method of God overturns

145. Rom 13:1–2.

146. Isa 32:4; Ps 33:15.

147. Schopenhauer, *Essays and Aphorisms*, 23.

148. For counter-arguments on the worries about libertarian free will, see Sullivan, "Problems for Temporary Existence in Tense Logic," 44–47.

149. Hart, *That All Shall Be Saved*, 183; italics in original.

what the Assyrian king had aimed for—and it did. The king succumbed to the will of the King of kings.

What Sennacherib had meant for evil, God meant for good. In the seizing of Jerusalem, this city had learned to humble herself before God. It was Sennacherib's contempt that brought the Jews to fear and panic. Nevertheless, it was God's concern that brought the Jews to faith and peace. This shows how God accomplishes his will without violating the human will. The latter capitulates to the former. We use currency, technology, and intelligence, whereas God uses economy, circumstances, and prescience. In other words, humans utilize things they can control, whereas God utilizes everything, for example, weather, pandemic, microbes, angels, and others, to his disposal.

However, how it works daily is quite difficult to figure out. The impossible to the beneficiary is possible to the Benefactor. This proves that God's way is indeed deep and wide, akin to a reservoir, and it also gives weight to the wonderfulness of divine counsel and the greatness of divine wisdom. It is within this mindset where the foundation of Israel is to be reviewed. In it, explains Barth, the foundation is "God's free mercy."[150] But such mercy does not connote ease or transparency but, instead, disturbance and unintelligibility, because, Barth continues, "The stone [God] becomes for it [Israel] an occasion of stumbling block and offense. Israel is necessarily destroyed by its sure salvation."[151] Unless God clarifies his strange approach to human beings, theodical contentions keep resurfacing. The truth is, God did clarify his outworking in Jesus of Nazareth. The problem is, more often than not, dissenters look elsewhere. A hypothesis can never be wrong or insufficient if it is situated Christocentrically.

Jesus Christ is not only *of* Nazareth, confined thus to this location or its culture; rather Jesus has cosmic relevance as the Messiah. On a macro-level, God makes nations great and God destroys great nations. He is very hands on in national affairs and international affairs. In Isaiah, Assyria, an imperial power, had been demolished; and Sennacherib, an emperor, had been deposed.[152] Moreover, Judah, an insignificant kingdom, had been

---

150. Barth, *CD* II/2, 242. Barth refers to Isa 28:16.

151. Barth, *CD* II/2, 242.

152. Isa 37:36–38.

spared; and Hezekiah, an ordinary king, had been preserved.[153] Time and again, the trustworthiness of God is underpinned.[154]

In being the great Sustainer, God provides through nature also; God uses the natural law to govern within the created reality. It is his pleasure to work with nature, hence to use, but not exclusively, natural *means*. In the divine providence, God wills to operate through natural incidents. Let us reconsider the healing of Hezekiah to cement the point. The prophet instructed Hezekiah to put "mashed figs" on his open sore.[155] Case in point: God could have miraculously healed Hezekiah by instructing the prophet to touch him or by some other extraordinary channel or technique. Rather, God used natural means to heal Hezekiah. The question thus emerges: why was the slaughter of Sennacherib's army not done through natural means? I propose the answer is located in divine essentiality—absolute autonomy. As God dictates the course of life itself, God's means cannot be strictly confined to natural means *only*.

On a micro-level, God is fully hands on in individual affairs. What is conceived as personal, in our standpoint, does not invalidate divine involvement. What is personal is *also* the Lord's business. Of course, since foreordination includes our agency, this means to say that God does not manipulate the details; God brings about things in a manner beyond the mortal mind, yet still concordant to his character. Thus, there are no straightforward explanations. What is substantive in this discussion is the outcome: God has the final say in our endeavors. One might curiously inquire: how is it so? I think the how question is a non-question in this reflection. What is relevant is to ask why? The rationale behind this is axiomatic in the human susceptibility to error and repeated mistakes.

3.2 Divine Supervision and Human Accountability

Adam and Eve conspicuously foreshadow the human race. The Isaianic narratives showcase that there is no confidence in humanity.[156] The non-aseity proposition, of course, does not attenuate the couple's culpability (and it is true as well to all human beings). What should be unattenuated is the role of foreordination in this regard. It must be displayed within the

---

153. Isa 37:33–35.

154. In Isa 36, God is the sure confidence of his people.

155. Isa 38:21.

156. Isa 39:1–4.

boundary of the hands-on model. True confidence is in God, and God is where it is rooted.[157] It is in the temple where people can be confident in God's grace. In the temple, people are far from getting lost.[158] God knows how frail and movable humans are, yet it is in humanness where God provides the most—in Jesus Christ.[159] Indeed, God is truly gracious to all; more importantly, God wills to see that his grace is for all.[160] In effect of grace in decolonization, Israel "will no longer be ashamed and disgraced."[161] In dispensing divine grace, the no (calamity, disaster, and misfortune) serves the yes (development, stability, prosperity).

Given divine providence, crucially, it behooves us in this study to stress that we remain accountable for our behaviors. Although I hold to the idea of the primordial ordering of actions and events, I also advance the notion of divine actuality. That frames the gravity and urgency of prayer: God sustains humanity in the eternal now. To emphasize this does not give room for human diversion from the divine master plan; albeit, humans, still, will stand in the trial in the eschatological judgment.

In such complexity, Proto-Isaiah grants the reader the non-negotiable: the fortitude (out of aseity) of the Sustainer. The fact remains: God made the Assyrian powerful; God made this army powerless. The rise of the Babylonian kingdom is contingent on God, likewise, its fall. What foreordination is not is God's being in view of humankind's act, generally speaking. Foreordination is about God's given *God's act*—specifically, in the person of the Messiah alone. There is simply a gap between being God and being human. Thus, there is also a disconnect between divine act and human act, for instance, the Messiah's leadership contrasting with Hezekiah's leadership. However, such disconnect is not to be taken simplistically. In the gracious providence, there is no hindrance in the sustenance of people.

In the treatment of the provisioned grace, it has been established that the Lord's method of discipline is not a sort that should breed suspicion but instead appreciation.[162] It makes true sense that the source of life is also the Sustainer. The idea of the Sustainer is always married to that

157. Isa 36:4b, 7a.
158. Isa 37:1, 6.
159. Isa 33:16; 37:27.
160. Isa 29:18b; 30:18a.
161. Isa 29:22b CEV.
162. Isa 38:16, 19.

of the foreordaining God. The act in the latter is the prelude for the act in the former. Moreover, the result of the former is predetermined in the latter. It is within this conception that the hands-on model of foreknowledge is fortified.

In the incredible assemblage of materials for the doctrine of God, the anomalies in conceiving of the divine ways and means are addressed; but I admit, the issues inherent in the subject matter, vis-à-vis theodicy, are not entirely resolved. We know very little of what is beneath the tip of the eschato-juridical iceberg. What is ascertained is the overtaking of our deficiency by divine methodology.

The problem adding confusion to the discourse on theodicy is the supposition that in sustaining Israel, God neglects Israel's enemies. It has to be spot on: God prospers Israel, as well as other nations, in fact, all nations. He blessed the Israelites; likewise, he blessed the non-Israelites. God is determined to reconcile all people to himself; God takes care of desolate land to make it into farmland.[163] God will never be arbitrary. He is always equitable in conducting his ways and dispensing his means. The fairness in fulfilling the decree tells about God's character. This gives weight to the impartiality of the eternal covenant as it affirms the integrity of God in it and confirms the legitimacy of human beings within the covenant.

After learning about God's macro- and micromanagement, we can now attend to the comparative study between Isaiah and Revelation concerning sustaining grace.

3.3 Reading Isaiah through Revelation

For the third time, we have to critically analyze Isaiah's testimony with John's vision to affirm the underlying argument in this project—that all peoples will be saved.[164] The prophet predicts,

> And the *ransomed* of the LORD shall *return*, and come to Zion with singing, with everlasting joy on their heads. They shall obtain joy and gladness, and sorrow and sighing shall flee away.[165]

---

163. God is the Restorer as depicted in Isa 35.

164. Isa 35:10; cf. Rev 7:17.

165. Isa 35:10 NKJV; italics added.

The "ransomed" refers to everyone who puts their trust in the LORD God for redemption.[166] The phrase "everyone will see" implies that the ransomed come from different ethnicities with a diverse social background.[167] The factors involved in the reunion of the ransomed are crucial, namely, how the ransomed return to the renewed Zion and the implication of their status.

Textual evidence shows that the ransomed will travel through the "highway of holiness" to their destination.[168] Based on the context, this highway is the "highway from Egypt to Assyria."[169] Even lexical tracing backs the notion, so, there is no escaping the fact that the highway towards Zion passes through Egypt and Assyria.[170] Another facet critical in this analysis is the status of the ransomed, which is somewhat incompatible with the language of holiness vis-à-vis the highway. The prophet makes a strong point: "Whoever walks the road, although a *fool*, shall not go astray."[171] To whom does the word "fool" pertain? As in the earlier exposition, it pertains to humanity in general—to whom aseity is absent, ergo, incapable of fulfilling their promises and unable to maintain confidence in God.

Having this thought as the foreground, with the Isaianic narratives as the background, we can deduce that the ransomed can be sketched, at least, into two categories, namely, their release from bondage (oppressed) and their deliverance from certain ruin (oppressor). Notwithstanding such distinction, both experienced utmost suffering, hence the terms "deserts" and "barren lands."[172] However, the prophet's depiction "deserts will bloom everywhere" signifies the people's grief and groaning will be replaced with exceeding happiness and exaltation because of the Messiah.[173] In specific terms, who are the ransomed? The context suggests

166. The Hebrew for the word *ransom* is *pâdâh* (פָּדָה), meaning "to release" or "to deliver" (*SECB*, h6299).

167. Isa 35:2c CEV.

168. Isa 35:8a NKJV.

169. Isa 19:23a NKJV.

170. In Isa 35:8a, the Hebrew *maçlûl* (מַסְלוּל) means "a highway"; cf. Isa 19:23a where *mᵉçillâh* (מְסִלָּה) also means "a highway." Noticeably, both Hebrew words come from the root *çâlal* (סָלַל), meaning "to cast up a highway" (*SECB*, h4547, h4546, h5549).

171. Isa 35:8c NKJV; Hebrew (הֹלֵךְ דֶּרֶךְ וֶאֱוִילִים לֹא יִתְעוּ) (Leningrad Codex; italics added).

172. Isa 35:1.

173. Isa 35:2a.

that they are witnesses to the glory and majesty of the Messiah; in the prophet's own words, these witnesses are "everyone."[174] The indefinite pronouns *everyone* and *everywhere* are not employed in Isaiah indefinitely but definitely. They are definite insofar as the number and the location are concerned. These pronouns are expressed ubiquitously, indicating the worldwide subjects of redemption and the global effect of redemption.

Similarly, we can turn to Revelation for further enlightenment, yet with discerning awareness packed with symbolism. The Isaianic description "sighing shall flee away" is retold in the Johannine description as "tears will be wiped away."[175] The redeemed will not suffer anymore, and they will worship the Lamb.[176] Moreover, the Lamb (Jesus Christ) shall lead the redeemed to the springs of life-giving water (Jesus Christ).[177] The Lamb will release those in bondage (Israel). The Shepherd will deliver those condemned for certain ruin (Israel's enemies). The Lamb as the Shepherd is vital in considering who the "redeemed" represent.

The unmistakable integer here is the twofold meaning of the life-giving water, its signification and its relevance. As shown in Johannine prophecy, the life-giving water does not only point to the redemption of the Son, but crucially, it also points to the *foreordination* of the Father, hence the "throne of God" as the source of the water.[178] What is truly remarkable is that the water, in a sense, nourishes the tree of life whereby its leaves are for the "healing of the nations."[179] The *nations* here particularly indicate *pagans*—worshippers of foreign gods.[180] These people are guilty of spiritual abomination and immoral intoxication. Nonetheless, King Immanuel overcomes them; his plan succeeds in the end.[181] Accordingly, divine restitution precedes human destitution: God pretemporally determined the Godself to be a gracious God even before humanity needed divine grace. In other words, when the Son of God becomes the Son of

174. Isa 35:2c CEV.

175. A paraphrase, Rev 7:17b.

176. Rev 7:10, 12, 16.

177. "For the Lamb who is in the midst of the throne will shepherd them and lead them to living fountains of waters. And God will wipe away every tear from their eyes" (Rev 7:17 NKJV). See also Rev 21:4.

178. Rev 22:1.

179. Rev 22:2c.

180. *Nations*, in Greek *ĕthnos* (ἔθνος), means "a multitude of people of the same nature" in the OT context, not worshipping the true God (*SECB*, g1484).

181. Rev 17:2, 14a, 17.

Man in eternity past, the provision of the water of life and the tree of life is sure. Jesus Christ, in a sense, is also the tree of life. He alone is life—the source and its upholder.

Thus by extrapolation, grounded in the designed pattern of Revelation, the subject "redeemed" cannot be used to refer exclusively to the Israelites, for textual and contextual evidence show that the beneficiaries of the water of life and the tree of life are the "ransomed." The evangelist's descriptive employment of the "four corners of the earth" and "from every nation, tribe, people and language" support a universalist version of the "redeemed."[182] In sustaining grace, the disconnect between God and his people is connected. Humans will be endowed with the ability to understand complex situations, such as the inclusion of the pagans. The prophet elucidates, "Then everyone who has eyes will open them and see, and those who have ears will pay attention."[183] Even so, the language connections imply that the evangelist's writings are not mere transcriptions from visions but an index to an "editorial activity" sourced from Jewish traditions, specifically here, from the prophet.[184]

Besides, the pagan nations anticipate condemnation on account of their idolatry and wicked acts, yet the Lamb will vindicate them by his sacrifice. These nations expect punishment, but the Shepherd will reward them with his compassion. Grief and groaning will disappear, and in place will be exceeding happiness. And by the same token, Israel will be filled with exceeding exultation over the great reunion in the renewed Zion. Therefore, tears of pain and tears of regret will disappear forever. The new order of things shall replace the old order of things.[185] The thought alignment we see in the prophecies of Isaiah and John helps the reader to see the divine perspective on the identity of the "ransomed" or the "redeemed."

There is still a lingering question regarding the foreordination of a *specific* group of people. Why is it that only Israel is considered elect? This concern somehow challenges the universality of the Lord's treatment of humanity. We will address it as we enter into Deutero-Isaiah.

182. Rev 7:1, 9; cf. Rev 7:4–8.

183. Isa 32:3 CEV.

184. Grabiner, *Revelation's Hymns*, 6.

185. Rev 22:2.

Chapter IV

ADVANCE YET REAL TIME

"I have sworn by Myself, the word has gone forth from My mouth in righteousness and will not turn back, that to Me every knee will bow, every tongue will swear *allegiance*."[1]

IN THE PRECEDING CHAPTER, WE STUDIED why God's ways and means in dealing with Israel (and other nations) are truly good. In this chapter, I shall argue that despite the concept of the predetermination of actions and events in time, God can also be in real time, at the present. To substantiate this, the motif of divine discipline will be discussed further as evidenced in Isaiah 40–48.

Here, the doctrine of election is studied within the doctrine of God. The electing God will be critically analyzed in the election of Israel. We will do so by considering election with attention to the honor, reliability, and integrity of God. The purpose of the analysis is to prove that the salutary eschatology is sure, as the One who promised it is eternal.

We now come to the fourth section of Isaiah with a keen eye on what it means for God to be eternal.

---

1. Isa 45:23 NASB; italics in original.

1. SUMMARY OF ISAIAH 40-48

Just as Isaiah predicted, about a century later, Babylon returned to sack Jerusalem and took her wealth, also carrying her noble men and women to exile in Babylon. All of the prophet's warnings of divine judgment had been fulfilled.[2] The fourth section, nonetheless, opens with an announcement of hope and comfort to embolden Israel. The Babylonian exile was over, and Israel's iniquities had been dealt with in a new era of beginning. In effect, Israel could return to Jerusalem, where God's glory encompassed all nations.

And so the prophet hopes that Israel will respond with gratitude by becoming the Lord's true servant. After experiencing the justice and mercy of God through his roller-coaster experience, Israel is summoned to begin sharing with his neighbors who is the true God. But unfortunately, that did not happen. Instead of witnessing to the world, the Jews complained against God by accusing him of turning a blind eye when Babylon took them to exile. They simply lost faith in the Lord God, even supposing that the Chaldean deities were more powerful.

Throughout this section, the setting is like a trial scene, where God is responding to the people's doubts and accusations. He does so by pointing out that their exile to Babylon was not proof of neglect but, rather, a divinely orchestrated wake-up call for Israel. God continues that it was for the sake of his people that he has raised the Achaemenid government to triumph over Babylon so the people could return home. The theme of hope after judgment is demonstrated surprisingly: judgment comes through the empire of Babylon that is to defeat Assyria and conquer Jerusalem; hope comes through Cyrus who is to defeat Babylon and let the Jews return to Zion. This is how God's rulership over his people is presented in Isaiah—something unconventional and indeed overwhelming.

The concluding part challenges Israel to see God as king of history, totally incomparable to Chaldean idols. God works the rise and fall of Babylon, also the exaltation of Cyrus for the good of Israel. All this evidence could have been enough to convince the Jews of God's majestic power and enduring compassion, but that was not the case. They remained rebellious and hardheaded, as their forefathers. As a result, God disqualified them as a servant yet without surrendering the mission to the world. Still, through Israel, he declared that the mission continued through his offspring—the Servant.

2. Isa 43:14; 48:14. See 2 Kgs 24-25.

Following the recap of the fourth section of Isaiah, it is expedient to examine why God is conceived as absolutely in charge as the Elector.

2. GOD AS ELECTOR

God as Elector is free in his choice, and God alone can exercise it. God is self-generated.[3] In being so, the divine foreknowledge is also self-contained; it rests in the being of God. In foreknowledge, God ordains. In prescience, God preappoints.[4] As the Isaianic message is retold in John the Baptist's preaching in the wilderness, so is the foreword about the Messiah is enacted in the enfleshed Word—Jesus Christ.[5] We have to deal with the concept of *foreordination*, since election is based on God's foreknowledge. God knows beforehand what is about to happen, as he has preordained things.[6] In pretemporality, God has appointed the actions and events in time, therefore, in the world. Here, God is not simply aware of the future, but instead, he makes humans aware of the master plan from beginning to end.[7]

In speaking of divine appointment, one cannot escape the fact that someone supreme, intelligent, and capable is behind such appointment for it to come to pass—the LORD God. It has been said, "To whom then will you liken God? Or what likeness will you compare to Him?"[8] God is intentional in causing and facilitating events in time, says Patricia Tull, yet she also believes that God is intentional in "responding to human behavior."[9] Such a belief is somehow problematic given the underlying Isaianic theme of pretemporal determination. Even in handling it alongside the real-timeliness of God, the word "response" is still a misfit in the equation.[10] Although the divine providence has cognitive and volitional aspects, human input is unnecessitated by it. More on this later.

3. Isa 40:5b, 8b.

4. Isa 40:13–14.

5. Isa 40:3; cf. John 1:23. Isa 40:4–5; cf. John 1:14.

6. Isa 40:9, 12.

7. Isa 40:10.

8. Isa 40:18 NKJV.

9. Tull, "God's Character in Isaiah," 201.

10. However, Tull indicates that God is "fundamentally incomparable" and is "most often described in human terms, doing things that humans do" (Tull, "God's Character in Isaiah," 202).

What is foreordained shall take place *in* time precisely because the appointment is done *before* time.[11] Inasmuch as the appointment covers eternity, whatever happens in time can never frustrate or stop it.[12] When God foreordains a person, people, or circumstances to accomplish the divine purpose, it is done (as appointed) and cannot be undone.[13]

The appointed figure is the elect, and so the elect is especially foreordained for a task.[14] The Elector appoints the elect in a predestined manner; that is, the generated and contained-in God is to be activated in the elect.[15] This means that the content of divine foreknowledge is to actualize in us what God *thinks* is for our good.[16] In addition, the discussion of predestination in light of foreknowledge is inevitable. In the grand scheme of things, the predestined is the being of God before the being of humans.[17] We may infer that the doctrine of election (or predestination) is all about God's self-determination; hence the doctrine focuses on God *pro nobis*.[18] This is the reason behind the repeated phrase "I will" in the Isaianic narratives, and the result is the resounding "You will."[19] Accordingly, God's self-determination is integral in the predetermination of humankind. The appointed figure will, by no means, deviate from the foreordained vis-à-vis actions and events in time.

The predetermination of actions and events is *not* determinism; it has no affinity with fatalism and Lao Tzu's "non-action" or "flowing with the moment" (*Wu Wei*).[20] The proper grasp of foreordination does not condone a consequent mindset of resignation or an attitude of passive acquiesce. Human freedom (to a certain degree) is possible and real in the world (as tackled in chapter 1). Although election is viewed pretemporally, God's activity in and through humanity is temporal—at present. It is emphasized here that the now of humanity is not detached from the eternal now of God. This is due to the utter dependence of the human

11. Isa 40:21.

12. Isa 40:28b. *Everlasting* in Hebrew is *'ôlâm* (עוֹלָם), meaning "permanent" or "antiquity and futurity" (*SECB*, h5769).

13. Isa 40:26; 41:4.

14. Isa 41:8; cf. Rom 8:28–30.

15. Isa 41:15–16.

16. Isa 41:17–19.

17. Isa 42:8–9.

18. In Isa 43, God is the Redeemer by gathering his people from exile.

19. For example, see Isa 41:10–16.

20. Watts and Huan, *Tao*, 78–80; Rice, "Divine Omnipotence," 124–26.

on the divine.[21] Moreover, any fatalistic injunction undermining the dynamic interconnection between God and humans is rejected. Determination *per se* is viewed strictly within the covenantal *relationship*.[22] In such a relationship, the negation of the negation is articulated in the implementation of that which is consigned—the commitment of the covenant members to the covenant Partner and vice versa.

In election, we are not powerless to do anything other than what is dictated by our nature; the Holy Spirit empowers us to do contrary to our natural inclination. The type of determination advanced here is closer to Molinism than the Spinozan concept of determinism because of the pronouncement of God's dynamic relation to the world (as seen in chapter 2) and God's active involvement in human affairs (as seen in chapter 3). God knows, therefore directs (in a nonabstract but personal fashion) future actions and events in an unconstrained manner made, however, in a set of appointed circumstances.[23] Human action is "free" since it is done in creaturely actuality, not forcefully determined. The Determiner, in this case, is also a friend. In other words, the freedom that humans have is freedom *for* God's appointment, not freedom from it. This is the human operation congruent to the divine operation.

The divine being is a category of its own—that is, in God's initiative and outworking. God makes sure that what is appointed comes to pass.[24] In being *sui generis*, God is unique in his category. He is the only being capable of enacting in the "pre" form: pretemporality, prescience, predestination, preordination, and predetermination. The fact that divine transcendence is upheld in the doctrine of God expounded here shows that God autonomously pre-acted as the Elector.[25] In being so, he chooses to be a God in time—a God *always advanced* in working things out for our benefit.[26] That is the Lord in Isaiah I aim to exposit; the "real God" as dis-

---

21. Isa 42:6.

22. Isa 42:6; 43:4a.

23. In Molina's assertion, God "wills to make a causal contribution that He knows with certainty will result in His chosen plan's being effected down to the last detail" (Molina, *On Divine Foreknowledge*, 4). Spinoza proposes that "in nature there is nothing contingent, but all things have been determined from the necessity of the divine nature to exist and produce an effect in a certain way" (Spinoza, *Spinoza Reader*, 29).

24. Isa 43:1b–2.

25. Isa 43:13.

26. Isa 43:14–15.

tinguished from the "textual God," according to Terence Fretheim.[27] The former underlines the deistic reality as distinct *yet* not detached from the latter, which is the deity of literary constructs. God could have otherwise been disengaged from us, but he rather decrees himself in a covenantal relationship with us. In the covenant, God for the people is said to be truly faithful in himself by being faithful to the decree.

In the covenant, the real God in the prophetic texts identifies himself with a negligible tribe.[28] It is written,

> But you, Israel, *are* My servant, Jacob whom I have chosen, the descendants of Abraham My friend. *You* whom I have taken from the ends of the earth, and called from its farthest regions, and said to you, "You *are* My servant, I have chosen you and have not cast you away."[29]

In one way, God has bonded the people of Israel to him.[30] Here, the descendants of Abraham, Isaac, and Jacob are kept to serve the Lord. God preferred these people (arising from an irrelevant ancestry) from among all people groups in the world as his own.[31] He makes the people acceptable before his presence, not because they are worthy of his acceptance, but because God treats their father Abraham as a friend—beloved.[32]

In another way, God has bonded himself with Israel. When God chooses Israel to be his people, he decides to be their Lord—the Custodian and Sponsor. Concerning God's treatment of his people, the notion of neglect or abandonment is dismissed, for they are the object of divine affirmation and assignment.[33] As the Custodian, God seizes Israel with the affirmation "I have redeemed you," and as the Sponsor, God fastens onto Israel with the assignment "I have summoned you."[34] These solidify the thought that Israel is the object of divine devotion. God determined himself to be *with Israel* without condition, as God determined Israel to

27. Fretheim, in Fretheim and Froehlich, *Bible as Word of God*, 116–18.

28. Isa 41:14.

29. Isa 41:8–9 NKJV; italics in original.

30. The Hebrew for *servant* is `ebed (עֶבֶד), meaning "bondman" or "bondservant" (*SECB*, h5650).

31. The Hebrew for *chosen* is *bâchar* (בָּחַר), denoting the idea of being "preferred" (*SECB*, h0977).

32. The Hebrew for *friend* is *'âhab* (אָהַב), meaning "beloved" (*SECB*, h0157).

33. Isa 44:21.

34. Isa 43:1.

be *with him* without constraint.[35] God demonstrated this by consigning the Son to be a Jew.[36] It is in the Jewishness of Jesus Christ that the
everlasting covenant with Israel is better appreciated. Israel is pivotal in
understanding the doctrine of election. But first, we have to probe the
meaning of the calling of Israel before we can apprehend his election.

2.1 The Calling of Israel

As is evident in Isaiah, God called Israel to be *his* covenanted people.[37]
The calling is an act of uncompromising commitment to the descendants
of Jacob. The divine commitment is immutable and unstoppable. Whoever is called, God alone can uncall; but he will not do so. God himself
declares,

> You are my *witnesses*, says the LORD, and my servant whom I
> have *chosen*, so that you may know and believe Me and under-
> stand that I am He. Before Me there was no God formed, nor
> shall there be after Me.[38]

Israel as elect (chosen) is called a bondservant, a *contracted* witness
for the LORD God. The people are to stand firm in their mission because
of who their God is—truly alive and powerful.[39] They can be confident in
their mission only by being certain of, hence quite acquainted with, the
One who chose and sent them. They have to "understand" whom they
serve by distinguishing the real from the unreal, the authentic from the
counterfeit.[40] God is saying here that he is incomparable to Bel and Nebo,
for God lords over these idols and their makers.[41] Per a deeper analysis,
Bel and Nebo are the Jews writ large. The idols were made, transported,
and used according to the pleasure of the people.[42] In consequence, the

---

35. Isa 44:1–2.

36. Isa 43:14a; 48:17.

37. Isa 43:10. The word for *called* in Hebrew is *qârâ'* (קָרָא), meaning "summoned,"
coming from the root "to encounter" (*SECB*, h7121, 7122).

38. Isa 43:10 NKJV; italics added.

39. The word for *witness* in Hebrew is *'ed* (עֵד), by implication meaning "to warn"
and "to stand upright" (*SECB*, h5707).

40. The Hebrew for *understand* is *bîyn* (בִּין), which connotes "separating mentally"
or "prudence in making a distinction" (*SECB*, h0995).

41. Isa 44:10–11; 46:1–2.

42. Isa 46:1.

idols serve their makers, as the makers, in a way, are held captive by the idols.[43] Thus the authentic ruler is the Lord God—sworn to no master and subject to no jury.[44] The Lord God makes things happen (basically for Israel); also, he does not make things happen (ultimately against Israel).[45]

God has called Israel from among the nations. How? God determined himself to meet with Israel in the covenant.[46] It is not a simple encounter, but rather, he sets an appointment with Israel *aggressively*.[47] God does it in the covenant wherein he appoints himself to be the God of Israel, as he appoints Israel to be the people of God.[48] So in speaking of election, strong intent and forceful readiness are central to appreciating the divine commitment.

Furthermore, God has summoned Israel from the "ends of the earth" to proclaim the true God to the ends of the earth.[49] It is a flagship concept in Isaiah that God is not limited in the area of Israel; God reaches out globally.[50] He has called Israel from the "farthest regions" as a witness.[51] In view of foreordination, we can deduce that God preferred the Israelites to serve as his ambassadors not because of their qualification but their location, not because of their disposition but their position. God aggressively pulls out these people from their previous settlements so they can eventually witness to their erstwhile fellows. Israel is incapable of the mission, yet God makes him capable. Israel is resistant to the mission, but God makes him willing. Above all, Israel is unworthy of the mission. God makes him not only worthy but desirable for it.[52] However, God fulfills his end of the bargain (in the covenant) indirectly—through King Immanuel.

In the meantime, the function of the elect is our immediate concern. The *elect* does not mean only chosen but, significantly, made fit

---

43. Isa 46:2.

44. Isa 45:11.

45. Isa 44:7, 11.

46. Isa 42:6; 44:21.

47. Isa 44:22.

48. Isa 44:1, 5.

49. Isa 41:9.

50. Davidson, "Universalism in Second Isaiah," 167–68.

51. Isa 45:22.

52. Isa 43:22–24.

to accomplish the divine purpose.[53] For instance, in being selected as a candidate for an electoral post, that person is elected (by the electorate)—authorized to serve (by the electorate). Respectively, the elected is made to function properly. From the biblical perspective, the chosen is made holy—*separated* for a specific purpose. The idea of holiness injected in the talk of election is foundational. The elect is holy not by the one chosen, but by the One choosing. Israel is made holy in the election to accomplish a holy purpose through the holy Sender. This is achievable by the outpouring of the Holy Spirit.[54] God chooses Israel, for God determines him to be holy as the Holy One of Israel.[55] This thought is the second application of what it means to be elect.

God is not tied to be God for Israel. There is a need to emphasize, in a sense, however, that Israel is tied to be a people for God.[56] God is not coerced to elect. It is equally true that he is indeed self-generated and self-contained in choosing Israel.[57] God is free in choosing Israel; therefore, he is also absolutely free to *continue* choosing him. In this continued choice, the people are made to remain covenanted with God. No matter how often they reject the Lord, God remains their Custodian and Sponsor.[58] Here, Israel is regenerated as God's partner and recontained in the covenant.

Now the continual choice of the human ought not to be taken negatively; such decision is a decision on behalf of Israel. It cannot be denied that there is no Israel without God choosing Abraham as a friend and, crucially, without God choosing to be the Friend of Abraham. Neither will the nation of Israel exist nor a single Israelite stand without persistent grace. Metaphorically speaking, Israel breathes and lives because of God. In that case, the people have no say in their subsistence and destiny. All of Israel and all about him are juxtaposed with the LORD God. Of course, such characterization is not static and paralyzing, as long as Israel is conceived within the covenant.[59]

---

53. Isa 43:25.
54. Isa 44:3b; 48:16b.
55. Isa 40:25; 48:17.
56. Isa 46:3–4.
57. Isa 46:12–13.
58. Isa 45:4–5.
59. Isa 43:4.

Perhaps the more pressing question is: why Israel? We have observed in Isaiah that Israel had failed God many times and in many ways. The truth is, God knew it beforehand.[60] So why would he *prefer* these hardheaded and ungrateful people from other tribes or nationalities? And to make this concern poignant—why would God commit himself to them despite the prescience of their noncommitment? The answers are from the self-election in the covenant.

In being a God in and of the covenant, remarkably, God determined himself to *be* faithful to the unfaithful.[61] In self-committing to the covenant, God chooses not to abandon his covenant partners bent on abandoning him. In the preservation of the covenant, God remains holy with those inclined to unholiness. In the spirit of the covenant, God voluntarily bonds himself to a people who long to be un-bonded since they despise servitude to the Lord. By being for us, therefore, God chooses to love the unlovable.[62]

In such an uncompromising commitment, the compromise of Israel is overridden.[63] In the covenant paradigm, Israel does not remain negligible and irrelevant due to his covenant Partner. God's self-appointment in the covenant is immutable insofar as his unceasing commitment is concerned, and the self-appointment in the covenant is unstoppable insofar as his strong intent and forceful readiness are concerned. Correspondingly, divine intent and readiness outweigh human irresolute and dullness. God is undeniably capable of turning the seemingly impossible into possible.[64] His intent is so strong that it overwhelms any discontent. Furthermore, God's readiness is so forceful that it overpowers any act of rebellion.

2.2 The Discipline of the Called

Some might wonder: if God elects Israel, does it mean that God favors Israel? Yes, God favors Israel, but he does not exercise favoritism.[65] The elect is tasked to introduce their God to other nations. If taken lightly,

60. Isa 44:6–7.

61. Isa 44:24–26.

62. Isa 43:11–12.

63. Isa 43:13.

64. Isa 48:3.

65. Papaioannou, *Israel, Covenant, Law*, 31.

then serious consequence follows.[66] Being elect has nothing to do with being treated as a VIP; instead, the elect is duty bound to undertake the commission. What is not apparent is the fact that the elect has to suffer. By suffering, the elect finds contentment and, ultimately, gratification. We can better grasp this notion if we view it coincident with judgment. The first application of judgment in the OT, I should say, is positive. When God says "I will judge my people," this conveys God's accompaniment of the people. The Judge is also the Vindicator; hence the frame of the verdict is: justice given equates to vindication spoken.[67] The second application of judgment is negative, which denotes the condemnation and punishment of the guilty.[68] But as long as God favors Israel, his condemnation is revoked. The punishment of Israel remains. This is not merely through the dismissed thought of favoritism but also to make the people just. The elect, by default, enjoys divine justice, so the elect is said to be under judgment. Such interplay of justice and vindication is evident in the covenantal paradigm.

Thus, the elect has its good times and bad times. The good times correspond to God—that is, commitment to the covenant. The bad times correspond to something other than God, opposition to the covenant. The tension between contentment and discontentment is constant in the covenant. God's partners are humans—highly volatile and treacherous due to self-centeredness.[69] The predisposition to self is what the Lord of the covenant consistently transforms into being other-centered: first to God, second to fellow human beings.[70] God does it through surgical means—painful but necessary.[71] We can see here the demonstration of the *realness* and *timeliness* of the foreordained. The discipline of Israel is through defeat and exile (painful). However, discipline is not a reaction on God's part but a preaction to activate the binding power of the covenant by actualizing the intended good for Israel (necessary).

In this light, the concept of favoritism within election is inviable, hence far from the truth. In fact, God did not leave the pride of Israel

66. Calvin, *Institutes*, 3.24.6.

67. Isa 43:25.

68. Isaiah 42 describes God as the Upholder of justice and righteousness.

69. Isa 47:8.

70. Isa 48:8–9.

71. Isa 48:10.

unchecked. God dealt with it with severity.[72] Crudely speaking, that is the flip side of being elect, quite the reverse of being favorite. The LORD God says,

> I will lay waste the mountains and hills and wither all their vegetation; I will make the rivers into coastlands and dry up the ponds. I will lead the blind by a way they do not know, in paths they do not know I will guide them. I will make darkness into light before them and rugged places into plains. These are the things I will do, and I will not leave them undone.[73]

Whenever the people of Judah become self-sufficient and slip into choosing gods of their own making, the Lord immediately disciplines them. Whatever their source of hubris, such as wealth, knowledge, security, God takes it without hesitation. In poverty, bewilderment, and uncertainty, they learn to remember God and renew their allegiance to him, hence the phrase "darkness into light." God so loves Judah that he will correct her, even if this is unfavorable. God is so committed to Judah that he will take her back, even if this is disturbing. God acts according to what he foreordains—to keep the people *in* the covenant. Thus it is written,

> Remember the former things of old, for I *am* God, and *there is* no other; *I am* God, and *there is* none like Me, declaring the end from the beginning, and from ancient times *things* that are not *yet* done, saying, "My counsel shall stand, and I will do all My pleasure."[74]

God is eternal. He is capable of completing the election congruent to his honor. Notice here the divine perspective of doing things: something appears inverted, "the end from the beginning" instead of the usual "from beginning to end." Critical to this framework is the vanishing point, the concealed, stacked up against the appearing point, the exposed. In God's exposé of humanity, humanity's condition is unpleasant; however, in God's disclosure of the appointment, the human condition is conditioned to be pleasant. In this case, human eschatology is the back end if the divine counsel is rightly conceived as the front end. That is to say that the *hereafter* is dictated by the *beforehand*. Also, this implies that the finale of all things is fixed but wrapped in dynamism in God's willing. It cannot be

---

72. Isa 45:7; 48:9b.

73. Isa 42:15–16 NASB; italics in original.

74. Isa 46:9–10 NKJV; italics in original.

swayed or altered by whatever happens in between the beginning and the end. In other words, from the beginning (election) God will reveal the end (consummation).

What God can, God will. He can transform his people from being proud to being humble, from being rebellious to being compliant. No one else can do it except the LORD God. When God elects the Israelites to be his people, it is binding; the Elector will see the election through. In spite of the ever-retracting, ever-repulsive nature of Israel, God is ever dedicated to be his Lord. The divine counsel "shall stand," for God "will do all" to keep Israel by his side. This is what pleases God—for the people to abide by the decree *because* he abides by it.

2.3 Election and Covenant

When I say abiding by the decree, this is feasible since God as Elector shapes the covenant. The Elector is in full management of his relationship with us because he directs it. Although our cooperation is necessary, it is not vital. What is vital is God's work to elevate his covenant partners.[75] Even though Israel has no say in the covenant, what God says to him is comforting: "Don't be afraid. I am with you. Don't tremble with fear. I am your God."[76] Notwithstanding the stubbornness of Judah to seek imperial insurance, God is also stubborn in reassuring her: "I will make you strong, as I protect you with my arm and give you victories."[77] When God makes a statement, it is self-binding and self-consummating.[78] It is self-binding, since the promise is real and enduring; also, it is self-consummating, as it is grounded in the eternal counsel.

I would argue that God's self-determination is like a bulldozer in which everything that comes in the way is demolished and pushed aside.[79] God will do so in accomplishing his purpose. Maybe that is an obstinate effort to disregard the divine message and others. In this line of thinking, God also pushes aside the manner and method of election prone to human conditioning.[80] Because of the inherent disconnect between

75. Isa 45:17.
76. Isa 41:10a CEV.
77. Isa 41:10b CEV.
78. In Isa 40, God is the Comforter because he renews the strength of the weary.
79. Isa 45:9.
80. Isa 45:11.

divine and human, the manner of election is unimaginable, as its method is unprecedented. The Elector is like no other.[81]

One indisputable exhibit of this is the election of Cyrus the Great. It is interesting to note that God refers to Cyrus as "anointed."[82] This is where contention about Cyrus originates, as it suggests, yet to a slight degree, that Cyrus is the promised Messiah as predicted in Isaiah.[83] My major argument against such a suggestion is in the concept of holiness. I argue that Cyrus is holy, worthy of God, not because Cyrus is in and of himself holy, but because Cyrus is *made* holy through election.[84] God anoints him to do the divine pleasure—liberate the people of God from Babylon and assist them to rebuild the temple of Jerusalem.[85] This is entirely different from the holiness of King Immanuel. That sort of holiness arises from and extends to eternity.[86] It means that that King is inherently and enduringly holy in and of himself. I equally stress that Cyrus could be referred to as *a* messiah, as a type of *the* Messiah. Another argument in favor of King Immanuel as the Messiah is the self-sacrifice he had to undergo for the sake of Israel.[87] Yes, Cyrus had his share of suffering by having to defeat the mighty Chaldean Empire and by freeing thousands of Jewish slaves, even in financing the rebuilding of the Jewish temple (which could have incurred a heavy toll on the treasury of the Persian Empire),[88] but that is nothing compared to the grievous and shameful death of the Messiah.[89]

Likewise, Cyrus could typify Israel as being primarily unholy but finally made holy by election. God used Cyrus (a heathen) to do his bidding. This indicates that God can use Israel even if he lived like a heathen.[90] It stimulates openness to the Gentile world instead of nursing Jewish particularism.[91] The point is, God is unconditioned in his election.

---

81. Isa 43:19.

82. Isa 45:1.

83. The term *anointed* in Hebrew is *mâshîyach* (מָשִׁיחַ)—the Messiah (*SECB*, h4899).

84. Isa 45:13a.

85. Isa 45:13b.

86. Isa 45:21.

87. This facet will be discussed in the next chapter.

88. Isa 44:28; see Ezra 1.

89. Isa 48:9; cf. 53:8.

90. Isa 45:13; 46:11.

91. Blenkinsopp, "Second Isaiah," in *Essays*, 50.

The conditioned in it are the humans determined to be God's and fulfill God's work on earth.[92]

After considering the nature and operation of election, we will now investigate who else is deemed the elect in the Bible.

2.4 The Elect

Aside from Israel and Cyrus, the rest of the elect vary in number and feature, namely, (1) citizens of Jerusalem,[93] (2) inhabitants of the new heaven and earth,[94] and (3) Jesus Christ.[95]

The reader might take it that the citizens of Jerusalem are redundant with Israel, albeit it has to be emphasized that the focal subject here is specifically the Jews. The role of Judah is fundamental in explicating the election of the remaining two elect. Isaiah says:

> Get you up to a high mountain, O Zion, herald of good tidings; lift up your voice with strength, O Jerusalem, herald of good tidings, lift it up, do not fear; say to the cities of Judah, "Here is your God!"[96]

The Lord summons, in particular, the people in Jerusalem to be bold in their mission because he abides with them. God has elected the Jews to continue the commission bestowed on their forefather Abraham.[97] Even if the Jews desecrated the holy city and the holy name of the Lord, God *reconsecrated* them to fulfill their calling.[98] This thought strengthens the argument that whoever is chosen is always made fit to pursue the purpose of election. Here we can see the reliability of the electing God by ensuring the integrity of the elected. The logical conclusion acceptable is that divine foreknowledge has everything to do with election.[99] In the permanent self-bonding with the Jews, God reinstated and reequipped

92. Isa 45:2–3.

93. Isa 65:9; 1 Pet 1:1–2.

94. Isa 65:22; Rev 7:3–4.

95. Isa 42:1; 1 Pet 2:6.

96. Isa 40:9 NRSV.

97. Isa 41:8, 18–20; cf. "As for Me [God], behold, My covenant is with you [Abraham], and you will be the father of a multitude of nations" (Gen 17:4 NASB).

98. Isa 40:1–2; 48:1–2.

99. God is capable of foreordination as the Alpha and Omega as elucidated in Isa 41.

them to remain as elect instead of abandoning and consigning them to incessant shame. Such preference is congruent with God's honor vis-à-vis Abraham. When God befriended Abraham, it goes without saying that God determined himself as the Friend of Abraham's descendants as well.

In such enduring friendship, it is likewise implied that the citizens of Jerusalem are forever covenanted. This is to state that in God's self-binding, the Jews are automatically bound for life to God. In this elaboration, the covenant members are affirmed and continue to be reaffirmed of their election. Subsequently, the Jews are fastened to their identity, no matter how stained their reputation, by the steady honor and integrity of the Elector.[100]

Secondly, the elect is the inhabitants of the new heaven and earth or, simply put, the inhabitants of the new Jerusalem. This explains why the specific role of the Jews has to be emphasized in the talk of election. The citizens of old Zion are converted into those of new Zion by election.[101] They are the undeniable testimony of the reliability of God as the electing God and covenant Partner. Whoever is elected is guaranteed progress. Isaiah says:

> I [God], *even* I, have spoken; yes, I have called him, I have brought him, and his way will prosper. Come near to Me, hear this: I have not spoken in secret from the beginning; from the time that it was, I *was* there. And now the LORD God and His Spirit have sent Me.[102]

Who is God speaking to? The immediate context tells us that God is in conversation with Israel, specifically the Jews; then God points out to the Jews what he has elected (beforehand) to happen (hereafter).[103] God says that he has chosen an ally against Babylon.[104] So the "him" pertains to Cyrus the Great, and as per election, he "will prosper" in his mission. Sure enough, Cyrus defeated Nebuchadnezzar, and this turn of events gives credence to the notion that the Elector is the King of history.[105] God has chosen Cyrus *for* Israel. God has selected Cyrus to bless Israel.

---

100. Isa 40:28.

101. Isa 40:31.

102. Isa 48:15–16 NKJV; italics in original.

103. See Isa 48:1, 6–7, 12.

104. Isa 48:14b.

105. Isa 40:9; 46:13b.

What does not come to the surface right away is the idea that God also used the Chaldean monarch to act out the divine will for Israel.[106] To a certain extent, I contend, Nebuchadnezzar is *selected* to demonstrate the divine discipline of the Jews. In other words, we can view here the election dialectically: Nebuchadnezzar is the no serving the yes who is Cyrus. The former is called to strike God's people, whereas the latter is called to heal them.[107] To that effect, Nebuchadnezzar's downfall triggers the rise of Cyrus.[108] Because things happen (in exacting detail) as predicted, the election of the people *for* the new Jerusalem is assured. The success of Cyrus is the progressive statement for the elect; ergo, the renewed "Jews" of the renewed Jerusalem correspond to the decreed result in the divine counsel. Accordingly, the residents chosen to bask in the new heaven and earth remain to be so. The human back end is set in stone.

After unpacking Cyrus's part in the passage, we have to establish the identity of the "Me" (whom the LORD God and his Spirit sent) as it introduces the final elect on our list. The passage itself hints at that the Me is someone *from the beginning*. Given the election, the writer of Deutero-Isaiah is called upon to magnify the primordial Elect—the ultimate Jew. The text in Isaiah unfolds,

> Here is my servant, whom I uphold, *my chosen*, in whom my soul delights; I have put my spirit upon him; he will bring forth justice to the nations.[109]

The servant is unique in status and purpose. This status is unique insofar as God's treatment is considered. The chosen is one in whom God "delights."[110] The servant is very unlike Cyrus or Israel/Jews because, to begin with, God is pleased with him; God accepts him favorably. The elect, therefore, is inherently pleasing and innately favorable, for these attributes are perpetual. Concurrently, the purpose is unique insofar as the scope of the mission is accounted for. Once again, the Elect is deviant

106. Isa 43:14. Notably, God referred to Nebuchadnezzar as `ebed, the same terminology as for the elect Israel and Cyrus. See Jer 25:9.

107. It is not surprising to know that Nebuchadnezzar (the epitome of human self-sufficiency and arrogance vis-à-vis Babylon being the golden head of the great image) was regenerated and recontained, evident in the book of Daniel. See Dan. 2:36–38; 4:34–37.

108. Isa 43:14–17.

109. Isa 42:1 NRSV; italics added.

110. The Hebrew for *delight* is *râtsâh* (רָצָה), literally meaning "to be pleased with" or "accept favorably" (*SECB*, h7521).

concerning Cyrus yet cognate concerning the Jews in terms of evangelistic territory. The mission of the former is confined to the ancient Near
East regions: the Babylonian kingdom and the Jewish nation. The mission
of the latter is unconfined, hence universal—to all kingdoms and nations.

The chosen One will "bring forth justice" worldwide because the
Spirit is upon him. This brings to mind what we analyzed in the previous
passage, that the Spirit sent the Elect. Although Cyrus is elect, there is no
biblical support for his full endowment of the Spirit.

Jesus Christ perfectly fits the above features not because he is made
fit, but rather, he *is* fit. The Spirit did not merely send Jesus Christ, but
crucially, he is *the* abode of the Spirit.[111] In retrospect, the following elect,
namely, Cyrus, Israel, and the Jews, are all types of the ultimate Elect.
Jesus Christ is the elected as the electing God. Karl Barth articulates that
"the Son of God given by the Father to be one with man, and to take to
Himself the form of man, He is elected."[112] Jesus Christ is not one among
the elect; instead, he is the first and last Elect as the Son of God—only a
God can finish the appointed revival of justice.

Again, Jesus Christ as elected also elects.[113] This is another reason
why Jesus is said to be utterly unique as the Elect. Christ can also elect for
the election to stand in covenantal terms. In a way, the Elect decides to
be with us in an enduring friendship by determining us to be like him—
that is, committed to such friendship. But Christ unprecedentedly and
unimaginably did it by being human. The Elect is the first as the Son of
God and the last as the Son of Man. The former embodies the vanishing point of predestination; the latter embodies the appearing point of
it. Here we can interpolate that the self-generation of God is activated in
the generation and regeneration of humanity. Rightly so, we can also interpolate that the Lord's self-containment is activated in the containment
and recontainment of humanity.

Even if the elect (human) fails in its commitment to the Elect (divine
and human), the former activates the binding power of the latter. Barth
comments, "It is in Him (Jesus Christ) that the eternal election becomes
immediately and directly the promise of our own election as it is enacted
in time, our calling."[114] What *is not* is that which corresponds to what is

111. Isa 48:16b–17a.
112. Barth, *CD* II/2, 105.
113. Barth, *CD* II/2, 105.
114. Barth, *CD* II/2, 105–6.

passing; what *is* is that which corresponds to what is succeeding. In other words, the strength of the covenant is independent of the members; but it is dependent on the Partner. The covenant is persistently robust, as the foundation of it is eternal.

We will now tackle why God is said to be eternal, in order to understand the reliability of election.

3. THE ETERNAL GOD

The terms self-binding and self-consummating are based on the eternality of God.[115] The decree is interminable because the originator and the lynchpin of it are forever existent.[116] God is diligent in guiding actions and events to coincide with the divine blueprint. Such outworking of foreknowledge can never be divorced from the eschatological role of the Elect.

Jesus Christ as the foremost and ultimate Elect provides true and lasting justice. Since the election itself is unconditioned, dispensing justice is also unconditioned. As the originator of the covenant, it is in Christ's divinity that justice emanates to be dispensed unconditionally. As the lynchpin of the covenant, it is in Christ's humanity that justice is said to have been dispensed unconditionally. Christ, the foremost Elect, has dedicated himself to stand in place of the guilty; in effect, the guilty is vindicated in Christ as the ultimate Elect. Here, justice is both served and executed.

Everything about election points to Jesus Christ. Israel, the citizens of Jerusalem, and the inhabitants of the new heaven and earth, even Cyrus function as analogical implements in highlighting how just and benevolent is the Elect. The ultimate Elect is the cornerstone of the elect. Without the Elect, the elect does not merely remain insignificant but also condemned.[117] Christ is the foundation of election. In him, all temporal actions and events are circumscribed within the everlasting covenant. Christ is so and can do so precisely because he is the Lord—the *always been* therefore *always is* God.[118]

---

115. Isa 44:6b, 8b.

116. Isa 45:8, 15.

117. Isa 42:1; 1 Pet 2:6.

118. Isa 45:18–19; 46:10a.

Furthermore, Jesus Christ as the Elect is the precursor of humanity. In the OT, the elect is Israel; whereas in the NT, the elect is the church.[119] Such categories speak of the categorical nature of Jesus, whereby the regeneration and recontainment of humans are activated. In view of predestination, Israel is the vanishing point, which accords with the church as the appearing point. The former is where people are regenerated; the latter is where people are recontained. However, as both appointed instruments are unreliable partners, the self-appointed Partner successfully activated what humans alone cannot achieve. In being the elected Human, the regeneration and recontainment of humanity are achieved due to the integrity and reliability of the Elect. This speaks of the reliability and integrity of the covenant as well.[120]

We can likewise interpose that the calling of Israel is with the calling of the church, given the covenant. Israel, as God's witness, is duplicated in the witnessing of the church. Unfortunately, there are also similar weak patterns between Israel and the church simply because of the human factor in both. To this David Bentley Hart reiterates that the church should remember why Israel was elected in the first place; that is, "its election [is] the concrete earnest of cosmic peace." Otherwise, the church would be diverted to worldly concerns.[121] Nonetheless, the beneficial result of the divine commission is *strictly* issued from the prototype—King Immanuel. The elected Human overcomes the weakness of the two human witnesses. Here the messianic initiative is given prominence. Through the faithful Witness (divine and human), that which is summoned to duplicate (human) is in turn duplicated.[122]

That is where Hart picks up his recommendation for the church. He alludes to "the Church [being] bound by its fidelity to the Abrahamic covenant to display in its practices the presence of the Kingdom within history."[123] A true statement, yet I have to add that it can never be true through human effort or perseverance. It can be true of the church *solely* by the election of Jesus Christ. In the messianic initiative vis-à-vis duplication, the "simulacrum" is therefore transformed into what has

---

119. Isa 44:1; 1 Pet 1:1–2.

120. God elects Israel to be the people of the covenant as underlined in Isa 44.

121. Hart, "Church and Israel," para. 5.

122. The *witness* language comes from the Hebrew root *'ud* (עוּד), entailing the idea of "to duplicate" (*SECB*, h5749).

123. Hart, "Church and Israel," para. 8.

been decreed—to mirror Jesus.[124] In this spectrum, the concept of the predestined restitution is better appreciated.

By holding to the covenantal relationship, we are also in a better position to continue the striking-healing theme with rigor. It is evident in Isaiah that God forgives Israel before restoration.[125] Even before repentance took place, God had already forgiven Israel. This does not mean, however, that divine discipline is unnecessary.[126] It is in such discipline that Israel is regenerated and recontained. What is unnecessary is the accusation of negligence and apathy against God.[127] But if that is so, the question immediately presents itself: who is actually on trial? In this account, the subject of the trial is Israel, not God. And in such a mode of reasoning, it must be restated that divine discipline is for the betterment of the one disciplined.[128] Divine discipline is the method by which the predestined restoration of Israel is reached; hence such method is part of the appointed good for humanity.

3.1 Unremitting Honor and Integrity

By looking at the above conception within the bounds of the covenantal relationship, it has to be said as well that God elects divine discipline principally for the sake of his honor:

> For the sake of My name I delay My wrath, and *for* My praise I restrain *it* for you, in order not to cut you off. Behold, I have refined you, but not as silver; I have tested you in the furnace of affliction. For My own sake, for My own sake, I will act; for how can *My name* be profaned? And My glory I will not give to another.[129]

The reason God disciplines Israel is to uphold his identity as the Lord. On the one hand, we can see that God indeed has no pleasure in striking the people. What pleases him is their transformation.[130] On the other hand, we can also see in Isaiah that Israel had failed in commitment

124. Isa 42:1; Rom 8:29.
125. Isa 44:21–22.
126. Isa 43:28.
127. Isa 40:27.
128. Isa 47:10; 48:17, 19.
129. Isa 48:9–11 NASB; italics in original.
130. Isa 48:18; Ezek 33:11.

to God and his commission. But God will act, and this will be with intense conviction and sincere devotion, which explains the double use of the "for My own sake" language. For his honor, as understood in covenantal terms, God reconciles the seeming gap between the predetermined continuity of Israel (being God's covenant partner) and his constant rebellion. This is by looking at the One whom God delights.

The unique status of Jesus Christ is not only confined to his delightful standing before God; the uniqueness of his status also has sway on his purpose. The rationale behind Jesus being a delight for God is because Christ is committed to self-sacrifice for us to be also pleasing in God's sight.[131] Christ, the ultimate Elect, is chosen to give his life for all (elect and others) to have life. This is what it truly entails to be the precursor of humanity: the elected Human is to lose so that humankind is to gain. God could have easily wiped out the rebellious and stiff-necked people, yet he would rather stick with them and, more significantly, be "in the furnace of affliction" to warrant the security of the covenant. In other words, it is in the offering of the Elect that the offense of the elect is overcome. It is plausible to accept that the calling of all nations, primarily via Israel and eventually via the church, means, in the end, all will acknowledge God.[132]

Nevertheless, for that matter, I am also aware that the idea of the reprobate (non-elect) is the gridlock in the doctrine of election.[133] The problem of the reprobate is undoubtedly *edgy*, as demonstrated in Christian church history. At the onset, I give credit to John Calvin for bravely engaging the concept of predestination as written in the Bible. Aside from reviving the doctrine of divine sovereignty, he is also instrumental in placing it on the pedestal of theology. Predestination, as Calvin presents it, remains mysterious, as it is rooted in the transcendence of God. As a result, it constitutes paradoxes and tensions.[134] In the spirit of nov-

131. Isa 48:11.

132. Isaiah 45 tells us that God blesses and also God curses.

133. Weber, *Foundations of Dogmatics*, 307.

134. The discrepancies will remain irreconcilable unless the following are resolved: (1) The doctrine of God with the *decretum* has no firm grounding to warrant positive divine aseity. I think what Calvin failed to do in the *Institutes* is to explain God's omnipotence without making him omni-causal. (2) Calvin's vertical understanding of the relationship between God and his creatures concedes to the double will of God. Despite Calvin's dismissal of "double ultimacy," his argument still creates the problem of inequality, let alone associating it with the "pleasure of God." (3) In an attempt to reconcile the bondage of the will to sin and the voluntariness of choice, Calvin's anti-anthropocentrism gives allowance to Molinism. (4) Calvin's position of God

elty, I will inspect the paradoxes and tensions concerning predestination in the context of Isaiah. For instance, it is clear in Isaiah that God sends pestilence and calamity to humble the proud.

In mortification, divine sovereignty has the final say if we look through Calvin's theological lens. Concomitantly, *only* the proud *elect* is corrected in the process and submits to divine rulership. In other words, the proud *non-elect* is deprived of correction; transformation is simply impossible. So if we apply Calvin's presupposition to the striking-healing theme of Isaiah, the result would be disastrous not merely to the doctrine of election but, more importantly, to the doctrine of God. Why? The problem emerges in how divine operation is articulated. The striking applies to both the elect and non-elect, yet the healing applies exclusively to the elect. Here, the non-elect is no doubt "the reprobate." God has no intention to restore the condemned. On a more somber note, the striking-without-healing of the non-elect is predetermined.

The kind of God pictured in this scenario is uncanny and suspicious. This is the deity the skeptics vehemently oppugn, and the believers silently impugn. This is the deity that makes theodicy stand on sandy ground. Calvin's God (though supreme and firm) invites more questions than answers, especially during the current pandemic. By contrast, Robin Parry's God (also supreme and firm) advances sympathy to *all* humankind. Concerning Second Isaiah, Parry argues that the thought pattern here is "doom-turned-to-salvation"—what seems hopeless is actually hopeful.[135] The God of Israel is not merely a mysterious Master, but a magnanimous Servant as well.[136]

That is central in reversing the distaste for the naked sovereignty of God. The paradoxes inherent in Calvin's presentation of predestination provide a valid deduction from an acceptable premise. In effect, the self-contradictory conclusions of predestination are adjusted into coherent formulations. For instance, when the LORD God proclaims his sovereignty to Judah, it should be taken seriously: what he desires comes to pass.[137] But then, God also declares, "Now I will keep my promise and do what I

---

determining the fall and the reprobate opens God's perfect image to suspicion. (5) The complexity of Calvin's arguments to suit a grand scheme of divine sovereignty makes his theological conclusion on predestination less definitive and indeterminate.

135. Parry, *Lamentations*, 163n6.

136. Parry, *Lamentations*, 166.

137. Isa 46:9–10.

planned."[138] What is the plan? God will rescue his people from Babylon and restore righteousness in them.[139] The amazing aspect here is that God had determined it for Judah despite her rebellion and unrighteousness.[140] Although the authority of God is in God's self, it is *for* the people regardless of their response. On this note, the work of the sovereign One dovetails with the work of the Servant.

To that end, the rhetorical expression of divine sovereignty in the *Institutes*, I observe, is magnificent yet inefficient. Be that as it may, contradictory elements in Calvin's thought must be settled to avoid the downplay of its majestic appeal.[141] With that, I propose: first, to renew the investigation of the decree itself to test its adequacy by the standard of the Bible; second, to correct the misconception of the "privileged" status of the elect and find solutions to the problem of inequality;[142] and finally, to treat dogmatics and ethics together, as both are founded on the same revelation—God's self-revelation in Jesus Christ. In Jesus Christ, argues P. T. Forsyth, "there is no dark decree lurking behind God's election."[143] What Forsyth does not seem to press further is why there is *absolutely* no dark decree in the first place. The solution we seek is not in resolving what is behind the election. There is none to be found behind it. The God of election is Jesus Christ—in him, there is no darkness; in him, we find hope past judgment.[144]

After analyzing Calvin's take on predestination, we should now scrutinize its impact on historical theology from his time and thereafter.[145]

---

138. Isa 46:11b CEV.

139. Isa 46:11, 13.

140. Isa 46:12.

141. According to Calvin: (1) God does not arbitrarily consign people to their respective ends, yet human choices are confined to what is contingent. (2) God maintains the concept of the fall in Eden, but it is part of his decree. (3) Jesus Christ's atonement is all-sufficient; however, it is only applicable to some. (4) God does bestow grace, albeit he is not gracious to all. (5) God's election renders assurance, yet without certainty. (6) God indeed loves; nonetheless, such love is selective (Calvin, *Institutes*, 3.21–23).

142. See Levering, *Predestination*, 21.

143. Goroncy, *Hallowed Be Thy Name*, 193.

144. See Lindsay, *God Has Chosen*, 35.

145. Boettner, *Reformed Doctrine of Predestination*, 23.

3.2 The Persistent Elector

Even if the Synod of Dordt had tried to minimize the tensions in Calvin's version of predestination, it failed to do so. Despite the efforts of Calvinists to "rationalize" the outworking of the Almighty, they still end up deficient in putting forward the relational God of the Bible.[146] Even though I insist on divine sovereignty, I also urge, in equal terms, on the firm yet compassionate act of discipline. I agree God will never waste time (despite being eternal) on a futile endeavor. However, the striking of people is simply not an end in itself. Respectively, the striking *always* leads to healing. God never wastes time. He is always on time in restoring all as decreed.[147]

In speaking of time vis-à-vis election, I also advance the notion of divine outworking in the present congruent to predetermination. The foreordained actions and events are to be in a dualistic schema. In it, the *actuality* of the elect consists of two modes, the present reality and the future reality. The present reality of the elect can be different from its future reality. The latter, however, dictates the actuality of the elect, not the former. To this effect, Forsyth distinguishes the experience of redemption from the experience of redeeming. As he puts it, "Because it is not the sense of the experience that is the main matter, but the source of the experience, and its content. It is not our experience we are conscious of—that would be self-conscious piety—but it is Christ."[148] Forsyth redirects the attention from the observer of reality to the giver of reality. For, in so thinking, the set reality of the Elect is actualized in the elect.

For example, when we look at the reality of the Jews as described in Isaiah, there is no doubt that most of them await an undesirable judgment. Their relentless insubordination towards God and cruelty towards their fellows are the reasons. But when we look closer to what is prophesied about the Jews in connection to the messianic initiative, their present reality is but intermediate. The set trajectory synchronizes with election.[149] The Jews are already redeemed and revived on the grounds of the certainty of the work of King Immanuel. We can say that their future reality (redemption and restoration) is underway (being redeemed and restored).

---

146. See Hunsinger, *Reading Barth with Charity*, xiv–xv.

147. Isaiah 46 expresses the thought that God's salvific act is not delayed.

148. Forsyth, *Positive Preaching*, 65.

149. Isa 48:1.

Of course, the condition of the Jews during the writing of Isaiah was far from the set trajectory; nevertheless, their status is solidly established in the identity of their Messiah, which is upright and steady. In other words, the messianic identity is applied as the actuality of the Jews by the messianic initiative alone. What is real for the Elector is true of the elect, but human perception is not on a par with the divine.[150] That is why I call human actuality advance-yet-real-time as I view it in the covenantal paradigm. The foreordained supersedes the conduct in time, because the covenant Partner is the guidepost to covenant partners. This is another way of demonstrating the truism of God's sovereignty.

True, divine sovereignty was the foundation for some of the major aspects of Calvinism, albeit we should not be misled by the usual stereotyping of divine sovereignty, as Philip Melanchthon rightly notes, to restrict it to predestination.[151] Indeed there is more to it. In the discourse on the restoration in and through Jesus Christ, Calvin had come somewhat close in that "God in Christ has taken man into his possession."[152] Unfortunately, Calvin could have widened his christological contemplation of predestination. He was impeded, however, by the intimidating sheer grandeur of God. All this said, though, it is necessary to stress that election is not arbitrary; in it, God is driven by *his* compassion.

At this stage, the *decretum* is worth investigating in a more comprehensive and meaningful tone. We can do this, I propose, by rigidly handling the doctrine of election inside the doctrine of God by making the eternal covenant the boundary and Jesus Christ the center. Talk about the "hiddenness of God" only brings ambiguity to the discussion; therefore, I hold to the Barthian conception that Christ is the electing God. Having Jesus as the placeholder, the synod could have continued the conversation through the intellectual cul-de-sac generated by the paradoxes and tensions in predestination. Calvin's ontological investigation of the known-about God is deficient simply because he falls short in locating the doctrine of election wholly in Jesus Christ—the *Deus revelatus*.

Using Christocentric parameters in approaching the doctrine of election, we can think and feel differently about the God of election and the outcome of predestination. By making the eternal covenant the borderline in revisiting the identity of the electing God, we can avoid

150. Isa 48:7b–8a.
151. Leif, *Practical Predestinarians in England*, 50.
152. Ritschl, *Memory and Hope*, 98.

the pitfall of jeopardizing God's image, owing to the enduring nature and operation of the covenant Partner. By taking Jesus as the center of election, we can place theodicy on unshaky ground over Christ's always-been-always-is status and purpose. This is not a skewed inference. The polemic against the Christocentric view of election inevitably falls into a conundrum of enigmatic theological dimensions as seen above.

In the wake of the interlocking intricacies, I would rather employ my own acronym, TUBIG: Total depravity, Unconditional election, Boundless atonement, Irresistible grace, and Guts of the saints (the courage of the believers), instead of TULIP (condensed form of Dordt's formulation).[153] Such a move is geared to the rigid Christocentric take on election, that divine atonement is for *everyone*. In the humanity of Jesus Christ, the entire humankind is represented, therefore, restored. I have to reinvent Dordt's theological articulation of election, not merely to be different from the Reform tradition but, critically, for the differences to outweigh the similarities with Calvin's teaching on predestination.

In utilizing the TUBIG formula, I can be confident that knowledge about God arises from knowledge about Jesus Christ. Despite the total depravity of the human race, Jesus uplifted humanity to be pleasing to God. This occurred when God exercised his unconditional election of humankind in Christ's representative election, in which the irrevocable effect is boundless atonement of all sinners. Humanity remains covenanted with God by the dispensed irresistible grace bringing about the guts of the saints to the end. In this case, we can say that the TUBIG formula is not that too big to comprehend; likewise, it applies to the present and future of humanity.

In addition, by holding to the TUBIG formula, the guarantee of already-but-not-yet redemption is better conceived. There is no security in humanity, only in election.[154] Redemption is *consummated* in the atonement. Also, it is not yet, as it is *completed* in the eschatological judgment.[155] The great hope for us is in the oversight of the King of history.

---

153. *Tubig* is the Filipino word for water. I adhere mainly to what is conveyed in TULIP (Total depravity, Unconditional election, Limited atonement, Irresistible grace, and Perseverance of the saints) except regarding the limitedness of Christ's atoning power. Furthermore, I disagree, to a great extent, with Dordt's stance on "the fall" of Adam and Eve. With supralapsarian underpinning, the eating of the fruit is indeed part of God's plan for humanity.

154. In Isa 47, God is the true security.

155. God is the Fulfiller of the eternal decree shown in Isa 48.

We can better appreciate this conception in our next reading of Isaiah through Revelation, having an eye for God's reward for humankind.

3.3 Reading Isaiah through Revelation

We will again critically analyze Isaiah with Revelation to advance the notion of Christian universalism.[156] Isaiah states,

> See, the LORD GOD comes with might, and his arm rules for him; his reward is with him, and his *recompense* before him.[157]

The setting of this pericope is eschatological, in which the LORD God comes with "might."[158] At first, the reader can easily picture a God with enormous power to rule using the "arm" of law or authority. The appropriation, of course, comfortably fits the judgment motif of Isaiah, where God's exacting punishment is sure. The original language, however, paints a different picture. His might is indeed demonstrated in his arm of rulership not to destroy but to *cure* or *repair*.[159] This is more coherent with the immediate and outer contexts. The coming God brings his reward and recompense. Interestingly, the word *recompense* in Hebrew is derived from the root "make" or "ordain."[160] If we put these thoughts together, it shows that such reward is not static but dynamic. In other words, the receiver of divine recompense is blessed in the cure of the wounded and the repair of the broken.

That constructed thought sits perfectly well with the striking-healing theme expounded in the study. God's power is for comforting the sinners; God's arm is for uplifting the hopeless.[161] The context reveals that the sinners and the hopeless refer to both the Israelites and non-Israelites with the mention of Jerusalem and Lebanon.[162] And last, but certainly

---

156. Isa 40:10; cf. Rev 22:12.

157. Isa 40:10 NRSV; italics added.

158. This event could probably refer to the second coming of Jesus Christ, given its correlation with Rev 22:12.

159. The word *might* is from the Hebrew root *châzâq* (חָזַק), figuratively meaning "cure" or "repair" (*SECB*, h2388).

160. *Recompense* is from the Hebrew root *pâ'al* (פָּעַל), meaning to "make" or "ordain" (*SECB*, h6466).

161. Isa 40:1–2, 9.

162. Isa 40:9, 16.

not least, God's recompense is universally applied.[163] It is the outcome of the messianic initiative to right the wrong—the mortification of the proud and the perfection of the imperfect—the purification of the people.[164] The best argument in favor of the coming God as Healer is God's eternal character portrayed in the entire book of Isaiah. As discussed in this chapter, the judgment is not only restorative, but more importantly, the Judge himself is full of honor and integrity. The sins of Israel and all nations are blotted out for *God's own sake*.[165]

Such eschatological description is repeated nearly verbatim in Revelation: "See, I am coming soon; my reward is with me, to repay according to everyone's work."[166] The thought pattern is almost similar to Isaiah's, except for the reward taken as correlative to individual actions. The quick impulse of the mind suggests the difference in culture: Isaiah (ancient Near Eastern) and Revelation (Graeco-Roman). Despite the awareness of that enclave, the fact remains: the reward is not some sort of satisfaction but scary, due to the evil nature of humanity. Again, the heuristic device in properly interpreting this statement is the lexical study. Sure enough, the *reward* is a payment viewed in a flexible sense (good or bad) depending on the nature of the work. Simply put, "What you sow is what you reap."[167] In the term *repay*, the negative connotation is replaced by something good vis-à-vis one's profit. Furthermore, the term also implies the idea of delivering things (a gift) promised under oath; it is unequivocally advantageous to the recipient.[168]

Even the background of the text supports the positive meaning of repayment for one's work. What we will get corresponding to our action is healing, as alluded to in the previous chapter.[169] God's reward has transforming power to completely change the heart of the awardee—from

163. Isa 40:17.

164. "Fill in the valleys; flatten every hill and mountain. Level the rough and rugged ground" (Isa 40:4 CEV). See also Rev 16:20.

165. Isa 43:25.

166. Rev 22:12 NRSV.

167. *Reward* is from the Greek *misthós* (μισθός), meaning "dues paid for work" (SECB, g3408). See Gal 6:7.

168. The term *repay* in Greek is *apodídōmi* (ἀποδίδωμι), implying the notion of a "profit." It is two words combined: *apó* (ἀπό), having the connotation of "completion" or "reversal," and *dídōmi* (δίδωμι), "commit" or "minister" (SECB, g0591, g0575, g1325).

169. Rev 22:2.

being unruly to being submissive.[170] Perhaps some might probe: why would God be unfair by rewarding positively those who do not deserve it? The answer is from the foreground of the text: the Rewarder is the "Alpha and Omega, the first and the last, the beginning and the end."[171]

The point here is, the divine repayment is non-contingent to actions *ad extra*, but rather, it is contingent on the reliable character of the One who repays. That is to say that God is not at all reactive in his recompense, but he is altogether *proactive* in dispensing his grace as foreordained. It is absurd to presuppose that the divine disposition at the beginning is incoherent with the divine disposition at the end, due to the necessity of equivalent recompense to the actual act. Here, it is necessarily thought that God's disposition to the innocent is unequal to God's disposition to the guilty. So my follow-up query is: who is not guilty? In the review of the being of humans, the answer is none. Who deserves God's reward? In the review of the being of God, the answer is everyone.

What is not absurd, theologically speaking, is that the Alpha is *exactly* the Omega. God's first intention (free to love) perfectly coheres with God's last intention (love for all). The divine repayment is contingent on actions *ad intra* (always been, therefore, always is), and the Judge will vindicate all in the final judgment, since the Judge is Jesus Christ.[172]

Having this concoction of ideas at hand as we tie Isaiah and Revelation together, we can construe that God's elect is not exclusive to Israel but also outside it. The calling of Israel parallels that of the church. Thus, the Jews and the pagans are to be transformed into the image of the covenant Partner. Since the elect are called to imitate the Elect by being a beacon to the world, this shows the universal intent of election. Given the eternal counsel, everyone will know the true God, and everyone will understand God's true character. As the language "my people" is not exclusive to Israel, therefore the language "my chosen" in the eschatos principally applies to Israel before it applies to all nations. We specifically deal here with *chronology*, not priority, in considering the doctrine of election.

Due to the failure of the elect to imitate the Elect, the Elect himself consummated the elected purpose. King Immanuel became *the* beacon to the world by informing us that he is the authentic God and his genuine character is everlasting love. The love of the King is indeed immutable

---

170. Rev 22:3.

171. Rev 22:13 CEV.

172. Rev 22:16.

and unstoppable until the entire humanity benefits from it. Hence the oath, "I have sworn by Myself [God's self], the word has gone forth from My mouth in righteousness and will not turn back, that to Me every knee will bow, every tongue will swear *allegiance*."[173] Now it has been clarified why God not only grants lasting justice but, crucially, irrevocable vindication. It is forever binding. The electing God is simultaneously the King of history. Amid the accounting of our work, what counts in the end is the work of the Elector/Elected. This makes the recompense not an occupational transaction but a covenantal exchange.

In the next chapter, we will scrutinize in more detail why redemption is for all, not to those *deemed* deserving only. Would it be unjust on God's part to redeem those who deserve some sort of punitive act? We will deal with this in the second half of Deutero-Isaiah.

---

173. Isa 45:23 NASB; italics in original.

Chapter V

KINGSHIP OF SACRIFICE

"But he was wounded for our transgressions, crushed for our iniquities; upon him was the punishment that made us whole, and by his bruises we are *healed*."[1]

PREVIOUSLY, WE STUDIED WHY GOD is understood to have been present in consummating preordained actions and events. A salutary eschatology is sure due to the eternality of the Elector. In this chapter, I shall argue that God does not relegate responsibility for the pain and misery his people experienced, and crucially, God does justify his actions. In this line of thinking, I shall also argue that striking-healing is congruent with the character of God.

To deliver these objectives, we have to consider the doctrine of redemption under the doctrine of God. Soteriology will be examined strictly with the formulation of the Servant-King as derived from Isaiah 49–55. We can do so by critically assessing passages emphasizing God's faithfulness, blessedness, purity, and selflessness. With these divine characteristics in mind, we then continue our discussion on theodicy with further intensity.

It is time to delve into the fifth section of Isaiah with special attention to the redemptive role of God.

---

1. Isa 53:5 NRSV; italics added.

1. SUMMARY OF ISAIAH 49-55

A figure who is called the Servant of God is going to fulfill the divine commission and do what Israel fails to do. God grants this Servant the title "Israel" and sends him on a mission, primarily to restore the people of Israel to their Lord. The second mission is to bring the kingdom of God to all nations in the power of the Spirit. It sounds exactly like the messianic King described in the introductory part of Isaiah, yet the Servant will accomplish the mission.

The Servant is going to be rejected, tortured, and eventually killed by his own people. In Isaiah, the Servant is accused and sentenced to death on behalf of the sin of his people. This shows that such death is a sacrificial atonement for Israel bringing about redemption. But after the Servant's death, all of a sudden, he is alive again! By his sacrifice, Israel is made righteous—in a right relationship with the Lord.

This section concludes by describing two ways people respond to the sacrifice of the Servant of God. Some will respond with humility and accept the sacrificial death on their behalf. They are the servants of God, the seed in the first section. They will experience the blessing of the messianic kingdom. However, others will reject the Servant as well as God's servants.

After the summary of the fifth section of Isaiah, we will now examine why God is conceived to be absolutely responsible as the Redeemer.

2. GOD AS REDEEMER

We have to continue our discussion of the eternal covenant because it is foundational in understanding soteriology in light of God's character. The first principle of the covenant is that it is God's.[2] The Lord initiates it, so he consummates it as well.[3] But although it is God's, it is made *with* humanity.[4] The second principle is that the covenant is permanent.[5] God is eternal; this goes with the thought that his covenant with humanity is also without end. When the Lord says he will be Israel's God, the commitment does not lapse; likewise, when God says Israel will be his people,

2. Isa 49:1.

3. Isa 54:10.

4. Isa 49:5; Gen 17:7.

5. Isa 49:8; Jer 32:40.

the appointment does not expire. We can see here the dual essence of the covenant: the divine role and the stipulation for the human.

We also have to be aware that what the Lord says is a command.[6] The stability and permanence of the covenant are rooted in the command. In the firmness and resoluteness of God, the covenant is said to last in time and even after time. As the commitment "I will" results in the command "you will" grants that the covenanted self of God produces the covenanted people, and in this way, the covenant transcends termination.[7] In the eternal binding of God to humanity and vice versa, we can derive the soteriological implication of the covenant. It is within the covenantal terms that the unfaithfulness of humanity is forgiven. It is also within it that the covenant members are made faithful.[8]

Significantly, it is in human unfaithfulness that divine faithfulness is best appreciated. The faithful pledge to send the Messiah is the guarantee of God's covenant with Israel.[9] God will not fail his people, for God does not forget them.[10] He will always be the Lord to the people. His command is irrevocable.[11] We have seen God's faithfulness to Israel by his being true to his promise to Abraham.[12] The faithfulness continues to the children of Israel, and more importantly, it is retained in the church—the spiritual descendants of Abraham.[13] But the greatest testimony to the faithfulness of God is shown in the identification of the Messiah with Abraham. Isaiah says, "You are My Servant, *Israel.*"[14]

In examining the context, there are four reasons why the Messiah is called Israel: first, to bring glory to God; second, to lead the Israelites back to God; third, to be a light to the gentiles; and last, to bring salvation to the whole world.[15] Israel, as a nation, should have brought glory, restoration, light, and salvation to the ends of the earth through personification. The people ought to *be* God's glory, restoring agent, light, and salvation. In other words, they can only act out the commission by

6. Isa 49:18b–19.
7. Isa 49:8b, 15b.
8. Isa 50:10.
9. Isa 49:3, 5; 50:4–5. Rom 11:25–27.
10. God is faithful as presented in Isa 49.
11. Isa 51:4–6; Rom 11:29.
12. Isa 51:2.
13. Gal 3:16, 29; Rom 9:6–8.
14. Isa 49:3 NASB; italics added.
15. Isa 49:3b, 5b, 6b.

their *being*. However, their being fell short before God which negatively impacted their duty. That is exactly why the Servant (Israel) is sent to fulfill the duty accorded to the servants (Israel): the efficiency of the former is to override the delinquency of the latter. This speaks of the firm and resolute covenant of God.

In contrast, when we make a promise, the promise is not guaranteed because of our limitedness.[16] We do not hold the future. We cannot fully control what is happening around us. We cannot even substantially prolong life. In other words, there are indeed many factors hindering humanity from fulfilling its promise. This explains that in the covenant, human beings will always fail God.[17]

It is plain in Isaiah that failure is incompatible with the Lord.[18] When God says Israel will *be* his people, this comes with the notion that God will never go against himself as the Lord of Israel.[19] In the covenant, the promise is also a divine command. The act is beyond revocation and termination as it arises from abiding faithfulness.[20]

2.1 Redemption through Offering

It is interesting to note that in Isaiah 1–48, the Messiah is portrayed as the "Lion" of Judah; remarkably in Isaiah 49–55, the Messiah is portrayed as the "Lamb" of Judah.[21] Such polarized messianic descriptions mark the dual roles of Jesus Christ. Like the Lion, Christ stands as the conqueror of the sin problem; as the Lamb, Christ stands as the offering for sins.[22] Crucially, we have to understand that the Lion and the Lamb are eternally paired, indicating that the conquest of sin is through the offering of the Conqueror. That is to say that the Messiah is sent to Israel to reign in the effect of self-sacrifice.

We discussed in the previous chapter that Jesus is *the* chosen One (Christ). In Isaiah, the chosen holy One is also the Redeemer:

16. Isa 51:18–19.

17. Isa 50:2a.

18. Isa 50:7; Rom 11:29.

19. Isa 52:5.

20. Isa 50:4b.

21. For example, Isa 31:4; 53:7; cf. Hos 5:14; Rev 5:12.

22. Rev 5:5–6.

> Thus says the LORD, the Redeemer of Israel and his Holy One, to one deeply *despised, abhorred* by the nations, the *slave* of rulers.[23]

The Holy One of Israel is held in contempt, regarded as utterly abominable.[24] God surrenders himself as an offering on behalf of the people as the next kin responsible to buy back or regain what was lost.[25] This sets the tone for the selflessness of God vis-à-vis Israel. By self-sacrifice, God reconciles with his beloved. The Lord treats Israel in a levelling up fashion—that is, from beloved friend to beloved kin. In the divine reality, the Beloved (Jesus Christ) is sacrificed for the good of the beloved (Israel). This epitomizes the reign of King Immanuel.[26]

Jesus Christ reigns over Israel when he voluntarily offers himself to pay the penalty of people. When Israel reached the peak of its self-centeredness, the Holy One of Israel had to overcome the evil of the human self by offering God's self.[27] As humanity is by nature selfish and in its humanity sins, Christ's selflessness overcomes it.[28] In Christ's being, our being is retained in the covenant. To elaborate, what is self-centered is made other-centered. Accordingly, the sacrificial act of the Son makes the covenant permanent. Here we can infer that the offering for sin is said to have successfully conquered sin.[29]

The ingenious metaphorical employment of the Lion-Lamb undergirds the initiation and consummation of the covenant. The Lion commands the direction set for the covenant members. The Lamb is the promise for the members to stay covenanted. In being covenanted, our failure is dominated and solved by the success of the Lord of the covenant. By extrapolation, through the divine-human (Jesus Christ), we are redeemed. The christologic conception of redemption is key in understanding why humankind anticipates a salutary eschatos. We can also deduce from the logical structure that the Lion-Lamb is undeniably the divine-human; and crucially, the messianic reign continues in the end-time judgment.

23. Isa 49:7a NRSV; italics added.

24. The Hebrew for *despise* is *bâzôh* (בָּזֹה), meaning "hold in contempt" (*SECB*, h0960). For *abhor* it is *ta'âb* (תַעֵב), meaning "utterly abominable" (*SECB*, h8581).

25. The Hebrew for *Redeemer* is *gâ'al* (גָּאַל), meaning "to be the next of kin" to buy back (*SECB*, h1350).

26. Isa 49:7; Luke 23:35.

27. Isa 50:5–6.

28. Isa 51:5a.

29. Isa 51:11.

Humanity is bound to successfully go through judgment due to the enduring character of the Redeemer. Jesus Christ the Redeemer is ever faithful to stand on behalf of the accused.[30] It is written in Isaiah,

> I gave My back to those who struck *Me*, and My cheeks to those who plucked out the beard; I did not hide My face from shame and spitting.[31]

The weight and severity of judgment should have been on humanity; instead, they are on the Lord. The Lamb is synchronous with the Lion. This shows how sin is overcome by the offering, in this case, strong and efficient. The offering is strong, as sin is no match compared to it. The offering is efficient, for sin is resolved.[32] How is this so? It is through the eternal resolve to be the Lord of people.

Let us put that to the test. If God is eternally firm in being the Lord of his people, then we can presuppose that the commitment "I will" can mean that God shall never abandon his people with the judicial decision—guilty. The verdict of the Judge (the Lion) against the guilty coincides with the vindication of the Judged (the Lamb).[33] In other words, the command "I will judge my people" is married with the promise "You will be vindicated." The eschatological scenario is where the Redeemer is conceived as ever faithful to stand on behalf of the ever unfaithful.[34] The comfort and assurance of the covenanted are grounded in the stability and permanence of the self-covenanted God.

2.2 Justice in the Covenant

The self-covenanted Deity, as indicated in Isaiah, is the self-sacrificing Deity.[35] This conception brings us to the rendition of the Judge (being judged) as the Servant-King. Jesus Christ is the Servant in taking the sin of the world. Jesus Christ is the King in taking sin once and for all.[36] It is apparent in the Isaianic narratives that God will vindicate, without

30. Isa 49:7.
31. Isa 50:6 NKJV; italics in original.
32. Isa 52:3.
33. Isa 51:4–5.
34. Isa 49:23b, 26b.
35. Isa 52:5–6.
36. Isa 52:7.

hesitation, the condemned.[37] That is not to say the guilty avoid condemnation. The accused shall suffer eternal death. The doctrine of God over
the doctrine of redemption implies an unimaginable and unprecedented
turn of events.[38] Instead of people bearing the penalty of death, the Re-
deemer-Judge willingly takes death.[39] Of course, this assertion has to be
in the covenantal paradigm. If not, then it will be untenable against the
challenge posed by the notion of *fair* justice and fairness to human choice
as in rejecting the offer of redemption.

Retributive justice, as affirmed worldwide, demands a fair sentence
equating to the punishment of the guilty and vindication of the innocent.
In this type of Cicerean justice, it is simply implausible, let alone appall-
ing, to suggest that the guilty is vindicated. Someone is willing to take the
punishment instead.[40] It is, generally speaking, unheard of in a proper
judicial system. We are to remember the strangeness and alienness of
God's ways and means tackled in chapter 3—also affording logic where
there can be none to locate in human terms. Beyond the narrower focus
on questions of jurisprudence, the proceedings and outcome of judgment
are totally unlike the finite judiciary praxis.[41] The underlying premise in
the human and worldly is the equivalence of the indemnification to the
offense. Yet as amplified in chapter 4, God's disposition against the guilty
coheres with God's association *with* the guilty. In which case, God freely
decides to be punished for the guilt of his people.[42] Does it mean that
God, together with the guilty, will be punished in judgment? The answer
is within the covenantal schema.

In keeping with judgment, it is apparent that the Redeemer had assumed the guilt of all.[43] Because Jesus Christ is the Son of God who is
always the Son of Man, what is ours is taken. The Athanasian formula
of what has been redeemed is vital in the discussion. Athanasius posits
that "the Logos has become man, and has not entered into a man" undergirds that the assumed humanity of Christ is of the human race (*humani*

---

37. As stated in Isa 50, God is the Vindicator.

38. Isa 52:9.

39. Isa 53:8.

40. See Cicero, *De Legibus*, I.45–48.

41. Isa 52:15.

42. Isa 53:4.

43. Isa 53:6.

generis).[44] The assumption of humanity is appointed beforehand due to its incapacity to remain in the covenant. Judah has to stay faithful and obedient to survive and thrive as a nation. However, we have also observed that Judah instead opted to worship and serve other deities. This transpired as the people were bewildered over God's dealing with them. In effect, they denied the LORD God and embraced Bel and Nebo. Judah is limited in discernment and incapable of enduring loyalty. To this end, she deserves punishment, not vindication.

But when Judah quitted on God, God did not quit on her, owing to his uncompromised lordship.[45] God acquitted Judah by assuming her penalty. The same motif is transmitted to judgment. The guilty will not suffer eternal damnation; the Judge suffered on their behalf.[46] This is not undermining fair justice *per se*. What is also irreducible is the firmness and resolve of the covenant. The true guilty did suffer under the command of the imposing Judge, albeit in discipline. This means that people suffer temporarily, so they do not have to suffer permanently.[47] The aim of divine discipline is reinstitution. In striking the guilty, the healing comes.

Reinstitution is the consummation of the covenant in which the stricken is healed.[48] What is healed, according to Gregory Nazianzen, is the *humani generis*.[49] It can be inferred here that the striking is temporary, and the healing is permanent. We are acquitted in the covenant, likewise, made worthy for the reward.[50] The traced soterio-eschatological pattern is sure, for the Vindicator is simultaneously the Redeemer.[51] In a sense, the covenanted lordship is truly enduring. The substitutionary sacrifice does not lapse; the appointed redemption does not expire. This is alluded to in Isaiah,

> The sky will vanish like smoke; the earth will wear out like clothes. Everyone on this earth will die like flies. But my *victory* will last; my *saving power* never ends.[52]

44. Kelly, *Early Christian Doctrines*, 284–87.
45. Isa 51:12–13.
46. Isa 51:22.
47. Isa 51:20b, 23.
48. Isa 52:4, 9b.
49. *Ep.* 101, 32; *Sources Chrétiennes* 208, 50.
50. Isa 49:4b, 5b.
51. Isa 50:2b, 8a.
52. Isa 51:6b CEV; italics added.

On the one side, what is God's never ceases; his victory over sin can be neither countered nor abolished. Respectively, Israel remains the people of God. This can never be negated nor invalidated. On the other side, what is not from God does not persist, let alone prevail. This proves that nothing can hinder the foreordained redemption.

2.3 The Redeemer and the Redeemed

No doubt, it is traditionally accepted that people can choose to reject the offer of redemption. The paradigmatic complexity in dealing with the people's response is in God's will against human choice.[53] If God is free in willing the redemption of humankind, yet God also accounts for human choice, what happens to his will? Does this imply that the covenant will have to surrender to human choice? And worse, is it how divine sovereignty expresses itself? But my follow-up concern is on the actual demonstration of the lordship of God over humanity. Is it to manifest God's will, or to respect human will, or both? The query is set in a multi-dimensional truth, never simply a given; but the harmony between God's will and human will develops from within the seeming contradictions themselves.

If people can nullify what God desires, then divine sovereignty is marred.[54] Thus the potency of our freedom is back on the agenda. Our potency, nevertheless, is that which is hostile to the advancement of the divine lordship and character.[55] But one might persist in asking: what need is there for choice if God so determined to redeem all? I would say, first of all, this undergirds God's choice for humanity and not vice versa. God has chosen to be in Jesus Christ to bring about reconciliation. God foreordains all unto himself. With this, the *free agency* and moral responsibility of humans still hold, yet subsidiary only to Christ's assumption of accountability for the negligence or misuse of them. I am not downplaying the proper accounting of human agency; Jesus nevertheless shows that only he can satisfy the tough demand of the righteous judgment of God.[56]

---

53. de Vera, "Controversy of Calvinist Theology," 12.

54. Isa 50:2b–4. Neither is God's freedom to sacrificially love advanced if God has given in to human choice.

55. Isa 52:6, 10.

56. Isa 53:10.

I belittle confidence in humanity because of my aversion to the overrated self-hinging on the Aristotelian potentiality. I laud God's accomplishment in Jesus Christ. The admittance effectively situates Christ's sacrificial act in judgment without detriment to either divine primacy or human integrity. It is a must to consider the doctrine of redemption under the doctrine of God. If not, the conversation will be more anthropocentric than theocentric. I advocate not just the theocentric conception of redemption but the Christocentric conception of it.

The discussion about soteriology should be rigidly Christocentric. Otherwise, there is a probability that the direction of conversation slips into Pelagianism or semi-anthropocentrism. Guards must be up in the philosophical-theological articulation of how human beings are viewed as restituted by a divine-human being. If one is unconvinced of the effectuality of the offering, one misses the point of the sacrificial act. Our nature will always find reasons for our contribution to redemption, since our nature is human accountability in the first place. When we are made accountable, by default, we are likewise made to correct our mistake or pay the penalty of our offense. Even though this sounds reasonable and just, it is not the case in redemption.

I know that human freedom has to be included in speaking of soteriology, but I also know, even better, that the divine freedom to save all has to be said more loudly and clearly. This will not undermine the justice of God. It is imparted to us in respect to the being of the Son of God. Likewise, it will not sidetrack the righteousness of God. Such righteousness is imputed to us—in respect to the being of the Son of Man. In other words, Jesus Christ in and of himself is the persistent voice of God's declaration that should not be silenced in considering our freedom.

Of course, I concede that the reader should be accorded due space to argue for one's disregard of the offered redemption. What I do not concede is that one's choice supersedes that of God's.[57] In the covenant, human destiny is congruous with human identity; and in covenantal terms, human identity is inseparable from divine identity; that is, the covenant members are God's.[58] That is to say that in covenantal partnership, we are made to identify with the Lord. As a result, such identification with God is shot right through our destiny as well.[59] Respectively, God has no

---

57. Isa 54:5.

58. Isa 54:17b.

59. Isa 52:12b; 54:15.

end, so neither does the covenanted. The ultimate destiny of humanity is dictated by what is penultimate: God's choice to be with humans forever. Such determination against the nature of human beings is expressed in Isaiah:

> How beautiful upon the mountains are the feet of the messenger who announces peace, who brings good news, who announces salvation, who says to Zion, "Your God reigns."[60]

As King Immanuel reigns in peace, the broken relationship between God and Israel is mended.[61] When Israel is forgiven, it is complete. It is not only executed, but significantly, it has to be proclaimed to the people. The good news is, God has overcome the offense against him by reconciliation: the offender is set free from guilt and from condemnation, too. Here, the old Zion is declared the new Zion, not because of the choice of its inhabitants; instead, it is the choice of its King.

Something does not add up if humanity is the placeholder in gaining peace with God. In the efficacy of the redemptive act, true peace has very little to do with what humans can do, as in the Epicurean sense, but it has everything to do with what God has done. There is not a reasonable explanation of this passage from Isaiah if the good news is announced only to some, while others are not privileged of regeneration. Though there is an obvious tension here that is problematic, a conceptual response is unaccommodated in the Christocentric view of redemption.[62] We need to uphold the Lord's commitment to *sacrificially love*. This eliminates the exploitation of one for another or the magnification of one over another. Moreover, human freedom and divine commitment need to be balanced to correct past mistakes and construct a way through deadlocks in the Reformed tradition.[63] Although apostasy is more likely the reality of being human, yet this reality should fall under divine reality (under righteous judgment). That is the true meaning of the ascendancy of God's choice over human choice. In the sacrificial act of Jesus Christ, God invalidates rejection by overriding the reality of humanity.[64]

---

60. Isa 52:7 NRSV.

61. *Peace* in Hebrew is *shâlôm* (שׁלֹם), denoting the idea of "completeness" or "making amends" (*SECB*, h7965).

62. "Problematic" means that it "has been understood as an intellectual mystery to which one can respond conceptually" (Gallaher, *Freedom and Necessity*, 227).

63. Muller, "Reception and Response," 196.

64. Isa 54:2–3.

Still, within this christological construct, I also give room to God's freedom not to redeem some people or even most people. This is something Karl Barth accords to God without reservation. Barth reiterates that "we cannot avoid to if we understand Jesus Christ and his work than to look for, yes, look for universal salvation," which means that we should not preach what we cannot be certain about. Barth adds, "Because salvation is an act and a decision of God's free grace . . . if we proclaim [it] . . ., then we take away God's freedom to do it."[65] I simply do not understand why the preaching of the *viability* of Christian universalism would violate God's freedom at all. When I attest to it, I also presume that I do not, in any way, obligate God (at least in my mind), to save all. I can see the practicality of not preaching what is inexplicit in the Bible. However, I can equally see the philo-theological viability and the magnanimity of the foreground of the redemptive act having the everlasting covenant as the background.[66]

That gives me the platform to accord God the freedom to pass over the denouncers of redemption but with reservation. In Isaiah, it is God's choice to be with Israel forever. Thus, I see the talk of divine freedom differently. So, in this regard, I part ways with Barth. The liberty not to save all is unremoved by pushing the covenant agenda. I simply present the philo-theological trajectory of the redemptive act. Moreover, what is biblically sound is that in speaking of divine freedom, what stands out is the God *pro nobis*.[67] I have sympathetic regard for David Bentley Hart's position that "the universalist understanding of its [Christian] message is the only one possible."[68] In deep introspection, to follow the Moltmannian spirit of embracing with joy the thought of universalism is not that difficult to welcome.[69] But it does not necessarily ensue that if a theological assertion holds to divine freedom, it necessitates limited atonement or the damnation of some. In navigating through Barth's reconfiguration of election, I am not convinced that he distances himself from the universalist argument. In fact, he reviews it with excitement.[70] Thus I align

---

65. Barth, *Gespräche*, 341.

66. Isa 54:5; 55:5b.

67. Isa 50:4a, 9a.

68. Hart continues, "And, quite imprudently, I say that without the least hesitation or qualification" (Hart, *That All Shall Be Saved*, 3).

69. Moltmann, *Coming of God*, 250.

70. Since Barth's impulse on reconciliation as universal rests on God's suffering love and freedom, then the universality of redemption, logically, is not merely an open

with Tom Greggs's observation that Barth's doctrine of election "tends very strongly in a universalist direction": the future reality of humanity is orientated by the simultaneity of election.[71] Even the "worst of our fellows" can be reckoned as saints in the coincident histories of God and humanity. Saints are made in the direction set by divine suffering.[72]

We will now examine why the Lord is said to be a suffering God, in order to comprehend the guarantee of redemption.

3. THE SUFFERING GOD

Redemption is guaranteed in the notion of the Suffering God. In suffering, God is the Lord; and in being so, the reconciliation of peace is warranted. The text states,

> He was despised and *forsaken* of men, a man of sorrows and *acquainted with grief*, and like one from whom men hide their face; He was despised, and we did not esteem Him.[73]

The Messiah is the utmost cursed. It is in this thought that Israel is blessed. What it entails concerns how redemption is enforced, whereas it does not deal with liability in terms of the sacrificial act. The Messiah suffered not because of his own sin but of humanity's. Concerning the

---

possibility. Universal redemption is not an event that might or could happen—that is, having a construct of conditionality. But crucially, people should "be open to it" which, for Barth, is a matter of fact given the redeeming sacrifice. The open possibility of universal redemption is understood as the eschatological reality in God, a reality of God's withdrawal of the final threat to humanity (condemnation) (Barth, *CD* IV/3, 478). Thus the "threat" in discussion remains a threat because it has no possibility of finally happening against what Barth calls the "super-abundant promise" of universal reconciliation (Barth, *CD* IV/3, 478). This validates Jesus Christ as the perfect Representative of all humanity. It is perfect in the sense that it is true and actual; after all, Christ's representation, is, in fact, irreversible and irrevocable, recalling God's commitment in and to the covenant.

71. Greggs, *Barth, Origen, and Universal Salvation*, 22–24.

72. Barth, *CD* IV/2, 433. Barth's distaste for any form of *-ism* emerges from his tough advocacy of the gospel. His attention is not on a certain theory or praxis but rather on the Subject of the gospel—Jesus Christ. Thus Barth says, "I do not believe in universal salvation, but I do believe in Jesus Christ the universal Saviour" (Dawson, *Resurrection in Karl Barth*, 190–92). For Barth, redemption (like predestination) is not a number game. The Subject of theology (Christ the substitutionary Sacrifice) matters, not theology itself. In this context, I understand that Barth simply refuses to be dragged into a static telos of God's redeeming sacrifice.

73. Isa 53:3 NASB; italics added.

substitutionary element of suffering, the idea of discipline is non-applicable. What is applicable is the redemptive effect of the substitutionary sacrifice for all. This particular human can be "the Godforsaken" for the "God-unforsaken."[74] Jesus is the former as the Reprobate, while Jesus is the latter as the Redeemer.

In the interest of the study of the suffering God, let us call this human the "unforsaken Sacrifice."[75] Jesus Christ is the unforsaken Sacrifice because he is the universal Identifier of humankind. The Son of God (in divine reality) cannot be the One who had been abandoned. Otherwise, this would implicate the divine abandonment of humans—an idea hardly accommodated in Isaiah.[76] In the Son of God as the Son of Man, the forsaken has become the unforsaken. Whatever the LORD God has renounced, Israel's continual wickedness and apostasy have been resolved (in their entirety) through the identified Reprobate. That in part provides a window in examining the healing of Israel vis-à-vis the self-offering of the Messiah. As stated,

> But He *was* wounded for our transgressions, *He was* bruised for
> our iniquities; the chastisement for our peace *was* upon Him,
> and by His stripes we are *healed*.[77]

The Messiah is beaten and battered for the reinvigoration of Israel.[78] In the suffering of the Servant-King, the faults and stubbornness of Israel are mended. The messianic initiative is unconfined to an evangelistic mission. It also stands as the quintessential contemptible or abominable mission. Here, it is reasonable to suppose that the Messiah is the ultimate Reprobate, so humanity might be complete in God's sight. While there may be other implications of peace, the best meaning of it, at least in this study, is the completeness or perfection of humanity.

By taking the soterio-eschatological implications of the identified Reprobate, I can say with confidence that the inconceivable has become conceivable and the impossible possible. When the Son of God is seen with the Son of Man, the inconceivable condescension (incarnation and crucifixion) of God becomes conceivable in Jesus of Nazareth. When the

74. de Vera, *Suffering of God*, 193.

75. de Vera, *Suffering of God*, 193.

76. Isa 49:15; 50:8–9.

77. Isa 53:5 NKJV; italics added.

78. *Wounded* in Hebrew is *chăburâh* (חַבּוּרָה), meaning "stripe" or "bruise" (*SECB*, h2250).

Son of Man is taken as the Son of God, the impossible exaltation (resurrection and glorification) of humanity becomes possible in that human as well. The guarantee and the realization of the redemption of all are in Jesus Christ's representation.[79] Furthermore, such representation cannot be nullified. What has been represented cannot be unrepresented. The represented stays as such; the Original is permanent in its nature and steadfast in its purpose.[80] This prefigures that the perfected remains perfect before the eschatological Judge. The integrity of the suffering God is uncompromised, as the effectiveness of redemption can never be minimized in scope. Even in an extended application, "redemption is a product of sacrifice."[81]

3.1 Suffering for All

We can value the universal application of the redemptive act in Barth's formulation of "the Lord as Servant" (regarding the *kenosis*) if we take it as Christ's fulfillment of the agreement for God.[82] Furthermore, we can better apprehend Barth's genius conception of "the Servant as Lord" (regarding human exaltation) if we take it as the fulfillment of the agreement for humanity.[83] In other words, the former indicates how God deals with sin, while the latter indicates how he triumphs over it.

When I say the covenant of God concerns all peoples, this expresses the universal efficacy of Jesus Christ's redemptive act.[84] God's love seeks all. God truly is free in his will if he chooses to redeem all.[85] The word *all* is descriptive of all human beings of all times and places.[86] The universal tone is amplified in the identity of Jesus Christ as a Jew. Subsequently, Christ's identification with the Jews does not show exclusiveness in God

79. Isa 51:16.

80. Isa 55:3.

81. Even if the background is political—the Spanish colonization—the underlying effect is similar. José Rizal (the national hero of the Philippines) once said, "Filipinos don't realize that victory is the child of struggle, that joy blossoms from suffering, and redemption is a product of sacrifice" (Rizal, "Como se gobiernan las Filipinas," para. 9).

82. Barth, *CD* IV/1, 157–60.

83. Barth, *CD* IV/2, 69–72.

84. Isa 49:7, 12.

85. Isa 49:8–9.

86. For example, Isa 52:10; 54:13; 55:12b.

but rather inclusiveness. God is all-inclusive in calling the human race back to him.[87] Also, the Jewishness of Christ somehow accepts the redeeming sacrifice: the passion and crucifixion are tied to Judaism. The creaturely categories, namely, gender, race, or even religion, are not issues for or against a person's reconciliation. The only advantage of being a believer, I think, is the thought that in Jesus, Christians are in solidarity with all other humans. Thus camaraderie and not sectarianism is the prominent theme of Isaianic eschatology.

Reinstitution is for everyone. The identification with Christ is open to all, across generations.[88] In freedom, God places the entire humanity under verdict. In love, God pronounces rapprochement to all.[89] When Jesus Christ is called Israel, he constitutes God's glory, restoration, light, and salvation—initially for the people of Israel and then for all peoples. Christ is said to have been successful in being; thus, the consummating act is successful as well. That is why I see no reason to shun the eschatological truth.

We can be modest in theology, but we can be bold, too, for the sake of the gospel—the triumph of Jesus Christ's redemptive role for all. Consequently, condemnation no longer exists at the end of God's history with humanity. The sinner is already destroyed and replaced. The sinner is destroyed in Christ's redeeming act, while the sinner is replaced through Christ's redeeming being. In the servanthood of Christ, the sinner becomes a saint. In the lordship of Jesus, the sinner is made just and righteous. Sin is not just dwarfed in this framework but eradicated in the immensity of the redeeming sacrifice. The gospel, therefore, amplifies the covenantal fellowship God has for us.

One could argue that an open reconciliation does not automatically equate to the universality of redemption. But these two notions are not irreconcilable positions in Isaiah due to the objective nature of the messianic sacrifice.[90] The objectivity is in strict conjunction with its Subject—Jesus Christ, the suffering Redeemer. Since the suffering Redeemer is also the sovereign King, we can derive that in the suffering of God, the suffering of humanity will cease in the end. Why? Jesus Christ redeems everyone. If this is not the case, Israel (the Servant) also failed

87. Isa 51:21–22.
88. Isa 52:10.
89. Isa 53:5–6. See Col 1:13.
90. Isa 53:3–6.

in his mission just like Israel (the servants) before him. But it can never be so; the being of the Servant is true to its commission. More generally, this heightens Israel's sense of his global mission. The efficiency of the Messiah overshadows the deficiency of the people. The Author of the covenant and the covenant itself have been proven firm and faithful.

Others simply do not need to take a stance in support (or not) of total redemption. Redemption is not about scope but *hope*; but I do need to take such a stance. My attention is not on the universal hope of redemption but the universal scope of the being in the act of Jesus Christ. Otherwise, the discussion tends to nosedive into the quagmire of hoping against hope itself. Jesus as the Son of God is universally applied in its determination to assume the being of humanity (unjust and unfaithfulness). Jesus's act as the Son of Man is universally applied in its actualization of the assumption of humanity (made just and faithful).[91] But what about those who will reject the redeeming sacrifice? My response to this comes back to God's character vis-à-vis the Isaianic theme of striking-healing.

God is faithful and pure. The despisers of the redeeming sacrifice shall be stricken; therefore, they will suffer the divine condemnation and punishment. Nevertheless, as the Lord is simultaneously selfless in blessing the object of his sacrifice, the stricken will finally be healed and restituted.[92] Robin Parry alludes to the healing of Israel in Isaiah, after the severe prophecies.[93] If God would only strike the guilty without the aim of healing them in the end, then God would be inconsistent with his character. Moreover, if the redeeming sacrifice is not efficacious to all (only to those who accept it in this life), the divine glory, restoration, light, and salvation failed in its content and purpose. Their intent is for all. At the apex of the discourse is the notion that universalistic ideas in Second Isaiah are related but distinct in terms of the Lord's dominion over the world, the heathen's recognition of God, and their salvific experience.[94]

The cosmic efficacy of redemption is not based on shaky ground. It is rooted in the stability and permanence of the covenant. The Partner already suffered in the covenant so that his partners would no longer suffer

---

91. Isa 53:12.

92. Isa 53:11; 54:1.

93. Parry, *Lamentations*, 162.

94. Gelston, "Universalism in Second Isaiah," 396.

by being kept in it.[95] It is preposterous to assume that the covenant transcends termination but not the lapses of humanity. It is equally absurd to suppose that Christ's apotheotic conquest of sin is discounted because of the weight of human action in the final judgment. The hope in Christ is fixed in the no under the yes of judgment.[96] In the soterio-eschatology of Isaiah, the positive dimension overtakes the negative.[97] Jesus Christ is the content and purpose, not merely of the Great Commission, but also of the great character of God.

3.2 Divine Suffering and Divine Discipline

The Isaianic drama presents the horrific-yet-magnificent act of redemption foreordained for humankind. In humility, the Messiah truly becomes the Immanuel.[98] In glory, the Messiah truly becomes the King.[99] We do well to review the Lion-Lamb paradigm in conjunction with the characteristic of King Immanuel to fully appreciate the doctrine of redemption under the doctrine of God. Here, the Lion bespeaks the mighty Deliverer, and the Lamb bespeaks the suffering Redeemer.

The Lion King typifies God's self-determination ending fear and shame of the people.[100] Israel is ordained for redemption when the Messiah is prophesied to rule with justice and righteousness.[101] The people have to anticipate it with endurance. It is in this anticipation where disgrace and humiliation are forgotten.[102] Because the King of Israel acts like a lion, this means that what God has predetermined shall be realized; and similarly, it implies that the people shall have what they hope and anticipate for.[103] As a result, the reproach of Israel is appointed to end.

The Lamb Immanuel typifies the divine self-determination to suffer without reservation over humanity's sin. Israel was ordained for redemption when the Messiah promised to rule with justice and righteousness.

95. Isa 54:4.
96. Isa 54:7.
97. Isa 54:6.
98. Isa 53:2; Phil 2:5–8.
99. Isa 53:12a; Phil 2:9–10.
100. Isa 54:4a.
101. Isa 54:10.
102. Isa 54:4b.
103. Isa 54:11–14.

The people received justice in foreordination and enjoyed righteousness in the promise.[104] Because Immanuel acts like a lamb, this indicates that the predetermined self-sacrifice of God is realized. Likewise, it denotes that the people already have what they had hoped for and anticipated. In effect, the reproach of Israel ended as appointed.[105]

The Lion-Lamb imagery is helpful in the handling of the striking-healing paradigm. On the one hand, it would be difficult to associate firm and unstoppable punishment with God if one fails to see God as the Lion. Israel must experience striking, as the Lion is the King. The King knows what is best for the subjects due to his irrefutable competence.[106] On the other hand, it would also be difficult to associate the requisite and sufficient self-sacrifice to God if one fails to see God as the Lamb. It is unequivocally essential for Israel to undergo healing, since the Lamb is Immanuel. Immanuel knows the best for the people due to his abiding companionship. It is in the reign of King Immanuel that Israel is truly blessed. God lifts his people; joy overtakes them.[107]

We can see God's blessedness before Israel by his reinstituting the people according to the promise. It is the appointed reality for Israel and all nations:

> Fear not, for you will not be put to shame; and do not feel humiliated, for you will not be disgraced; but you will forget the shame of your youth, and no longer remember the disgrace of your widowhood.[108]

In blessedness, the people have peace; the then is overrun by the now. In and through the LORD God, peace replaces fear. Their supposed destiny (condemnation) is no longer real; their identity is with their Lord. In this framework, God had assumed shame and humiliation. Disgrace and reproach can no longer haunt them as God already determined it for himself. Accordingly, in the divine self-humiliation, Israel will not be humiliated. In peace, Israel has no reason to fear. This, however, does not negate the implementation of divine justice through divine discipline.

---

104. Isa 54:16–17.

105. Isa 51:7b, 54:4b.

106. Isa 54:17b; 55:3a.

107. Isaiah 51 tells us that God is the One who genuinely blesses.

108. Isa 54:4 NASB.

When Immanuel offered himself as King, this speaks of God's self-taken responsibility for Israel.[109] God does not have to dodge the theodical questions thrown at him because of the sufficiency and efficiency of his self-sacrifice. Also, God defends the way he disciplines his people. God can empathize with them. As attested in Isaiah, God had suffered for them before they suffered under his care. It is a major reconfiguration in how we think about the atrocities of war in the Isaianic narratives. Such thought is sustainable if the spotlight is steady on Jesus Christ.

The decisive Christ is in the covenant. He upholds the covenant by leading Israel to justice and righteousness by being the Son of God. The Son is the Lord of humanity as God rules over Israel. In such rulership, human beings are made ready for redemption.[110] As long as we stay within the covenant, redemption is guaranteed. There is nothing we can do to thwart the salvific trajectory. The One who has the final say in the covenant is its Lord.[111]

When the great Lion offered himself as the meek Lamb, this speaks of the divine self-taken accountability for Israel.[112] God justified the way he disciplines his people because God unreservedly sacrificed for them. Here we can see how obedient Jesus Christ is in the covenant.[113] Christ preserves the covenant by being the justice and righteousness for humanity as the Son of Man. The Son is the Servant because of his sacrificial act. In such an act, humans are redeemed.[114] The covenanted are redeemed. Redemption is final in the covenant, for the offered Servant is also the offering Lord.[115] In this articulation, we can deduce that the operation of God's self in and through the covenant is a kingship of sacrifice.[116]

We are accounted as redeemed since the Messiah is truly stricken.[117] The Messiah is the quintessential afflicted. It is indeed unfair to accuse God of negligence or apathy in considering the afflicted people of God.[118] The God-self originally and chiefly endured the sorrows and griefs

109. Isa 55:10–11.

110. Isa 54:14.

111. Isa 55:13.

112. Isa 50:1–4a.

113. Isa 50:6, 53:7b.

114. God is a suffering God alluded to in Isa 53.

115. Isa 49:26b.

116. Isa 49:1–3.

117. Isa 53:4b.

118. Isa 53:4b.

people had to endure.[119] God is first and utmost sorrowed in the person of the Messiah before Judah experienced terrible sorrow in her captivity. God is first and most grieved in the person of the Messiah before Judah experienced prolonged grief in her exile. Correspondingly, in the notion of divine discipline, it was God who fundamentally suffered; yet he had to be firm in dealing with his people. In a sense, God would rather suffer with his people than to completely let go of them to suffer indefinitely.[120] God's self-sacrifice is the definite no to our imminent unending suffering. The offer of redemption is the definite yes to the imminent end of our suffering in the eschatos.

In the end-time, Jesus Christ is the Eschaton by representing the entire humankind. As Jesus is the One judged guilty of sin, we are judged innocent; and as the One convicted to death, he did die. Therefore, we are set free from such conviction.[121] Having that in mind, I would say that Jesus is not only the temporal sacrifice at Calvary, but crucially, he is also the post-temporal sacrifice in the final judgment. Jesus is the exact exponent of God's pure character by being blameless as a sin offering. The offering is the decisive judgment of God against sin, for Jesus stands as the ultimate Reprobate.[122] This shows that Jesus is the Archetype of the entire humankind. This is what John Calvin missed in his exposition of predestination; he believed that there are vessels of honor (elect) and vessels of wrath (reprobate). In concurrence with Barth, I react to Calvin's presupposition by saying that the vessel of wrath is ultimately Jesus.

Concomitantly, the integrity and scope of the redeeming sacrifice are not subject to human conditioning—that is, through the potency of choice and the actuality of the rejection of redemption. The covenantal appointment of humanity has no expiration. This brings us to P. T. Forsyth's reflection on Isaiah 53 when Forsyth points out, "Christ is to us just what His cross is. All that Christ was in heaven or on earth was put into what He did there . . . . You do not understand Christ till you understand His cross."[123] In the initiation, action, and consummation of God, no one is left unhealed; what the Lord does is based on his persistent grace. Here,

119. Isa 53:4a.
120. Isa 49:4; 53:9a, 12b.
121. Isa 52:2; 53:8–9.
122. Isa 53:3; Gal 3:13.
123. Forsyth, *Cruciality of the Cross*, 44–45.

the healed becomes pure, as the Healer and the healing reshape the discussion on theodicy.[124]

Though God is within his rights to condemn and punish the sinners, he rather assumed the condemnation and the punishment; hence, the free love of God overrules.[125] This is how God is covenanted: eternally willing to suffer despite his due right as the Lord. It is the supreme and true right of the LORD God.[126] Despite having the right to be vengeful against the people, God has rather sworn not to be angry with them.[127] We can read,

> For a brief moment I abandoned you, but with *great compassion*
> I will gather you. In overflowing wrath for a moment I hid my
> face from you, but with *everlasting love* I will have compassion
> on you, says the LORD, your Redeemer.[128]

The passage gives us a convincing theological argument in support of theodicy—a theodicy that is not theoretical, since we can grasp its telos with lucidity. It has been shown that God admits that he "abandoned" his people and "hid his face" from them. It explains the terrible pain and dragging sorrow under God's care. However, such wrath is overruled by compassion and love: in the greatness of compassion, God has gathered his people, and in the everlastingness of love, God has forgiven them. This conveys that what God has sworn to himself is beneficial to the offender. The Redeemer vindicated the offender via justification.

3.3 The Completeness of Justification

We now embark on a study of justification in connection with the redeeming sacrifice. Complete forgiveness and renewal of the redeemed is the justifying effect, not merely of God's discipline but of the covenant itself as well. In other words, the true beauty and power of the redeeming sacrifice are evident in the justification of the sinner; and such justification is comprehensive given the covenantal appointment. It is comprehensive

---

124. God indeed reigns on the earth, as shown in Isa 52.

125. Isa 55:6–7.

126. Isa 55:4–5.

127. Isa 54:9. The term *sworn* in Hebrew is *shâba'* (שָׁבַע), literally meaning "to take an oath," but its primitive root also connotes "to be complete" (*SECB*, h7650).

128. Isa 54:7–8 NRSV; italics added.

insofar as justification is accomplished "once and for all."[129] Justification, therefore, is already consummated and efficacious for humankind. This is the entity with which God has partnered within the covenant.

In love and compassion, God calls us to live a life of completion. This does not prefigure that the justified life is incomplete, but rather, the justified life is complete at present *and* yet to be completed in the future. Even if justification is already binding at present, it is so in the future. This is better understood in God's invitation for Israel:

> Ho! Everyone who thirsts, come to the waters; and you who have no money, come, buy and eat. Yes, come, buy wine and milk without money and without *price*.[130]

The invitation does not indicate that Israel is, in essence, far from God—not at all. If it does, the notion of King Immanuel is dismissed. Rather, it implies God's *enduring companionship* with his people. It is an indication of God accomplishing his desire for them: to seek him and turn from their evil ways.[131] The justification of Israel is already complete by the being of the Servant (Jesus Christ), and it is yet to be so by the free pardon of God in the eschatological judgment.[132] It explicates why people can drink wine and milk without paying a cent. Redemption is free, and the Lord is free to redeem. Hart remarks, "The only Christian narrative of salvation that to me seems coherent is the one that the earliest church derived so directly from scripture: a relentless tale of rescue God conducted, without requiring any tribute to win forgiveness or love."[133] God desires to rescue all from damnation, and such desire is irreducible in the OT and NT.[134] Rightly so, the justification is already binding for Israel because of the act of the Servant; it is binding in the eschatos. The purpose of God is achieved.[135]

God's anger is consequential, and God's compassionate love is eternal. The covenant is truly permanent in substance and execution.[136] The concept of sanctification is in the permanence of the covenant. Or else,

---

129. Heb 7:27; 9:12.

130. Isa 55:1 NKJV; italics added.

131. Isa 55:6–7a.

132. Isa 55:7b.

133. Hart, *That All Shall Be Saved*, 27.

134. For example, Ps 98:3; Ezek 33:11; Zech 8:7; cf. Rom 11:32; 1 Tim 2:4; 2 Pet 3:9.

135. Isa 55:11b.

136. Isaiah 54 categorically shows that God is love.

the talk on sanctification would divert, if not subvert, the concept of justification. The sanctification of the covenant members is only the *fruit* of the identification with Jesus Christ.[137] So the idea of particular redemption becomes implausible in Isaiah's schema on the messianic initiative.[138] When God declares a person righteous, this same person is called to live out the declaration of God—to live in righteousness.[139] God is the One who sanctifies through and through; this means to be wholly sanctified.[140] Looking for redemptive assurance elsewhere (not in and through Christ) will naturally lead to self-reliance and epistemological relativism. That, in a sense, falls within "rationalistic Calvinism" (a tendency for extreme outcomes such as limited atonement), something I consciously avoid throughout the enterprise.[141] Divine sovereignty is the superstructure of the main aspects of foreordination and redemption. If reworked Christocentrically, this makes our participation (though important) subsidiary, given the eschatological hope.[142]

Remarkably so, there is no injunction of the process of acquiring sanctity or holiness in the course of thought vis-à-vis Isaianic expression of foreordination.[143] What is upfront in Isaiah is that justification and sanctification are interlinked in the predetermined revival of Israel. God's "I will" results in the "you will" of Israel. When it is said that the Lord is the God of Israel, this connotes that Israel is the people of God at the moment of declaration. Any suggestion of a process of becoming, especially in the form of acquisition, is altogether dismissed. In this respect, Israel is not becoming God's people; instead, Israel is *already* God's people under the divine command, not human pursuit. Therefore, the already-but-not-yet applies exclusively to the absolute consummation of the sacrifice, not to the identity of its object.

In an unconditioned kingship, God dispenses his universal mercy in his redemptive act. It is in this context where the suffering God is understood as the impetus for the redeeming God. The question thus arises: if we are already redeemed, why is there eschatological redemption?

---

137. Isa 51:1.

138. Isa 51:4-6.

139. Isa 51:6b, 9a.

140. Isa 51:16a; 52:1-2.; cf. 1 Thess 5:23.

141. See Hunsinger, *Reading Barth with Charity*, xiv-xv.

142. Dixon, *Practical Predestinarians in England*, 50.

143. Isa 53:11b; 54:10b; 14b.

Redemption has begun and is still underway. This is the elegance of Isaiah's eschatology in connection with the substitutionary sacrifice.[144] Redemption, I propose, is conceived in terms of the not yet and already so. Such thought is in tune with the actual reality humanity has in Jesus Christ as articulated in chapter 4. Although redemption is largely implied as futuristic, however, when the repristination of Israel is considered with finality in divine history, then the not yet *becomes* the finally so. This is the rationale for seeing people to have been redeemed in the eventual redemption.[145]

That is not wishful thinking in theological sense. It is not even an overstretched idea but rather a synthesis resulting from the shared history of God and humanity. We need to view the shared history against the judgment event itself to grasp why justification-sanctification is soterio-eschatologically significant. The futuristic view of redemption is the "enforcing, emphasising and unfolding of truth already perceived and known."[146] In other words, the hope of redemption arises from the reconciliation Jesus Christ has achieved.[147] This is the reason for coining the term *tadhana*, exposited in chapter 3, that provides us with the essential grammar to attenuate the confusion in the not-yet-and-already-so of redemption. In this way, it is doable to articulate the guaranteed redemption in the primordial self-sacrifice.

The tone here is set for a dynamically self-offering God. The Holy One of Israel can be affirmed as unbridled in delivering salvation to the world expressed in the meaning of Isaiah ("salvation of Yahweh").[148] This is why I understand divine freedom as none other than "the freedom and power of God's mercy."[149] As such, that divine freedom cannot be inferred somehow counters the redemption of all. Even when we conceive of divine freedom against any suggestion of contingency upon God, we still cannot extrapolate that the suffering God is inclined to a particularist judgment. There is danger in forgetting the fact that the freedom

144. Isa 54:16–17a; 55:3a, 6–7.

145. Isa 51:16.

146. McDowell, "Learning Where to Place," 337.

147. Isa 53:5, 12b.

148. Brown et al., *Brown-Driver-Briggs*, 441.

149. Nimmo, "Compassion of Jesus Christ," 78. See Barth, *CD* II/1, 372.

inherent in God is always alongside his everlasting mercy. The covenant is everlasting, too.[150]

The freedom of God is demonstrated at the crucifixion.[151] Golgotha, therefore, functions as the center point where people understand the content and purpose of the redeeming sacrifice. That is to say, in covenantal terms, the covenanted self of God produces the covenanted people. Philosophically speaking, that which is covenanted *remains* covenanted—forged in the blood of the Lamb.

Justification and sanctification are not in dichotomy in the treatment of the striking-healing paradigm. Since people are already healed (not being healed) in the wounds of the Messiah, then the sense of progression is irrelevant. *Progressive understanding, however,* is vital: Jerusalem is rebuilt through destruction.[152] In a sense, God demolished the old Zion for the new Zion to rise. From the rubble emerges the majesty of Israel; the nation enlarges far and wide.[153] As the majesty of Israel (the Servant) is revealed, the Israelites will acknowledge him as their Lord, and all humankind will know him as the Redeemer.[154]

In a later setting, but no less impressive, is the apostle Paul's rendition of justification. It appears that in Pauline theology, justification and sanctification happen coincidentally.[155] The two are a one-off event insofar as the atonement is concerned.[156] In that respect, sanctification is a single event, not a progressive event as located Christocentrically. Since God will not remember the sins of humanity in the covenant, the covenant members are associated with the being and act of the covenant Partner.[157] It is apparent here that forgiveness is contingent on the Forgiver, not on the forgiven. Through the Messiah, Israel is pardoned and reinstated as per decree.[158] This is sure and active in the covenanted via King Immanuel.[159]

---

150. Isa 55:3b, 13b.

151. Lewis, *Between Cross and Resurrection*, 209–11.

152. Isa 49:21.

153. Isa 54:2–3; 55:4.

154. Isa 52:6; 49:26b.

155. Rom 8:30; Eph 5:26; 1 Thess 5:23.

156. Titus 2:14; 2 Cor 5:21; cf. Heb 10:10.

157. Isa 55:7b; Heb 10:16–17.

158. Isa 51:15; 53:1.

159. Isa 51:11; 52:13.

The suffering of God is efficacious; once executed, it does not need reenactment.[160] The Lord is at amity with us, making us blameless. As Barth reiterates, "Our chastisement was upon him, that we might have peace."[161] In the covenant, the hard-heartedness of the covenant members is overridden by the tender-heartedness of the covenant Partner. God has "perfected for all time" the covenant members; they have been redeemed.[162] The uncertainty of redemption can be traced back to the progressive concept of sanctification. If a person fails to catch up to its daily and continuous demand, then justification is jeopardized. And of course, if that happens, then glorification is merely wishful thinking.[163] The prominent contributory factor here is human choice over foreordination. Thus the proper conception of sanctification is pivotal in soterio-eschatology, for it is not merely feasible but also sustainable if reapproached christologically.

Surely, God accomplishes what he desires: the justification-sanctification of sinners mirrors the healing and revival of the Israelites.[164] I have to spotlight the exclusive right and exercise of the messianic initiative to cripple any thought of human contribution to the discussion of redemption. Human participation cannot warrant any soterio-eschatological assurance; it only robs the surety of reconciliation in Jesus Christ.[165] The integrity of God is not put under suspicion by the exemplification of Christ's justifying and sanctifying sacrifice. Dogmatics must be anchored in God's kingship of sacrifice. The conditionality of faith is secondary to the predetermined *pro nobis*. In this manner, reconciliation and the response of faith will not be contradictory but complementary. Here we can say that identification with Jesus Christ truly brings solid hope.

The key is the reality behind the anticipation. In God, as indicated in Isaiah, whatever is anticipated is already so.[166] Thus, the not yet is not a potentiality in God; instead, it is sure to happen. Nothing can avert or divert what the Lord has planned for us.[167] R. N. Whybray's contest

---

160. Isa 55:11; Heb 9:12.

161. This is in reflection of Isa 53:5 (Barth, *CD* III/4, 282).

162. Isa 51:14; Heb 10:12–14.

163. We will discuss how a person is glorified in the last chapter.

164. Isaiah 55 showcases God's universal offer of redemption.

165. Beeke, *Quest for Full Assurance*, 42.

166. Isa 49:22–23.

167. Isa 55:8–9.

against the universalist interpretation of the world's acknowledgment of the Lord God not equating to redemption (because other nations are not on an equal footing with Israel), I would say, is a misguided inference.[168] As argued above, unless the call to the nations and the response to it is *within* the eternal covenant, any conclusive statement on the topic would be anti-universalism, due to the seemingly opposing proclamation in Isaiah.

The fact that the sacrifice and death of God are so overwhelmingly profound logically requires an outcome of equal degree. The universal scope of redemption fits this category. What is the effect of the sacrificial act in Christ? Drawing on Isaiah, humanity might have genuine and lasting peace.[169] The peace arising from the suffering God permanently shuts the entrance to obscurity and opens wide the gates of certainty.[170] It is even understood that peace from redemption is eternally real. Its validity takes place before our response, and more substantially, it is irrevocable. Only in this *proactive and invasive* grace do we find assurance, hence it is called redemptive grace.[171] It is not a mere postulate. Its locus is based strongly on the firmness and resolve of the Sufferer in the covenant.

Having these in mind, therefore, my unequivocal answer to the question on universalism has nothing to do with securing the eternal freedom of God but rather in highlighting it with compassionate love.[172] God can (if he desires to) redeem all, if he decides to (already a done deal in the covenant). The positive view of the redemptive act and the negative view of universalism can be rendered as distinct yet compatible positions if they do not violate the sovereignly wounded nature. The Godhead itself was wounded in the agony of Jesus Christ at Calvary; Forsyth puts it, "Our redemption drew upon the whole Godhead. Father and Spirit were not spectators only of the Son's agony, nor only recipients of his sacrifice. They were involved in it."[173] If God gives all to humans, it grants that the yield is all of them as well. We can expect too much from God without claiming too much from it. We can firmly hope, nevertheless, for

---

168. Whybray, *Second Isaiah*, 62–65.

169. Isa 49:20, 54:2.

170. Isa 49:7b, 8–9.

171. Isa 49:1b, 3, 6.

172. Isa 49:15.

173. Forsyth, *Missions in State and Church*, 29.

the eschatological implication of the eternality of the sacrifice.[174] In our retake of Deutero-Isaiah, the efficacy of the sacrifice tips the scale in favor of a universalist reading. There is even a viable absent of consensus regarding the co-equality of Israel with other nations.[175]

We can better appreciate this conception in our next reading of Isaiah through Revelation with attention to God's reward for humankind.

3.4 Reading Isaiah through Revelation

This is our second last critical analysis of Isaiah with Revelation to understand why Christian universalism is conceivable in the Bible.[176] It is prophesied in Isaiah,

> They shall neither hunger nor thirst, neither heat nor sun shall *strike* them; for He who has *mercy* on them will lead them, even by the springs of water He will guide them.[177]

The objects of God's mercy are those who suffered in want and affliction. God decides to show his compassionate love to the stricken. Notably impressive, mercy is shown not because the stricken returned to him, but rather, it is "the time of God's favor."[178] In other words, such mercy is out of the messianic initiative; also in it is preserved Israel as a covenanted people.[179] The LORD God sets the captives free of their humanity, that is, wickedness and apostasy, through Christ's mediation as exposited in chapter 3. In Christ, the stricken are renewed, in which their joy "burst[s] into song."[180] This is a metaphorical description of the stricken being comforted.[181] The portrait of Isaiah is astonishingly comprehensive, to help us appreciate its overwhelming beauty. It is like Claude Monet's depiction of Rue Montorgueil, Paris (festival of June 30, 1878), in which you have to view it from afar in order for it to have its greatest visual impact.

---

174. Isa 49:16.
175. Van Winkle, "Relationship of the Nations," 446.
176. Isa 27:13, 19:23–25; cf. Rev 7:16.
177. Isa 49:10 NKJV; italics added.
178. Isa 49:8a.
179. Isa 49:8b.
180. Isa 49:13a.
181. Isa 49:13b.

The source of the astonishing impact of the eschatos, of course, is in the Eschaton.

The magnificence of what is to come is repeated, almost identically and in the eschatological sense, in Revelation, which says, "They shall neither hunger anymore nor thirst anymore; the sun shall not strike them, nor any heat; for the Lamb who is in the midst of the throne will *shepherd* them and lead them to living fountains of waters . . . ."[182] The evangelist is specific in the identity of the "he" in Isaiah—the Lamb of God. Once again, the Lamb is also the Shepherd alluded to previously. The Shepherd is the Servant-King whose compassion is great and whose love is everlasting.[183] How do I know this? The immediate context renders the Lamb-Shepherd as cautious not to harm the people until the people are secured (sealed) of redemption.[184]

The Lamb-Shepherd, moreover, is responsible for making God's people righteous by substitutionary sacrifice.[185] At a glance, the Johannine text is not beyond reproach in advancing universalism. The sealed people are Jacob's descendants.[186] The subsequent text, however, shows that the redeemed are from "every nation, tribe, people and language."[187] Perhaps the reader might yet insist: still, it does not unequivocally say that all peoples will be saved. The solution to this pressing concern is in the outer context showing that inhabitants of the earth (and the heavens) are invited to rejoice as the enemy (the devil) is condemned for punishment.[188] The invitee refers to God's people (Israel) and the afflicted others (gentiles).

In my counterpoint, the divine compassion would not be "great," and the divine love would not be "everlasting," if they were only for some, not all. Not surprisingly, if we take a closer look at the Isaiah collection, the offered redemption (and restitution) is double-sided.[189] Though Isaiah begins by ensuring God's freedom in forgiving, it likewise indicates

---

182. Rev 7:16 NKJV; italics added.

183. Isa 54:7–8.

184. Rev 7:3.

185. Rev 7:14.

186. Rev 7:5–8.

187. Rev 7:9.

188. Rev 12:12; 18:20. These texts are in parallel with Isa 49:13, which says that the Lord comforts his people and will have compassion on his afflicted ones.

189. Isa 49:14; cf. 49:15b; 54:7–8.

a God who is free to supply it to all.[190] If we put the two together, we can sense an interest in the universality of salvation. Such interest is derived from the freedom to splash forgiveness to all—cohering with God's superabundant mercy depicted as refreshing water, hence the phrases "spring" and "living fountains." The "incipient universalism of the prophecy in the light of the Christ-event" results in total forgiveness and rejuvenation, according to Barnabas Lindars.[191]

Despite the forgiveness in the superabundant mercy of God, we still cannot conclude without a doubt that we can read in Isaiah, specifically in this section, a resounding yes favoring a universal redemption. I find this strange, in company with Parry, since it is an idea derived from the Bible; similarly, its essence *per se* is not officially declared or at least deemed heretical in Western tradition, even in the modern period.[192] The promise of healing for the afflicted is indeed for *all*—eternally guaranteed in the covenant. This is not but a spurious idealism. The guarantee of *shâlôm* is from the kingship of sacrifice. In the eschatos, therefore, the Eschaton is not antithetical to both divine choice and human choice. The parched (deficiency of humans) eventually is refreshed (efficiency of God). In the exercise of his infinite judicial power, God pardons us without reservation. With that mindset, the paradoxical injunctions in Isaiah and Revelation are married in the new eon.

In the final chapter, we will investigate the reason for the glorification of the undeserving. This brings our attention to the closing section—Third Isaiah.

---

190. Isa 49:26b, 52:10, 55:1.

191. Lindars, "Good Tidings to Zion," 496.

192. Parry, "Is Universalism Heretical," para. 7.

Chapter VI

EXALTATION OF
THE UNDERSERVING

"Arise, shine; for your light has come, and the *glory* of the LORD
has risen upon you."[1]

IN THE PENULTIMATE CHAPTER, WE STUDIED God's self-taken responsibility for Israel's suffering in the disciplinary action. This chapter will
further show the impact of divine sovereignty on eschatology by inspecting God's equitable treatment of humanity. I shall argue here against particularism. In the end, everyone is exalted in and through Jesus Christ.

To prove my case, we will tackle the final human state with the covenant with Israel, the promised rest, the call to the world, and the favorable judgment. This is to show that the renewal of Zion and the service
of Jerusalem signal the deliverance and glorification of the human race.
We turn now to the ending section of Isaiah with emphasis on God the
Glorifier.

1. SUMMARY OF ISAIAH 56-66

In the ending section, the chapters are designed to bring symmetry to the
Isaianic themes. In the very heart of this section are three beautiful poems describing how King Immanuel announces the good news of peace

1. Isa 60:1 NASB; italics added.

and prosperity to the poor and weak. All promises of hope are reaffirmed from predictions earlier in the book, for instance, the coming new age for Israel. The Lord's servants will live in the new Jerusalem, and from this place, justice, mercy, and blessing flow out to the whole world.

Surrounding these poems are two long prayers of repentance where the people confessed their sin as they grieved over all of the evil around them. They asked for forgiveness and that God's kingdom would come here on earth as in heaven. On each side are collections of poems contrasting the destiny of the servants with that of their persecutors. In the end, the Lord judges the defilers of the world with their selfishness, exploitation, and idolatry and removes them from the new Jerusalem forever. In contrast, the humble and repentant are forgiven and inherit the new Jerusalem, depicted as a renewed creation where death and suffering are forever gone.

That description brings us to the very outer frame of the section where the kingdom of God is the focus. People from all nations are invited to come and join Israel to form the covenanted people, so everyone can know their Creator, Sustainer, Redeemer. The Isaianic narratives end with a grand vision of the fulfillment of God's promises. The elected is eventually glorified through the ministry of the Messiah. The sovereign God creates a glorified family from the ends of the earth, as indicated in the introductory part of Isaiah.

After the recap of the concluding segment of Isaiah, we will now look at one aspect of God seldom magnified—being the Glorifier.

2. GOD AS GLORIFIER

Before we discuss the being of God as the One who glorifies, we have to know what glory is as defined in Trito-Isaiah. The concept of glory has both positive and negative definitions. Glory is synonymous with honor, reverence, splendor, and abundance, yet synchronously, it also connotes heaviness, affliction, grievousness, and burden.[2] In apprehending the dual meaning of glory, it is necessary to engage with how it is articulated in the Isaianic narratives. Also, in this milieu, we can know how God is said to glorify and be glorified.

---

2. The Hebrew for *glory* is *kâbôd* (כָּבֹד), meaning "splendor" and "abundance," yet it bears the root meaning "to be heavy or grievous" (*SECB*, h3519; h3513).

The LORD God tells the people to practice justice and righteousness so that deliverance and prosperity will occur.[3] With this statement alone, we can deduce that the former entails sacrifice on the part of the leaders and the rich in Jerusalem. The leaders will have to abandon graft and corruption. The effect is the loss of political connection and likewise, of easy money. The rich will have to stop exploiting the poor and weak. This will result in the loss of advantage in business, also of sizable income. But because of the revival of social justice, the latter will follow—begetting honor and satisfaction. That is to underscore the heaviness of practicing justice and righteousness, but in effect, deliverance from adversaries and the prosperity of their endeavors will happen.

As discussed in chapter 2, the *shabbât* is attainable if the fractured covenant between God and humans is rectified.[4] The covenantal aspect of the *shabbât* is reinforced at this juncture.[5] The *shabbât* observance is strict, hence burdensome to keep.[6] However, if the people keep it, there will be no affliction in the land—instead, splendor and abundance.[7]

The blessing of the *shabbât* is not only for the Jews but non-Jews, too.[8] In handling prophetic ethics, we should not uplift the Hebrews by making the gentiles the disadvantaged. Accordingly, all peoples are foreordained to worship the true God; it shall transpire, for the sovereign One has declared it.[9] It is worthy to note that the genuine keeping of the covenant (and the *shabbât*) is ascribed to the Messiah, hence the phrase "I will."[10] The rectification of the relationship between God and humans is the messianic work primarily and ultimately because the Messiah himself is the promised rest.[11]

The Hitchenian thought is a case of deficiency of acumen in looking at glory. It hints that God somewhat craves for glory, making God

---

3. Isa 56:1.

4. *Sabbath* in Hebrew is *shabbât* (שַׁבָּת), which comes from the root meaning "to cease" or "to rest" (*SECB*, h7676; h7673).

5. Isa 56:4.

6. Isa 56:2. Aside from the Sabbath of the fourth commandment, there are other types of sabbaths. For example, see Deut 15:1–18; 16:9; Lev 12:2; 23:15–21; 25:2–7; Num 28:9–10.

7. Isa 56:5; 58:13–14.

8. Isa 56:3a, 6.

9. Isa 56:7–8.

10. Isa 56:5, 7a, 8b.

11. Isa 57:13b.

egocentric.[12] Such an idea is initially dismissed if glory is understood in its dialectical meaning and purpose. Even Karl Barth says that the divine does not require glory, the human does.[13] From a christological perspective, glory is demonstrated in the nature of Jesus Christ. In the heavy affliction and grievous burden that the Son of God bears in the Son of Man, humanity acquires honor and splendor. There is little said (or otherwise contorted) of this in Christopher Hitchens's outlandish play on words.

In Jesus Christ, God is fully glorified, and God fully glorifies humanity. This is true as well with the city of God. In anticipating the promised Messiah, the old Jerusalem experienced heavy affliction. Nonetheless, in its actualization, the new Jerusalem experienced reverence and abundance.

Another facet of glory that needs unpacking is about "the death of the righteous."[14] The Socratic method of eliminating self-contradictory hypotheses helps validate our beliefs about the subject matter. We need to understand why some godly people die early. Unless this is taken seriously, the negative aspect of glory inundates its positive aspect. Those walking upright have peace by finding rest. This has to do with the *shabbât*. The rest here is congruous with the final separation from evil.[15] We can see, concomitantly, the interplay of the dual meaning of glory vis-à-vis the *shabbât*: there is heaviness of grief in the death of the godly, albeit in it they find an abundance of peace. What appears detrimental is, in reality, profitable. The death of the righteous is not death *per se* compared to that of the ungodly. Their life already descended to the "realm of the dead"—the lowest possible degradation of a person.[16] It is a life of worry and weary—the complete opposite of the final abode of the godly, where liberty and prosperity last.

---

12. Christopher Hitchens thinks that the God of the Bible somewhat suffers from megalomania. See Hitchens, *God Is Not Great*, 12, 37, 71.

13. Barth stresses, "But it is not the Son of God who is *glorified*. He who humbled Himself according to the decree of God had no need of glorifying. He does not experience glorifying, but rather, in the power of His deity, He realises and accomplishes it. The *glorification* is of the Son of David. His is the justification, His the salvation from death, His the exaltation to fellowship with God . . ." (Barth, *CD* II/2, 173; italics added).

14. Isa 57:1a.

15. Isa 57:1b–2.

16. Isa 57:9b.

In the Bible, the *shabbât* is tied with Jubilee.[17] As stated in Isaiah, liberty and prosperity are unachievable by turning to idols, like Molech.[18] In seeking their rest and peace, the Jews waste their energy and resources. Whatever they do or wherever they go, they will only grow weary without seeking the Lord.[19] Through the messianic initiative, whatever hinders them from turning to God is removed.[20] It is written:

> For thus says the high and lofty one who inhabits eternity, whose name is Holy: "I *dwell* in the high and holy place, and *also* with those who are contrite and humble in spirit, to revive the spirit of the humble, and to revive the heart of the contrite. For I will not continually accuse, nor will I always be angry . . . ."[21]

The reverence and splendor of God are for those sorrowful of sin. The burdened and grieved are relieved and refreshed owing to forgiveness and restitution. What God does not desire is to be continually against his people. God rather shows mercy and compassion. The gracious act overflows. Even if the people continue their idolatry and greediness, God is determined to heal and comfort them.[22] With their disloyalty, God repays with his loyalty. With their rejection, God repays with his restitution.[23] The *shabbât* cannot be divorced from liberty and prosperity. God wills it for the people.[24]

It has become apparent that the glory of God is exhibited in his character.[25] The *šekīnah* shines in the darkest place and time testified in Isaiah. In glory, God is merciful and compassionate yet, at the same time, does not excuse the guilty.[26] Again, we can see here the striking-healing schema: the Lord punishes Judah for her sins, and also the Lord heals Judah of her sins.[27]

---

17. Isa 57:2; Lev 25:8–13.

18. Isa 57:9; cf. Ezek 23:14–16. Molech is the Canaanite god associated with child sacrifice. See Lev 18:21; 20:2–5.

19. Isa 57:10.

20. Isa 57:14.

21. Isa 57:15–16a NRSV; italics added.

22. Isa 57:18.

23. God is rest, as connoted in Isa 57.

24. Isa 57:19.

25. See also Exod 33:18–22; 34:5–7.

26. Isa 57:20–21.

27. Isa 57:17–18.

John Flett reacts: "If I hear the striking and healing thing, I also hear domestic violence."[28] The rationale you get from it, he expounds, is that you can beat someone, for instance, a wife, for her benefit. The feminist voice to warn against imitating God in this manner or being the interpreter of the will of God is crucial indeed. In a patriarchal mindset in Christendom, exemplifying a male God subordinating his subjects is worrisome. To counter this, Elizabeth Johnson and Rosemary Radford Ruether argue that the Church must reimagine a feminist interpretation of God.[29] In this regard, it does not take much to envision God as a female. The God of Isaiah is also depicted in female imagery, like a human mother or a mother eagle.[30]

Concerning domestic violence, the articulation of the doctrine of atonement becomes a hot topic. Darby Kathleen Ray explains how the ransom model posits Jesus Christ's submission to the cross, encouraging instrumental-calculative violence. It could promote the infliction of pain as something redemptive, as this fosters women's submission to men's castigation for a *worthy* cause.[31] This androcentric portrayal of God makes the convenient connection between superiority and violence. Margaret Miles puts it, "The twin assumptions of male supremacy—through self-identification with God—and women as male property constitute patriarchal order. Rationalized as loving protection of the ruled, the bottom line of patriarchal order is the use of violence toward and even murder of the ruled for their protection."[32] Violent means, therefore, are justified to deliver a good end. To this, I insist that it is profitable to look at the striking-healing paradigm *within* the doctrine of God. To justify beating a wife for a good cause is simply problematic due to the corruption of human character. Avoid confusion and regain the integrity of women (also of the disadvantaged) by retrieving "the feminine imagery" and separating the divine from the human.[33]

---

28. John Flett is a professor at Pilgrim Theological College within the University of Divinity, Melbourne, Australia. He reacted upon the presentation of this project in the Parkville Seminar at the Trinity College Theological School lecture theatre held on April 12, 2021.

29. Johnson, *She Who Is*, 241–43; Ruether, *Sexism and God-Talk*, 68–71.

30. Isa 42:14, 49:15; 66:13.

31. Ray, *Deceiving the Devil*, 121.

32. Miles, "Violence against Women," 17.

33. Moder, "Women, Personhood, and Male God," 88.

If God is likewise a female, then male dominance is unsustainable. Further, humans cannot imitate the striking-healing method, as they are susceptible to mistakes, unlike God. This is true as well in interpreting the will of God. Humans are limited in apprehension, unable to fathom the mystery behind the strangeness and alienness of the divine operation.[34] In the case of the atonement, the sacrifice in question cannot infer violence (by a ruler) for altruistic purposes (for a subject), as Jesus Christ is both the Lord and Servant as the Creator-creature. In other words, what is ascribed to Christ's activity cannot be done so to any human action, even if it appears beneficial.

In retrieving the personhood of women (and all humankind), forgiveness is at the core of the reinstituted people of God. Interestingly, forgiveness covers three phases of spiritual fall: iniquity (turning from the truth), transgression (rebelling), and sin (being astray).[35] The people expect justice and righteousness, yet they mock God with their injustice and unrighteousness.[36] Their fasting has become an iniquity before God; they continue exploiting the poor and weak.[37] That is why it results in quarrels and bigotry instead of in being just and right.[38] They rebel against God with their idolatry.[39] And the worst part is, they are unaware of the fallacy and vanity of their deeds, showing they are indeed astray.[40] This proves that humanity, on its own, is not free from the bondage of sin. By the messianic initiative, however, humans are deemed away from the point of no return.

We can further explicate how God is said to glorify and be glorified in the kind of fast he recommends. God is glorified if the poor and weak are cared for and not exploited.[41] In other words, true fasting entails self-sacrifice for the needy. As a result, God will glorify his people through liberty and prosperity.[42] The covenantal relationship is in play in the operation of glory and the sharing of it with humanity.[43] In this way, we can

34. See Isa 28:21b; 38:15–17.
35. Isa 58:1–7; cf. Exod 34:7a (*SECB*, h5771; h6588; h2403).
36. Isa 58:2, 4b.
37. Isa 58:4a.
38. Isa 58:1–7.
39. Isa 57:3–8.
40. Isa 58:2a, 3a.
41. Isa 58:6–7.
42. Isa 58:8–9.
43. Isa 58:10–11.

better understand why the human will is wholly in bondage to sin before divine deliverance.

2.1 Glory and Liberty

It is outstanding in the previous chapters that human will is subservient to the divine will, and human freedom originates from the suffering of the Messiah. In God's self-bondage to sin, we are deemed free from the shackle of sin. This is the underlying truth in God's glorification of humanity: the human is made to *be* with the divine because, in Jesus Christ, both are inseparable. What is sensible is that the mystery of God does not remain mysterious for God's self; it is in the promised Messiah.[44] What is nonsensical is that in it, our destiny remains a mystery. As we have understood that the Lord is highly active in working out his foreordination at present, it is irrational to presuppose that only some, let alone few, will taste glory.

In the covenant, the promised glory is sure, hinting that the eschatological judgment is favorable for humanity.[45] It is true; divine wrath is upon idolatrous Israel, yet God forgives to ensure a life of peace.[46] Israel mirrors the church. Praise and dignity are determined likewise for believers.[47] In the messianic initiative, the glory given to Israel is the same glory given to the church. In it, the dual meaning of glory is manifested as well. Now, what does it mean for believers to be glorified? The answer is the foreordained glory for humanity founded in the *glorious suffering* of Jesus Christ.[48]

The prosperity coming from glory is better appreciated in the review of the *shabbât*.[49] In remembering the *shabbât*, the focus should not be on observance but on its Lord.[50] Glory is the by-product of what God has done, not what humanity has done or will do. People glory in success stories, such as from rags to riches, especially when self-made. People fancy

---

44. Isa 59:20–21; 1 Cor 2:6–7, 10.

45. Isa 58:9.

46. Isa 58:8.

47. *Glory* in Greek is *dóxa* (δόξα), which means "praise" and "dignity," having the base meaning "to determine" or "to be accounted" (*SECB*, g1391; g1380).

48. Isa 59:20; 1 Cor 2:2, 8–9.

49. Isa 66:23.

50. Isa 58:13; cf. Mark 2:23–28.

associating themselves with a successful figure and sometimes dream of becoming one.[51] The eschatological glory, however, is not a dream, not self-made but God-made. The attention should be on the Glorifier—Jesus Christ. Without him, there is no glorified humanity.

2.2 Glory in the Apocalypse

The glorious suffering of Jesus Christ cannot be divorced from his triumph for us vis-à-vis predestination. It is unlikely that we would end with an ambiguous eschatological outcome, as we begin and end with Jesus Christ. In speaking of this, the end is no longer unknown. What used to be veiled has been unveiled—the accurate definition of *apocalypse*. Furthermore, the apocalypse does not necessarily convey the destruction of this world or the end of the human race, hence all doom and gloom. Even though ambiguity is somewhat compatible with what David Bentley Hart thinks of the apocalypse, I do not share his pessimistic view; he refers to it as "an intricate and impenetrable puzzle, one whose key vanished long ago."[52] In my assertion, the key is in the Christocentric articulation of the eschatos.

Be that as it may, the apocalypse is all good news—God sharing glory with all peoples. Such glorification is certain, as it is done through the Holy Spirit,[53] and it has now been made known to all nations.[54] I compare it to God's love letter for us, open to read, and it has to do with what God has in store for his loved ones. I therefore call it an open mystery, which, I suppose, is also perceived as foreordination. It is revealed in Third Isaiah,

> Then your light will break forth like the dawn, and your healing will quickly appear; then your righteousness will go before you, and the *glory* of the LORD will be your rear guard.[55]

---

51. For instance, the legendary boxer Manny Pacquiao, dubbed the *pambansang kamao* (the national fist), is emulated by almost all youth in the Philippines.

52. Hart holds that the book of Revelation is not about the end of time but rather about the "inauguration of a new historical epoch where Rome will have fallen, Jerusalem will have been restored, and the Messiah will have been given power 'to rule the gentiles with a rod of iron'" (Hart, *That All Shall Be Saved*, 108.)

53. Isa 61:1; 1 Cor 2:10–11.

54. Isa 61:2; Rom 16:25–27.

55. Isa 58:8 NRSV; italics added.

The act of glorification is compared to the sunrise. The awareness of this act gradually increases as God unfolds his master plan through Jesus Christ.[56] As depicted here, glory coincides with healing. It is secured, as the human destiny is in God's hand. Every hindrance to returning to God is removed. Every yoke is broken. In this manner, God altogether satisfies the people.[57]

The removed and broken testify to the power of the Spirit.[58] The Spirit is upon the Messiah. Jesus Christ is the Rebuilder and Restorer of humanity.[59] In Christ, the being of humans is glorified. In being Israel, the people of Israel are predestined to resemble the Messiah.[60] On the same note, the church is predestined to resemble its head—Jesus Christ. Unless spiritual Israel breaks away from thinking in nationalist terms, any universalist stance is undermined. Thus the way forward is to think of global interest. The vocabulary of the pericopes engaged in Isaiah is vigorous enough to be "universal, ultimate, and radical."[61] It is the epitome of this formula: the glorifying God in the God glorified.

As genuine honor and prosperity are sourced from God alone, the success of the instrument is grounded and generated by its Maker and User.[62] The pots have an entity owing to the entity of the Potter. One might insist that not all are bound for glory; it is explicit in the Bible that there are "vessels of wrath."[63] I would like to address this concern with the use of my own tale of two pots.

The tale of two pots accounts for the pot for honor (or mercy) and the pot for dishonor (or wrath).[64] They are God's instruments intended to contain the riches of divine glory. The pots are mutable; the function is amendable—from honor to dishonor or vice versa. Its objective is to keep the glory intact, ready for dispensation. In like manner, the "riches" of God's glory are indeed wealthy—deep and wide. They are deep insofar as the essence of glory is appraised; they are wide insofar as the proportion is assessed. The depth and width of divine blessing parallel that of our

56. Cf. 2 Cor 4:6.

57. Isaiah 58 shows that God answers the prayer of Israel.

58. Isa 59:21.

59. Isa 61:1–2.

60. Isa 58:12; 61:4.

61. Kim, "Eschatology in Isaiah," 352.

62. Isa 63:7.

63. Rom 9:21–23.

64. Isa 64:8; Rom 9–11.

need. The glory of God is immeasurable, without bounds, without limits. That is why the glory is rendered as surpassing, by the supereminence of Jesus Christ.[65]

Correspondingly, the disobedient (non-Israelites) will become obedient by the disobedience of the Israelites.[66] The obedience of the gentiles is in the effect of God's mercy, and the same mercy is shown to the disobedient people. Here we can see the universal dispensation of divine mercy. The Lord has consigned all to be a pot of dishonor so that all may be a pot of honor.[67] This is the splendid twist in the reality of humanity and the operation of the glorifying God. God is glorified as God glorifies whom he uses—the elect (people).[68] In a sense, there is no non-elect. Everyone is predestined to contain the glory.

In continuing our discussion on people containing God's glory, we have to rework the theological construct of the vessels. This will elucidate why the concept of election and reprobation is not the sort to be afraid of or avoided, because it is unfixed. What is fixed is God's mercy to all. It conveys the thought that whoever is deemed reprobate (present) is also deemed elect (future) as foreordained. So in the end, we have only one type of pot—of mercy. Whether the pot is used for either honor or dishonor, the fact shines out brightly: the pot is God's. It holds the glorious mercy. Moreover, whatever God utilizes is holy—that is, separated for a divine purpose. In other words, even the pot for dishonor, though used to demonstrate the divine wrath, in this sense, is *still holy*. The open mystery is the glorious mercy dispensed to all through the glorious suffering of Jesus Christ.

If we push the argument to its logical conclusion, the tale, in actuality, is about the Potter, not the pot. It is the story of Jesus Christ, how he served the twofold purpose: he has contained the riches of glory in *being* an instrument of mercy and wrath. By Christ bearing the divine wrath (Reprobate), we find mercy; by Christ bearing our dishonor, we become God's honor (elect).[69] The truth concerning the glorifying God in the God glorified is to be revealed to the ends of the earth. The text shares,

---

65. 2 Cor 4:7.

66. Isa 63:4–7; Rom 11:32.

67. Isa 63:15–16; Jer 29:11.

68. Isa 65:18.

69. Isa 62:12; 63:8; Rom 11:32.

So they will fear the name of the LORD from the west and His *glory* from the rising of the sun, for He will come like a rushing stream which the wind of the LORD drives.[70]

Its fulfillment coincides with the work of the Spirit. Glory shall sweep the world like a raging flood. I envision it like the flood during Noah's period, wherein the whole earth flooded according to the decree.[71] Akin to the great flood, the Spirit shall envelop all human population.[72] As the will of the Lord always prevails, the glorification of humanity is assured. It is the demonstration of the faithfulness of God to his covenant partners. The Spirit will never leave until all share in the glory.[73] In this case, the gap between God and us is bridged, as the separation is unsustainable within the covenant.

Within the covenant, the reconciliation of all is possible: the divine glory overwhelms human stubbornness.[74] The human, in the end, succumbs to the divine.[75] When this occurs, God's call to the world is triumphant, in the sense that all will acknowledge and worship the true God.[76] In this line of thinking, Israel (Jesus Christ) is duplicated by Israel (the physical and spiritual descendants of Abraham).[77] The glory shines as God glorifies his people as spoken in Isaiah:[78]

> No longer will you have the sun for light by day, nor for brightness will the moon give you light; but you will have the LORD for an everlasting light, and your God *for your glory*. Your sun will no longer set, nor will your moon wane; for you will have the LORD for an everlasting light, and the days of *your mourning will be over.*[79]

Glory will dwell in people *forever*. Mourning is gone—replaced by rejoicing. Although repentance and submission are needed, God had caused and facilitated them. He planted righteousness in humans, which

---

70. Isa 59:19 NASB; italics added.

71. See Gen 7:17–24.

72. Isa 63:11b; 65:1.

73. Isa 59:21; 61:8b.

74. Isa 59:1.

75. Isa 59:20; 60:2.

76. Isa 60:14.

77. Isa 60:5–6.

78. Isa 60:7, 9, 13.

79. Isa 60:19–20 NASB; italics added.

marvelously explodes into glory.[80] God works out his glory in people via striking-and-healing.[81] And if ever the reader is tempted to presuppose human contribution in glorification, let the employment of the imagery "brightness of the sun and moon" serve as an aide-mémoire. People only benefit from the light in heaven. There is no way they can contribute to its brightness.

2.3 The Target Glorification

The main thrust of the Bible, I think, is not redemption but glorification. The focus is on the former if a theological construct begins with temporality (creation); however, if it begins with pretemporality (precreation), the focus is on the latter.[82] I professed in chapter 3 that I have no concept of "the fall" *per se*, since the perfection of Adam and Eve is not at the beginning but the end; and suffering is God's means of achieving it. In other words, critically speaking, there was nothing from which to fall, simply because Adam and Eve were at the bottom of the perfection process. Likewise, the concept of restoration (reboot), in the strict sense of the word, is irrelevant in the pretemporal construct; the trajectory is progression, not a system recovery. Of course, something was lost, such as innocence and the Edenic life, when they ate the forbidden fruit. Nevertheless, what was lost is contributory to what is to gain—glorification. So in the interest of this book, it is appropriate to use the language *glorification* in place of perfection and restoration.

When temporality dominates the theological discussion, creaturely reality serves particularism or exclusivist soterio-eschatology. However, if the discussion is grounded in pretemporality, then universalism becomes compatible with glorification. Why should there be a need for it if glory were native in Eden? And if glorification is congruent with resurrection, then logic dictates that glory follows suffering as death precedes resurrection. In my postulation, the primordial couple was deficient in

80. Isa 60:5–6.

81. Isa 60:10b.

82. This assertion resonates with the Eastern Orthodox "creation-deification arc." Andrew Louth posits that deification (or *theōsis*—union with God) is the climax of creation, not just mending what was broken in Eden. See Stump and Meister, *Original Sin and the Fall*, 7, 90.

knowledge *about* Jesus Christ—the suffering Redeemer. It is in knowing him that eternal life is obtained.[83]

Our remaining task now is to grasp the implication of that knowledge. With it, we have to investigate the epistemic background of the creation of Adam and Eve in the image and likeness of God. If this God is Jesus Christ, then the intent for Adam and Eve is humility, obedience, and willingness to sacrifice; all these are non-operative in their situation, simply because Adam and Eve are in a paradise.[84] The said attributes are possible only, philosophically speaking, in a post-Edenic environment, as they involve actual suffering. For such a lack, we can interject that the couple was deprived of knowledge of the glorious Sufferer. With surprise, I discovered that Augustine holds to the idea of the *permitted fall* of humans when he posits that God allowed the eating of the fruit of knowledge, for God foreknew that great good could arise out of it through Jesus Christ.[85] To this supposition, Karl Barth reasons, "God *wills evil* only because He wills not to keep to Himself the light of His glory but to let it shine outside Himself, because he wills to ordain man the witness of this glory."[86] In other words, the threat of negation from eating the forbidden fruit can never inundate the aimed glory which comes with it in the end. This assertion reinforces the argument for the necessity of the knowledge of good-and-evil as unpacked in chapter 3.

Suffering is also essential in being perfect as the Father.[87] The perfection of the Father is exhibited in the equitable treatment of the righteous and the wicked.[88] The suffering of God is congruent with perfection. Furthermore, it serves as a model in the talk of glorification. In God's impartiality, all shall transform into the image of Jesus Christ. The process is through striking-healing, in which human beings are humiliated to be exalted.[89] What does it mean to conform to the image of Jesus Christ? As Christ's image exemplifies humility, obedience, and willingness to sacrifice, so will we become humble, obedient, and selfless for the good of others. In other words, what King Immanuel embodies will also be in us. We

---

83. Gen 2:17; cf. John 17:3.

84. Humility, obedience, and willingness to sacrifice are all together in Jesus of Nazareth, as discussed in ch. 5.

85. Augustine, *De Dono Perseverantiae*, 7.14 (citing Eph 1:11).

86. Barth, *CD* II/2, 170; italics added.

87. Isa 64:8–9; 65:2; Matt 5:48.

88. Isa 65:16–17; Matt 5:43–45.

89. Isa 57:18–19; Rom 8:29–30.

are fashioned after the Partner—the epitome of the covenant. In it, God is triumphant in sharing his glory. Foreordination shall come to pass.

3. THE INCLUSIVE GOD

With Christocentric spectacles, it is not that difficult to see the all-inclusive God. As evident in Isaiah, God embraces all who call upon his name and live within the covenant.[90] Now we have to reconsider God's call to the world vis-à-vis the favorable judgment by inspecting the Isaianic prophecy:

> Nations shall come to your light, and kings to the brightness of your dawn. Lift up your eyes and look around; they *all gather together*, they come to you; your sons shall come from far away and your daughters shall be carried on their nurses' arms.[91]

The inclusivity of God's glorification is noticeable as "all gather together" in the new Jerusalem. The mood is worship, and in this instance, God is pleased with the offering.[92] It implies that social justice is revived and violence finally ceased, because the Jews and the gentiles are harmoniously praising the LORD God in the temple.[93] There is a similar prediction indicating a favorable judgment of the world:

> For Zion's sake I will not keep silent, and for Jerusalem's sake I will not rest, until her vindication shines out like the dawn, and her salvation like a burning torch. The *nations* shall see your vindication, and *all* the kings your glory; and you shall be called by a new name that the mouth of the LORD will give.[94]

God will not rest until his people rest. In the purview of Third Isaiah, the eschatological court shall bring forth peace unto rest. God will do so by his mercy and compassion on Zion (the Jews) and Jerusalem (the non-Jews). The result will be a bursting forth of righteousness from God to the people. Moreover, salvation blazes like a "burning torch," suggesting that all will witness it. Salvation is not only for some, due to the

90. As evidenced in Isa 56, God is inclusive in his approach to human beings.
91. Isa 60:3–4 NRSV; italics added.
92. Isa 60:7.
93. Isa 60:16, 18.
94. Isa 62:1–2 NRSV; italics added.

universal character of the prophecy. Hence, the "new name" signifies the renewed status of humankind—from dismay into delight.[95]

This displays the glorifying God in the human glorified; the glorification is solely in the divine hand.[96] As people are afflicted and grieved in God's pursuit of righteousness for them, it is only proper to anticipate splendor and abundance from the same God. The stricken are healed.[97] In fact, the healed Jerusalem gives the Lord so much delight that he treats her as a bride.[98] Such imagery fortifies the covenantal paradigm inherent in the talk of redemption unto glorification. Here, humanity is glorified like the Glorifier. Redemption is a prelude to glorification; the latter is the icing on the cosmic wedding cake. This finds support in Isaiah when it says, "They must remind the LORD and not let him rest till he makes Jerusalem strong and famous everywhere."[99]

Below is another text proving the exaltation of all:

> Oh, that You would rend the heavens *and* come down, that the mountains might quake at Your presence—as fire kindles the brushwood, *as* fire causes water to boil—to make Your name known to Your adversaries, *that* the nations may tremble at Your presence![100]

No one can withstand the glory of God. Each nation, each person that witnesses it shall be transformed through the glorious mercy of the Lord. The proud shall be humbled, and the rebellious shall submit through the glorious suffering of ʾel šaddai. In this proclamation, even the enemies of the Lord will eventually succumb to his majesty.[101] In the end, there will be no adversary, as adversaries will be converted into a family. P. T. Forsyth enunciates, "The sinless certainty of Jesus was the result of constant thought, passion and conflict as to His course and victory . . . for *the overthrow of God's enemy* through the redemption of the race, the forgiveness of its guilt, and its moral re-creation."[102] The Glorifier truly creates a glorified family gravitating from the ends of the earth. People are

95. Isa 62:4b.

96. Isa 62:3.

97. Isa 62:4a.

98. Isa 62:4b–5. Isaiah 62 sketches God as the Bridegroom.

99. Isa 62:7 CEV.

100. Isa 64:1–2 NASB; italics in original.

101. Isa 64:6, 9.

102. Forsyth, *Revelation Old and New*, 124–25; italics added.

reclaimed as part of God's cosmic household via the messianic initiative.[103] The bridegroom (God) so loves the bride (humankind) that compassion and mercy are always readily available.[104] Despite people being unfit, the covenantal God made glory fit for them.[105] These things shall take place by the triumph of King Immanuel.[106]

The King extends his arms of peace as his comforting hands reach out to the undeserving.[107] Who else needs it the most? Of course, the Israelites. They rebelled against the Lord, then the non-Israelites; they rejected the true God. As this concept intersects with the locus of the dispute against the call to the nations, I insist not only on Israel's mission to the gentiles but, pivotally, on its success.[108] So far, I have qualified the seeming exclamations contra the universalistic stance of Isaiah. This affirms the divine charge to missionize all. In other words, amid what sounds like clashing statements hardwired into the genetic code of Isaiah, what stands out is the divine peace offer for the covenanted human race.[109]

We now come to the last evidence of the favorable judgment for all:

> I know everything you do and think! The time has now come to bring together the people of every language and nation and to show them my glory by proving what I can do. I will send the survivors to Tarshish, Pul, Lud, Meshech, Tubal, Javan, and to the distant islands. I will send them to announce my wonderful glory to nations that have never heard about me. They will bring your relatives from the nations as an offering to me, the Lord. They will come on horses, chariots, wagons, mules, and camels to Jerusalem, my holy mountain. It will be like the people of Israel bringing the right offering to my temple.[110]

Tarshish, Pul, Lud, Meshech, Tubal, and Javan represent the corners of the earth (in reference to Jerusalem), implying that glory is demonstrated to all—the prelude to total reconciliation. The wonder lies in the sophistication of the divine roadmap to outreach. The LORD God, in a

---

103. Isaiah 64 points out that God is the reliable Helper. See also Isa 65:1.

104. Isa 65:2.

105. Isa 65:3–7; cf. 65: 8–9.

106. Isa 66:1–2.

107. Isa 66:12–13; cf. 66:3–4.

108. For insights regarding the dispute on this matter, see Kaminsky and Stewart, "God of All the World," 139–40.

109. For example, Isa 65:1, 6–7; cf. Isa 65:17. See also Isa 66:2, 4; cf. Isa 66:18.

110. Isa 66:18–20 CEV; italics added.

way, deployed the lost tribes of Israel to the far ends to evangelize the Gentile. As a consequence, all will worship God in the new Jerusalem. This is pleasing to God, not merely due to the camaraderie between nations but, substantially, because they *are* considered "the right offering" before the Subject of worship. This shows that what used to be detestable is now acceptable, since the wicked are made righteous. In other words, as Israel announces God's glory, the people, in turn, are glorified.

In glory, the human act is a delight to God, and it is in this sense that the covenant is conceived of as glorious. In the equitable treatment of all, everyone is exalted unto the final Jubilee. After the reunion of the dispersed tribes of Israel, observes Malka Simkovich, "Jerusalem will become a centripetal force for all of humanity."[111] The eschatological scene is made possible in and through Jesus Christ—the foundation of peace and essence of rest, for he is the *shabbât shalom*.[112] Jesus Christ is so: first and foremost, he revives the relationship between God and humanity; secondly, he rebuilds what has been damaged in humanity. In this way, universal regeneration is executed, and its effect is everlasting.[113]

With this repertoire of supporting evidence for God's absoluteness and all-inclusiveness, philo-theologically speaking, I am not doubtful of the viability of universalism. Although the above catalogue of supporting evidence is not foolproof, what is disputable in Isaianic prophecy can be approached with ease if seen within the striking-and-healing paradigm and the eternal covenant.[114] This, I think, is the way forward in dealing with the material intricacy and perplexing content of Isaiah.

3.1 Universalistic Eschatology

I also think that most Christians, if not all, are hoping for salvation not just for themselves but also for others, especially for family and friends. That hope is extended to all regardless of belief or unbelief (in the meantime). In this manner, one can be referred to as a *hopeful* universalist. There are, of course, Christians not shy to admit that they are *convinced* universalists. They do not see a gap or an allowance (in the eschatos) for

111. In reading Isa 66:18–23 (Simkovich, "Origins of Jewish Universalism," para. 11).

112. Isa 66:23.

113. Isa 66:21–22.

114. For instance, see Isa 66:24.

everyone not to be saved, due to the inclusive and uncompromising merit of Jesus Christ. This sort of believer has unwavering confidence in the universal application of the glorious mercy.

In the grandness of foreordination, the Lord makes Israel fall in order to realize his fault. The Spirit will not forsake him; Israel is sure to rise.[115] There is indeed a period of refreshing—that is, the reconstitution of all things (*apokatastasis*).[116] When the language *all* is mentioned in the OT, it connotes "exceedingly full" or "many and more."[117] In the NT, it refers to everyone or its entirety.[118] God willed his people to disperse, so likewise, God willed for them to cluster. In that case, the divine is amplified and the human is diminished as described in Isaiah; the light of God shines brighter in the darkness of the world.[119] Moreover, all shall be magnetized to the Messiah—the light of the world. Perhaps one might probe: if universalism is truly convincing, then why is it not part of mainstream dogma? I posit that it has to do with Augustine's teaching.

It was just after Augustine's period that human will began forming a stronghold at the expense of God's will.[120] I suppose the misinterpreted Augustinian formula on human will is that which was funneled through the Western Christian tradition. As expounded in chapter 3, the human will is in bondage to sin, which sits well with Martin Luther's thought on the topic.[121] If *free* will is to be insisted on, I would say, arguably, that there were only three people who had it: Adam, Eve, and Jesus of Nazareth. Apart from them, no one can be deemed (indisputably) to have the freedom to choose.

The deteriorated human will is in harmony with the Reformed concept of total depravity, albeit what has been passed throughout Christendom is the potent will that can frustrate the eternal decree.[122] The impact of such misinterpretation is profoundly catastrophic to universalism. The

115. God is the all-sufficient God in Isa 59.

116. Isa 65:17–25; Acts 3:19–21.

117. For example, Isa 53:12; Lam 3:23. *All* in Hebrew is *rab* (רַב), meaning "exceedingly" or "full," from the root meaning "increasing in number" (*SECB*, h7227; h7231).

118. For example, Matt 5:11, 20; 22:14; 2 Cor 9:19. *All* in Greek is *pâs* (πᾶς), meaning "everyone" or "whosoever" (*SECB*, g3956).

119. God is light, as shown in Isa 60.

120. See Augustine, *De libero arbitrio*, II.10.54 (Couenhoven, "Augustine's Rejection," 281–82).

121. Luther, *Bondage of the Will*, 70–73, 236–37.

122. See Baker, "Why Christians Should Not," 463–64.

rejection of redemption overshadows the foreordained salvation. What I advance here is the unbound divine will as opposed to the bound human will. The latter can never overturn the former. The sort of universalism I put forward here walks arm in arm with what is usually attributed to Gregory of Nyssa. Greogry argues that though some unregenerate need a longer period of purification, eventually "no being will remain outside the number of the saved."[123] This is due to the unity of Christ's humanity with *humani generis*.[124] Surely, in the end, the evil in and of being human is overcome in Christ the Victor.

This platform is presumed in Third Isaiah, wherein God is conceived as "the mighty to save"; therefore, the divine victory over the human is set in stone.[125] God will not remain quiet and distant in response to the ongoing wickedness of Israel.[126] God rebuilds Jerusalem and revives her glory in double portion—underscoring the exaltation of the bride.[127]

It appears that the biggest challenge posed against universalism is the "lake of fire" cited in Johannine prophecy.[128] At the outset, I would state that the lake of fire does exist, hence is real, and its consuming effect is equally real. As rendered in Isaiah,

> For the LORD WILL COME IN *fire*, and his chariots like the whirl-wind, to pay back his anger in fury, and his rebuke in flames of fire. For by fire will the LORD EXECUTE JUDGMENT, and by his sword, on *all* flesh; and those slain by the LORD shall be many.[129]

In fiery wrath, the LORD God himself sanctifies and purifies the people. This is in direct retort to those who attempt it on their own.[130] If one hints that the fire here annihilates, then one should rethink it, since the fire is paired with the sword. It presents a problem: either all or only some (in this case—many) are subject to the eschatological judgment. As "all flesh" will go by the sword, then it is fair to assume that all flesh will go by the fire. If the judgment is universal, then why is it that the slain are not all but many? The issue lies in the word *many*.

---

123. Gregory of Nyssa, *Illud*, 17; 21 (in reference to 1 Cor 15:28).
124. Gregory of Nyssa, *On the Song of Songs XV*, 154.
125. Isa 63:1b.
126. Isa 62:1a; 63:3–6.
127. God sets the year of the Lord's favor, as attested in Isa 61.
128. Rev 19:20; 20:10; 21:8.
129. Isa 66:15–16 NRSV; italics added.
130. Isa 66:17.

When *many* is used in the OT, it denotes multiplication by the myriad or connotes the spread of something like water brought about by copious showers.[131] In lexical terms, *many* carries the idea of *fullness* rather than greatness in number; it coheres with the object "all" of humanity. Thus when it is said that many shall be slain, it means that all shall be slain. Furthermore, the word *slain* comes from the root meaning "pollute" or "defile," hence it is more logical that it prefigures a cosmic purification, since the whole of humankind is defiled.[132] Hermeneutically speaking, the many in this context far exceeds what is usually understood. It implies *all and more*. Such implication can be taken as a generalization in an object-oriented framework, signalling a broad envisioning or a prevailing trajectory. As God's purifying act is for everyone, he wills the fullness of purification unto glorification.[133]

I am not swayed by Tertullian's assertion of unending conscious torment, let alone John Stott's extinction model.[134] Thus I stress the purification view of the lake of fire accentuated in chapter 1. What is not yet made clear in the study is the substantive evidence for that view. I once believed that in the profundity of love, God (in the effect of the eschatological verdict) gives what some people desire: total independence from God. And so he will ultimately leave them to disintegrate. This is the natural cause of being detached from the source of life. The disintegration process, however, is gradual, as it depends on the gravity of the sinful life. Correspondingly, the last human to vanish is the most wicked, followed by the vanishing of the fallen angels. The final being to be extinguished is Satan—the champion of evil.[135] When that occurs, evil, sin, and sinners are extinct forever.[136]

131. The Hebrew for *many* is *rᵉbâbâh* (רְבָבָה), denoting "increase" or "multiply by the myriad," from the root meaning "to spread" and "copious showers" (*SECB*, h7231; h7234; h7241). For example, Isa 59:12; Eccl 5:11; Jer 46:23. In Greek, it is *polýs* (πολύς), showing "greatness" in number or degree (*SECB*, g4183). For example, Mark 10:45; 13:26; Heb 3:3.

132. *Slain* in Hebrew is *châlâl* (חָלָל), meaning "pierced" or "profaned," from the root "pollute" or "defile" (*SECB*, h2491; h2490).

133. Isaiah 66 shows that God rules in heaven and on earth.

134. See Vincent, "Salvation Conspiracy," para. 20; Pinnock, "Conditional View," 162.

135. This study limits itself in the treatment of humanity; anything about the enemy and demonic spirits is out of scope, because it requires separate research.

136. Isa 65:17b; 66:5b–6.

That is the problem arising from the short-sighted view of glory. It is narrowed to mean "value in weight" as in the weight of gold or silver.[137] Here, God is said to be glorious, and his glory shines the brightest when all his enemies are finally vanquished. I am not suggesting that such an interpretation should be discarded. What I do suggest, with vigor, is to present glory as portrayed in the Isaianic narratives (and in other parts of the Bible). It shines the brightest by transforming the evil into the holy—that all sinners are turned righteous. It is not my intention to apply the Bultmannian demythologization technique in this matter. I arrived at such a conclusion mainly through lexical and hermeneutical means. Philosophical reflection was secondary. At any rate, I am deeply worried by the insistence of the majority of scholars that in the final day of judgment, the *weight* of the divine smashes into smithereens the *weightlessness* of the human.[138]

No matter how cogent that might be, it cannot be sustained against the sheer grandeur of foreordination. Yes, sinners will be thrown into the lake of fire for purification. This is due to the enormity of God's love for those unworthy of it. In his tender kindness, God vehemently refuses to turn a blind eye in handing over the wicked to their self-destruction. The Bible attests that no one or nothing can separate us from the love of God—not even the desire to be independent of God.[139] That is to show how profound divine love is and how superficial human rejection is.[140] Above all, the inkling of human freedom prompting the decimation of some, frankly, is nonsensical.

On the one hand, it would be easy to accept the eternal torment view of the lake of fire (or hell) as it leaves room for the possibility (which is very possible) of an end to it. On the other hand, the concept of annihilation, no matter how rhetorical it sounds, closes all possibilities of total reconciliation. As argued, it already lapsed in time—before the Parousia. It is encapsulated in the phrase *when mercy ends, justice begins*. But is this truly coherent with the entirety of the Bible? I do not think so. God's mercy never ends, it constitutes God's justice; the latter is the climax of

---

137. Piper, *God's Passion for His Glory*, 191–92. For an alternative insight on the weight of God's glory, cf. C. S. Lewis, *Weight of Glory*, 39–40.

138. See Morgan and Peterson, *Hell under Fire*, xxi; Date and Highfield, *Consuming Passion*, xi–xii.

139. Isa 65:1–6; Rom 8:35–39.

140. Isa 66:1–2; Eph 3:18.

the former. Besides, God is not reactive but proactive. The so-called *lapse in time* is inconceivable, especially given the decree.

It cannot be further argued that there is such a thing as righteous indignation, that is, thrusting unrepentant sinners into the fiery lake of retribution precisely because the reprobate Christ had borne the fullness of God's anger. In this respect, I agree with Barth when he avers, "Predestination means that from all eternity God has determined upon *man's acquittal* at His own cost . . . in the place of the one acquitted He Himself should be perishing and abandoned and rejected—the Lamb slain from the foundation of the world."[141] Reduction to eternal punishment is not healing. In reconciliation, the assumed cannot be sent back. We can no longer take our condemnation; Jesus Christ already took it from us. Even if we would like to take it, it is no longer possible. The Son of God has been afflicted by our affliction as the Son of Man.[142] In the wonder of God's glory, that which suffered is also glorified.[143] In this frame of mind, the apocalyptic fire must be reimagined.

3.2 God as the Purifying Fire

As we walk through the Isaianic pathway, we have good reason to assert that fire is not merely the divine means of purification, but crucially, the purifying fire is God himself.[144] Specifically in the NT, fire is one of the symbols of the Spirit.[145] Notably, those baptized in the fire were not decimated but, instead, cleansed and empowered. God is the fire, so it is eternal.

The fire in Revelation is symbolic. The entire text is peppered with imagery designed to convey a pattern of thought. For instance, the churches symbolize the diverse conditions of Christians; the trumpets indicate the proclamation of God's plan; the beast stands for a world system in opposition to God's servants; and so forth. It is a case of *lost in translation* if interpreted otherwise or with a lack of exposition. If objects or events are taken metaphorically, why not apply them as well to the lake of fire? So it is not philo-theologically sound to think that the lake

---

141. Barth, *CD* II/2, 167; italics added.

142. Isa 63:9.

143. Apparent in Isa 63, God is the glorifying Father.

144. Besides what is discussed in the last section of ch. 1, see Isa 4:4; 6:6–7; 10:17.

145. For example, Matt 3:11–12; Luke 3:16–17; Acts 2:3–4; 1 Thess 5:19.

of fire is literal. To know its meaning and implication, we must decode the imagery.

I advance the notion of purification because the fire, biblically speaking, does not necessarily consume its object. For instance, the fire did not consume the bush in Moses's account, and the fire did not devour the Jewish satraps in Daniel's account.[146] In these circumstances, the fire did not harm its objects simply because the fire *is* God, or God is *in* it. These explicitly show that the concept of purifying fire is not alien to the Bible.

Put in other terms, perhaps one might quickly ask: what makes the lake of fire in Revelation a purifying fire? The weight of the evidence is in the evangelist's employment of the image "lake." Rather than calling it the river of fire or the sea of fire, it is called the lake of fire, due to its circular enclosed shape. It pictures a *crucible*, wherein fire and sulfur are used to subject a metal to very high temperatures in burning its impurities. The Hebrew thought of refinement unto perfection (discussed in chapter 1) is strengthened in Revelation.[147] I am persuaded that purification is an ongoing theme in Johannine eschatology through the recurrent use of crucible imagery. It would be a category error if the fire were understood as a destroyer rather than a purifier. In this regard, the notion of torment can be accommodated not for punishment *per se* but, rather, for purging the dross of sin.

The word *torment* communicates a twofold idea of testing the purity of metals and forcing a person to divulge the truth.[148] The former is functional in exposing the image and likeness of God in humanity, while the latter is functional in confessing that "Jesus Christ is Lord."[149] These operations illustrate the refinement unto perfection motif and, in a way, the glorification of people.[150]

In the overriding argument about the lake of fire, I am happy to adjust my previous belief (annihilation) into an inclusive covenant-friendly stance (purification). So in divine love, God will eventually render people

146. Exod 3:2; Dan 3:27.

147. "Buy your gold from me. It has been *refined in a fire* . . ." Rev 3:18 CEV; italics added. See also Rev 1:15.

148. The Greek for *torment* is *basanízō* (βασανίζω), primarily meaning "to test the purity of metals: gold or silver," which comes from the root meaning "torture by which one is forced to divulge the truth" (*SECB*, g0928; g0931).

149. Isa 45:23; Rom 14:11; Rev 5:13.

150. Isa 66:7–11; Phil 2:10–11.

what they ought to be: *gloriously righteous*. He shall conclusively refine the unregenerate through the holy fire (the Spirit). This is where I locate the epic showcase of the glory of God—the "immoral, murderers, idol worshipers" and the rest of the wicked are meant for purification.[151] As the lake of fire is the Refiner's tool, any defilement is burned before the habitation of the new Jerusalem.[152]

Another salient point needing clarification is about the regenerate. The purified in this life do not need purification in the afterlife. This is the framework where the striking-healing paradigm is well situated. Some are purified by suffering in this world, others by torment in the lake of fire.[153] Common sense dictates that it is logical to presuppose that the purified are exempt from the final torment, hence the *shabbât* in relation to the "death of the righteous." Nevertheless, in speaking of apocalyptic portraits, the fire is not isolated from the sword. Even the regenerate undergoes a sort of final refinement—*dinalisay*.[154] All human beings, in a way, bear the *scar* of sin. Here, the *šekīnah* overcomes the shadow of death. The Spirit, of course, effects the prevailing trajectory: the glorified humankind. That is the fullness of purification unto glorification—the broadly envisioned state of humanity. As all are foreordained to inhabit the new Jerusalem, everyone is *dinalisay*.[155] This is in company with Hart's take on the new epoch. He points out that the text hints at "adumbrations of a larger set of eschatological expectations."[156] In the new heaven and earth, "everything of the past will be forgotten."[157] No one will bear even a slight memory of sin; this is the will of the LORD God.

In which case, we have two options: be purified temporally or post-temporally. This conception does not condone, even to some degree, complacency—that is, as if we can defer the process of moral and spiritual purification. Urgency is not frivolous in this context, since voluntary submission is indispensable. That is why I emphasized, on the onset, the Lord's hands-on oversight of our affairs. The timing of purification is not our decision; it is totally and exclusively the Lord's. So, the idea of

---

151. Isa 66:3–6; cf. Rev 22:15

152. Isa 66:15–18; Rev 22:14.

153. Isa 48:10; 66:15–16.

154. *Dinalisay* is a Filipino word that means "to refine."

155. Isa 66:18; cf. Rev 13:8; 21:27.

156. Hart, *That All Shall Be Saved*, 108.

157. Isa 65:17 CEV; cf. Isa 43:18; Rev 21.4b.

procrastination is dismissed. In this context, what we do and what we cannot do are not in our hands. Accurately speaking, in matters of our transformation from unrighteousness to righteousness, or from rebellion to submission, the Lord has the final say, not us.

Well, if there is a temptation to think otherwise, then Jesus's description of the punishment would make any critique rethink. In the end, the wicked will undergo "weeping and gnashing of teeth."[158] This appears to be an expression of extreme remorse and regret by the disciplined. In the context of the fiery lake, the wicked have to bear it excruciatingly for a period equivalent to one's sin, devoid of any clue of the duration of the purification process.[159] In my evaluation, the weeping indicates repentance and the gnashing of teeth regret. The former shows the realization of one's guilt vis-à-vis an action—what I should not have done—while the latter shows the realization of one's fault vis-à-vis an omission—what I should have done. In the afterlife, the greatest remorse and regret would be the missed opportunity, namely, recognizing Jesus as Lord, as it is inevitable in judgment; also, rewinding time (in the hopes of serving him) is impossible.

3.3 Glory after Death

What about the mention of the second death in the apocalypse? The second death has binary implications—the end of evil and sin as it pertains to the end of death itself and Hades.[160] It is ridiculous to assume that death consumes another death, amplifying the need for decoding. It simply means that death becomes unreal. *Thánatos* signifies the power of death; *háidēs* signifies the territory of death. God conquered both.[161] When Jesus of Nazareth died, the notions of impotency and immobility were precluded. He even went down to Hades to manifest his glory,

---

158. See Matt 8:12; 13:42; Luke 13:28. This is a piece of additional evidence that the wicked thrown into the lake of fire are not disintegrated, whether sooner or later.

159. It is surprising to note the strand in Islam advocating the "remedial nature" of hell. See Maulana, "Hell Is Meant for Purification," para. 7.

160. Isa 65:8, 20; cf. Isa 25:7–8; Rev 20:14.

161. *Hades* in the OT is *Sheol* (Isa 28:8, 57:9). *Death* in Greek is *thánatos* (θάνατος), meaning "the life on earth ended because the soul separates from the body," while *háidēs* (ᾅδης) means "the place of departed souls" or "grave" (*SECB*, g2288; g0086). See 1 Cor 15:55–57.

known as *descensus Christi ad inferos* (Christ's harrowing of hell),[162] in which the descent into Hades is triumphant because Jesus managed to get out of it accompanied by imprisoned spirits.[163] This becomes evident in Jesus's death. At that time, some rose from the grave.[164] From this, we may infer that in the resurrection of Jesus, the power and territory of death are truly "swallowed up in victory."[165] With this backdrop, we can appreciate properly what it means for Jesus Christ to be the "firstborn of the dead."[166] That is to say, to some degree, that the death of death transpired when he rose from the tomb.

Still, the LORD God is analogized as a "strong soap" aside from being a purifying furnace.[167] This reinforces the concept of *dinalisay*; royals and commoners formerly unfit were made fit due to the glory of the divine mercy.[168] The Christocentric vision of the lake of fire proves immensely significant in accepting a salutary end. For the future, we can exclaim that in the purity of Jesus Christ, the impurity of humankind is removed.

Death has become powerless and pointless before the glory of God. The glory of the Son emanates from the Father. The glory of humanity emanates from the Son through the Spirit.[169] The refusal of the Trinity to surrender humans to death is exemplified by Stanley Hauerwas, who claims, "Just as there is no God who is not the Father, Son, and Holy Spirit, so there is no God who must be satisfied that we might be spared. We are the spared because God refuses to have us lost."[170] God does this exactly through the cleansing blood of the Lamb.[171]

In the covenant motif, we are deemed glorious due to the faithfulness and sacrifice of the author and preserver of the covenant—Jesus Christ.[172] Before the Glorifier, the enemies are no more. They are rather glorified. What could be more glorious than to witness the mending of

162. Isa 62:1; cf. 5:14–16; Eph 4:9; 1 Pet 4:6.

163. Isa 57:16–19; 61:1b; cf. Rom 8:10; 1 Cor 5:5; 1 Pet 3:19. See Warren, "Harrowing of Hell."

164. Matt 27:53.

165. Isa 61:2–3; cf. Isa 25:8; 1 Cor 15:54.

166. Isa 64:3–4; Isa 53:10–11; Rev 1:4.

167. Mal 3:2–4.

168. Isa 64:6, 66:19; Rev 19:19; 20:8–10; cf. 21:24–26; 22:2.

169. Isa 60:1; 63:14, 16; Col 3:2–4.

170. Hauerwas, *Cross-Shattered Christ*, 66.

171. Isa 61:10–11; cf. Rev 22:14.

172. As demonstrated in Isa 65, God is the Preserver.

broken hearts and the resuscitation of comatose spirits?[173] Even the most corrupt leader or the greediest entrepreneur is still a son or a daughter of God. In projecting the foreordained, the children of humanity finally become "children of God."[174] In the end, all acknowledge the triumph of the Lord. Those in heaven, on earth, and beneath it, in turn, are glorified.[175] Respectively, humankind is truly God's—his covenanted family.

The glory of Jesus Christ, indisputably, is meant for all peoples. What Adam and Eve longed for in Eden has been actualized in the death, resurrection, and glorification of Christ. Critically, Christ is the *prōtótokos— what he is, is what we become. Holding that in mind, predestination is good news to be heard.*

We can better grasp such formulation in our next reading of Isaiah through Revelation.

3.4 Reading Isaiah through Revelation

In our closing evaluation of Isaiah with Revelation, we will discover why the human race is saved in the final reckoning of God.[176] It is proclaimed,

> Therefore your gates shall be open continually; they shall not be shut day or night, that *men* may bring to you the wealth of the Gentiles and their kings in procession.[177]

There will be a triumphal procession in the new age. All types of people—rich and poor, strong and weak, leaders and subjects, Jews and gentiles—will come to the new Jerusalem. The entrance is wide open to all; all are *dinalisay* through the glory of God. In glorious suffering, all will be made humble. In glorious mercy, all will be made worthy. King Immanuel is the everlasting light all peoples are attracted to; in his glorious brightness, the stricken are healed in the end. The former rebels are now servants.[178] All are made righteous; therefore, everyone is made

---

173. Isa 59:19–20; 60:1–3.
174. Isa 62:4, 12; 63:8; Ps 82:6.
175. Isa 63:15; 66:20–22; Phil 2:10.
176. Isa 60:11; cf. Rev 21:25–26.
177. Isa 60:11 NKJV; italics in original.
178. Isa 60:19–20.

glorious.[179] There shall be no more social injustice, for the splendor of the Lord is manifest in all the inhabitants of the revitalized city.[180]

That proclamation is echoed in Revelation: "Its gates will never be shut by day—and there will be no night there. People will bring into it the glory and the honor of the nations."[181] Here we have the evangelist once again drawing inspiration from Isaiah.[182] The universal dispensation of mercy and compassion is beyond denial in this context. The subject (people) and the object (nations) are the éthnos (multitude of heathens), synonymous with gôy (a massive number of gentiles) in Isaiah.[183] That is to say that all Israel and all non-Israel shall worship King Immanuel after the eschatological judgment. Surely nothing impure will ever infiltrate the new Jerusalem. Everyone in convocation has been *dinalisay* in glory.[184] This is the effect of the sword of the LORD God. And since the Lamb is also the Shepherd, what has been struck down has been healed.[185] No wonder, compliments to St. Jerome, Isaiah is known as the "Fifth Gospel."[186] Carroll Stuhlmueller's inference that Second Isaiah "broke the impasse between election and universalism" is a bit of a stretch. In my conviction, the entirety of Isaiah did it.[187]

The coming down of the glorious city on the recreated earth marks God's dwelling with humankind, as Robin Parry illuminates that the new Jerusalem "is not merely a city that contains a temple (like Jerusalem), but the city *is* a temple . . . the biblical cosmos what the temple writ large. In other words, in the world of the Bible, the cosmos *is* God's house."[188] I am happy to side with Parry on this matter; however, I find his thought on glory (still in this context) deficient, articulated in a mystical rather than practical fashion. Even if he somehow associates the talk of glory with the story of Jesus, Parry nevertheless slips into presenting it as the

179. Isa 60:21.

180. Isa 60:22.

181. Rev 21:25–26 NKJV.

182. For additional references to the common grounds between Isaiah and Revelation, see Moyise, "Isaiah in New Testament," 538–39.

183. *SECB*, g1484; h1471.

184. Rev 21:27.

185. Rev 19:15; cf. Isa 63:3.

186. Sawyer, *Fifth Gospel*, 1.

187. Senior and Stuhlmueller, *Biblical Foundations for Mission*, 100.

188. Isa 65:17 (Parry, *Biblical Cosmos*, 139, 148; italics in original).

"grandeur of God."[189] It would be better if Parry unpacked the notion that the unseen glory is manifested through the seen. As explained in this chapter, ubiquitous glory is seen in the acceptance of peoples, regardless of their offense against God.

Anyway, the message that is sent here is that everyone is in the glorious family of God; everyone interconnects in a quantum world. In the kingdom of God, the covenant with Israel extends to all. There is no retreat to this pact, because the *shabbât shalom* is predetermined for all. The outcome of the eschatological judgment is indeed marvellous: the wicked become righteous, the impure pure, and the unworthy glorified.

Such thought could be unnecessary and therefore unlikely to pass Ockham's razor. But I persist in testing the known against the grand theme about God. The gamut of common objections to the purification model of the fiery lake needs reconsideration in the wonder of God's glory. The favorable judgment showcases that whatever is human is eclipsed by the divine. The *šekînah* saturates the entire cosmos as foreordained.

The glory in and of God is captured, not without entertaining the plausibility of universalism. In other words, universalism is the medium in conceiving the true essence of glory. Having imposed this thought on the study, unlike Gregory of Nyssa, I have no intention to "dampen down" (to minimize the shock of my take on eschatology), let alone to mute the universalist stance of the Isaianic message.[190] I intend, rather, to raise the banner of God's glorious act in and through Jesus Christ. Thus in this treatise, my background music is Mozart's Symphony No. 40 in preference over Bach's Cello Suite No. 1.

Truly, the compounding weight of God's love, power, grace, eternality, and sacrifice reveals its loftiest value in the exaltation of the undeserving. After all, a Christian reading of Isaiah has been proven scholastic *and* practical.

189. Parry, *Biblical Cosmos*, 147, 152.
190. Ludlow, "In illud," 423.

CONCLUSION

IN NAVIGATING THROUGH ITS ANTHOLOGICAL AND CRYPTIC character-istics, Isaiah's comprehensive shape features the God of Israel. In the locution evident in this prophetic book, the reader is challenged to see the whole picture or else dismiss it as a literary blunder, for it seems unsystematic. I took the former stance to peek into God's splendor in the magnificence of his plan. This was done through deconstructing the arbitrary signifiers (complicating the prophecy) to reconstruct a positive approach to the end of things.

In aiming to construct eschatology from the Isaianic prophecy, I began with the big question of human suffering despite the presence of God. Throughout this enterprise, I have argued for the sovereign God who loves unconditionally. This God, however, is often misconstrued over the strangeness and alienness of his method. In the talk of theodicy with the doctrine of God, evil cannot be easily associated with God. The thought of an evil God of Israel is inviable in the spectrum of the eternal covenant. Evil is undeniable in the striking of people, yet it is knocked out in their healing.

The constancy of the divine operation has emerged as the reliable predictor in speaking of God. Such constancy is evident in God as King Immanuel. I have shown that God is King in terms of having full author-ity and responsibility regarding Israel, and God is Immanuel in terms of the ever-present ministration to Israel. By contemplating the divine sovereignty testified by the prophet Isaiah, the tight relationship between the end of the history of Israel and humanity has been established. In this respect, Jerusalem stands as the center of eschatological hope as preordained.

Pretemporality has been identified as the locus of divine activity. Temporality has been understood to be where the actualization of this activity is located. The objective is to disengage human activity from that of the divine, but the result is harmony of the two, not union. Without losing sight of the oracles of Isaiah, I have made it plain that whatever is foreordained can never be frustrated, let alone diverted by creaturely reality. It has been validated in Isaiah that an *invisible hand* had been orchestrating individual actions and world events. In clarification, however, human accountability still holds, making Israel liable for his sins. In the end, I have also contended that all condemnatory weight shall be on the suffering Messiah.

In the first chapter, we have seen that the Lord is sovereign in love. Despite Israel's greed and idolatry, God did send the Messiah as promised. I have continuously used the term *messianic initiative* to point out the determination of God in rescuing his people. This strengthened the argument for the calling of Zion and her success in fulfilling the call through the Holy Spirit. The refining power of the Spirit purges Zion's impurities. Hereafter, the Messiah as the *šekīnah* was shown to prompt Zion's role as a beacon to the world. God's dealing with Israel, therefore, can be conceived as altogether an act of love. Predestination, in its truest sense, is not troubling but comforting. What is alarming is the hopelessness interjected in the discourse due to the stubbornness of people to obey God. That does not apply to the God in Isaiah. God's stubborn love short-circuits any attempt to distort the covenantal relationship.

In the following chapter, the unwavering compassion of the Creator God is safeguarded. The sacrifice of Jesus Christ fixed the fractured covenant. I have maintained that whatever Christ has done can never be undone. As far as God is concerned, that which is foreordained is set in stone. God's faithfulness to what he has foreordained mirrors God's faithfulness to himself. People who should have received indignation rather received mercy—proof of the dynamic grace of God. The rebel city (old Jerusalem) has become the servant city (new Jerusalem). In creating the world, God has in mind for humanity to achieve the pinnacle of its design. The predetermined actions and events are sourced from God's self-determination as the Lord of creation. Whatever is created is eternally attached to the Creator in the covenant. The sound of the *shofar* united the tribes of Israel and all the tribes in the world.

I have explained in the third chapter the graciousness of God in sustaining Israel against the seemingly harsh discipline involved. In reinspecting the covenantal promise, the Messiah's rod of punishment is also the guiding instrument. This gave a window on the turning of grief and groaning into happiness and celebration. All tribes are set for a great reunion in the new Jerusalem; the new state of things replaces the old. Tears of pain turn into tears of joy in the new world order. The overflowing grace is always available for humanity—the crowning act of the triune God. By the authority of the Father and power of the Spirit, the Son provided for humans to reflect his being. This is the guidepost for advancing the notion of maturity or perfection. The introduction of suffering in the equation reconfigures the conception of the fall. The suffering unto perfection paradigm reconstituted the doctrine of humanity and therefore put the strict view of restoration (the return to Eden) inviable.

In the fourth chapter, I have continuously stressed that the electing God is consistent in correcting Israel through King Immanuel. In the development of this train of thought vis-à-vis the eternal decree, it has been demonstrated that the Davidic figure is *the* beacon to the world. By informing all peoples of God's everlasting will, the entire humanity comprehends the decree and benefits from it. I have also clarified that lasting justice means the irrevocable vindication of all in the forever binding covenant. The recompense for human decision and action accounts for the merit of Jesus Christ. Thus, what humanity gets is not a payoff but a *buy-off*. In the retake of the doctrine of election, I have rendered God's commitment to the covenant as eternal. Salutary eschatology is guaranteed not because humans somehow managed to be faithful to the covenant, but rather, God is ever faithful to it. I reject the notion of particularism and any eschatological separation of the wicked from God. All humanity is elected for eternal life in and through Jesus Christ.

I have highlighted in the penultimate chapter that the redeeming God is indeed selfless. In the atrocity of the Son (being like us), humans gained indemnity. Excessive forgiveness in the superabundant mercy is ready not only for the chosen people but for all. The object becomes destitute and distraught in the way God strikes whom he loves. Nonetheless, God's promise of healing is sure afterward. I have also unpacked the guarantee of *shâlôm* emanating from the kingship of sacrifice. The Eschaton—Jesus Christ—is the Lord of the eschatos, and this formula is endemic in Isaiah. What had been prophesied shall be consummated in full in the new eon. When the doctrine of redemption is reexamined in a Christocentric dimension, it eliminates any doubt about the final status of human beings. Although God's ways and means are strange and alien, these are designed to uplift and rejuvenate the object. The objective orientation of the striking unto healing method is beneficial. This is to bring out true humanity, not from Adam but from Jesus Christ. Any soterio-eschatological pronouncement must not be made without spelling out first the selfless character of God.

That brings us to the concluding chapter that exemplifies the glorifying God in the inclusive treatment of humankind. Favorable judgment is given to the shamed. The saturating lovingkindness of God eclipsed the darkness enshrouding humanity. The glory in and of God is understood in the acknowledgment of Christian universalism. God unconditionally forgave and accepted his masterpiece—the human race. The exaltation of the undeserving is not an overstatement if anchored in the messianic initiative. Little wonder, then, that God takes responsibility for disciplining humans. Whoever is subjected to striking is therefore subjected to healing. The telos of it all is to share glory with people. God's readiness and willingness to reunite with people are traced to people's bearing God's image and likeness. All are bound to the final refinement (*dinalisay*), including those purified on earth through suffering.

More generally, I have discovered that the scroll of Isaiah is a sort of symphony—full of repetition with variation in mood and tempo. In its process of repeating, recycling, and developing the plethora of themes, the unmitigated divine outworking for the advantage of humankind is solidified. I have been careful tackling theodicy, balancing my way along a tight rope, which, of course, is conclusive yet not without criticism. My reading of Isaiah through Revelation is not a razor-sharp proposal; however, it is not a hodgepodge of thoughts patched together to come up with the desired conclusion. As exhibited in this project, there is a convincing underlying tone of universal healing in the wake of the final judgment.

If one thinks that reading Isaiah through Revelation is simply an untenable task given the two distinct texts, I suggest, think again. The uncertainty is resolved not in the anthropology and sociology involved (for the texts vary in these respects) but rather in the sure character of the LORD God in both accounts. The God in Revelation is the same God in Isaiah—One who is ever true to the decree. God has foreordained himself to be God for humanity. Whatever we do will not affect him being God for us. In one way, this reading can be canonical as it communicates with today's community of believers. In another way, this reading can be non-canonical as it detaches itself from a general rule (or acceptable procedure) in considering these texts. What has been rigidly argued is the unbreakable train of thought concerning God's equitable treatment of all peoples. This is feasible despite the purported incompleteness of Isaiah as a manuscript. I admit to its unsettled authorship; therefore, the content remains under scrutiny. But the fact stands: there is a way to read Isaiah *with* Revelation and vice versa, and the way proposed here is well grounded.

In company with Karl Barth, I have asserted (on various occasions) the definite act of God in King Immanuel. Furthermore, I reiterated that God's being is not in human activity, simply because God's action is solely in God's being. The disconnect between the divine and human has been made obvious. Human activity is not according to the divine being; therefore, such an act cannot have a lasting impact on the grand scheme of things. Given foreordination, the divine self-determination to overcome human self-aggrandizement is outstanding. It demonstrates itself in the tremendous outgrowth from the "stump" and the awesome flashing of the "beacon."

In rigid consideration of the doctrine of God, I sided with David Bentley Hart as regards God's intrusive intervention in human affairs. This is done, however, not without God's supreme love. The idea of capriciousness and indifference is out of the equation. What is *not* here, in handling the notion of predestination, is exclusivity in dispensing grace. What *is* here is universal access to it.

As shown thus far, foundational to the discussion on divine sovereignty is as follows: (1) God is the only sovereign; (2) God's self-determination towards us is unchangeable; (3) God's masterplan is impeccable; (4) God empathizes with our suffering; (5) God has fully revealed himself in Jesus Christ; and (6) all creation is in, through, and for Jesus Christ. With these, theodicy is in a better position to withstand the attack of the skeptics.

What are horrible are sin and its effects (not God). We are challenged to reboot our philo-theological conception of God, repaint our theological landscape, and rethink our eschatology. These recommendations, which Robin Parry shares, are supported biblically. The crux of the OT is located in the NT (specifically in the Gospels). This is true even if the latter springs from the former (Isaiah in particular). It has come to light that the Second Temple Jews had missed the suffering Messiah, and contemporary Christians somewhat overlooked the almighty Messiah. The Anointed One who rules by condescension is magnified throughout the study. This is the ground where I have dug out a theological construct about the Lion and the Lamb. Accordingly, the grandeur and effectivity of the striking-healing paradigm address the concerns of theodicy. We do not have to sanitize the picture by downplaying or skipping the recurring violence in Isaiah. What we have to do is to take the "I am what I am" alongside the "before Abraham was, I am."

The Son is the sanitized God, yet no matter how troubling it may appear in the OT, he *is* the creator of the forbidden tree, the bringer of the plagues, the accuser of immoral cities, the organizer of ethnic cleansing, and the dispatcher of the great flood. What could be more persuasive than to show that the *'el šaddai* on Mount Sinai is the "man of sorrows" in Isaiah? I have tried to be coherent about God's all-out embrace of humanity amid pestilence and disasters. In agreement with P. T. Forsyth, the unadulterated picture of the LORD God is located in Jesus Christ alone. In Christ, clouded impressions and convoluted expressions are made intelligible and clear.

In advocating precision in theodicy, the following have been established as false teachings. First, God's will is not sovereign; the human will is. Second, God's mercy ends in the final judgment. Third, we are the masters of our destiny. Fourth, the doctrine of universalism is unbiblical. Last, the Edenic freedom of choice is biblical. In my estimation, those who hold these viewpoints imagine a deity who sits well with modernism.

In contrast, as posited in Isaiah, we see that (1) God's will is sovereign over human will, yet human accountability also holds true; (2) God's justice is subservient to God's love; (3) God is the Master of our destiny and the destiny of creation; (4) God desires for us to grow in Jesus Christ; (5) God does not infringe on our freedom, as he is the Liberator of humanity. With these, the argument for the supremacy of God does not fall prey to secular humanism and anti-theism. By pairing divine sovereignty with universalism, the dogmatic bigotry between the Arminians and Calvinists is somewhat deescalated.

But then the question arises: if God exceedingly loves by sacrificing for all, why does the certainty of redemption stay elusive? I think the question which ought to be asked is: now that people are aware of God's eternal intention for all, can they un-know what they already know (vis-à-vis the new reality), or can they nullify what is already done? Unless, of course, if they disagree. We can state with confidence only that which is revealed in Isaiah (paralleled with Revelation). That is situated in the evangelical spirit of the Isaianic predictions exemplifying the love of God in the end. The messianic initiative punctuates the freedom of God where assurance is maintained. Despite maintaining human accountability, I have decided to refrain from unnecessary *guilt trips* to block any anti-climax on the eschatological horizon.

As it stands, universalism is an optimistic estimate of Jesus Christ as the universal sacrifice. But can we overestimate the suffering God in this regard? In the talk of the ultimacy of reconciliation, it is legitimate to be optimistic about the future. It is not because of humanity but God. The covenant Partner is eternally inseparable from the covenant members. As I have put it bluntly, it is not too much to expect from God. We can trust God superabundantly with concrete hope. Since there is no Achilles heel in the covenant, therefore God's relationship with humankind is forever intact.

As the eternal covenant is woven into the very fabric of Reformed theology, it is not too ambitious to push for the universality of vindication. I do not intend to dance around the topic but to emphasize its plausibility in the Bible. The sheer force of foreordination treats the discussion on universalism as an intellectual cul-de-sac, in which engagement with it proves nothing. Also, the mountainous challenge against universalism is insurmountable. There is a path to make the discourse profitable; the way forward lies in the eternality of God's suffering. In contemplating this, no one fades into oblivion in the grand scheme of things. With the mystery of the final judgment, the foreordination *pro nobis* serves as a boundary marker between what is accommodated and what is not.

Though a universalist pre-perception of events is a hard topic, I have entered a field where many have trodden before me. The real obstacle is novelty, not so much as arguing against cynicism. I was presented an op-portunity to offer fresh insights into the debate on universalism in detect-ing a gap in the Isaianic prophecy about Jesus Christ as *the Israel*. To this, I continued the inquiry on the eschato-juridical outcome that resonates today more than ever.

By exploring the colorful themes of Isaiah, I am therefore convinced that multifunctional methods and a diachronic approach to things bring a unified purpose: to amplify that Isaianic theology is Christology. The readers will soon notice that the light at the end of the tunnel is Jesus Christ. In judgment, we shall all confess, in a crescendo of praise, that Christ is Lord. In raising the stakes on the debate on universalism, I would state that there is no spiritual handicap with King Immanuel. The pierced hand of God covers any deficiency in humanity. This is directly informed not by soteriology but by the doctrine of divine sovereignty—in which case, the theological bastion is located in pretemporality. The covenanted before creation remains as *is*, since the Subject of theology (the triune God) is manifested in the Subject of Christology (the Son of God as the Son of Man). In other words, the evoked can never be revoked.

What has been outstanding, so far, is the eternal efficacy of the redemptive act. This, in turn, serves as an overture for the glorifying act. As I have argued in philo-theological terms, the spotlight is on pretemporal eternity. The endpoint of God's operation is the unmerited glorification of human beings. Of course, the burden of proof is on the predestination in and of Jesus Christ—that which I meticulously articulated in more fluid linguistic forms. It may be arbitrated that my standard of proof falls short of degree insofar as the Bible is concerned, yet the level of proof for universalism is what is intensified, at least in expositing Isaiah. This, however, grants the elusiveness of the subject matter. Since there are no easy answers, the reader is then challenged to rethink eschatology. The reading of Isaiah through Revelation is more subtle and complicated. This reading may appear crooked and overstretched; nevertheless, it is unfair to discount it as mere speculation. In the parallel reading of the two, theologically speaking, the former is the superscript and the latter is the subscript.

In sum, God's dealing with Israel is *in* the preordination of love. God knows best, for he has planned the journey and destination. The utmost concern of God is ascertained even amid suffering, as long as grace is in the equation. God's ways and means, however strange and alien they might seem, are uncompromisingly good. Election delivers a salutary end through divine commitment. The system of striking-healing is congruent with God's character. God's self-taken responsibility for our discipline does not preclude God's equitable treatment of us all. Our deliverance and glorification spring from the death and resurrection of Jesus Christ. Confronted by these statements, it would take a heart of steel to resist.

The findings from this study make several contributions to the current literature. (1) The distaste for predestination ceases against the sovereignty of God's love. (2) The sustained are later glorified. (3) God's pre-decision is consummated in the now of eternity. (4) Providence is inimical to particularism and annihilationism. (5) The final refinement removes the scar of sin. (6) The concept of the fall is unsustainable in light of foreordination. (7) The weight of God's glory is in the transformation of the wicked. (8) The idea of restoration is incompatible with the purification unto perfection model. (9) In the end, there is only one type of vessel, that of glory. (10) The major thrust of the Bible is glorification, not necessarily redemption. Armed with these assertions (with nuances), we can conclude that the covenantal theme is a vital component in accommodating universalism. It aids our understanding of the plausibility of the salvation unto glorification of all. Besides, further research is needed to crack the enigma inherent in the final judgment.

Returning to the question posed at the outset, I can claim with confidence that the God of discipline and compassion is the God amid COVID-19. He is the Lord who heals people after striking them. Our breakdown jumpstarts our glorious transformation. As we look back to the history of Israel, Isaiah directs us to fix our eyes upon Jesus Christ—the *shabbât shalom* yesterday, today, and tomorrow.

BIBLIOGRAPHY

Adams, Marilyn M. *Horrendous Evils and the Goodness of God*. Ithaca, NY: Cornell University Press, 2000.

Alexander, Joseph Addison. *Commentary on Isaiah*. Grand Rapids: Kregel, 1992.

Allen, Leslie C. *A Theological Approach to the Old Testament: Major Themes and New Testament Connections*. Eugene, OR: Cascade, 2014.

Allen, Wayne. *Thinking about Good and Evil: Jewish Views from Antiquity to Modernity*. Philadelphia: Jewish Publication Society, 2021.

Baker, Lynne Rudder. "Why Christians Should Not Be Libertarians: An Augustinian Challenge." *Faith and Philosophy: Journal of the Society of Christian Philosophers* 20 (Oct. 2003) 460–78.

Barth, Karl. *Church Dogmatics*. 4 vols. Translated by G. W. Bromiley and T. F. Torrance. Edinburgh: T. & T. Clark, 2009.

———. *Gespräche*, 1959–1962. In *Gesamtausgabe* IV.25, edited by Eberhard Busch and Karl Barth, 339–45. Zürich: Theologischer Verlag, 1995.

Beale, G. K. *The Book of Revelation*. Grand Rapids: Eerdmans, 1999.

Becker, Uwe. "The Book of Isaiah: Its Composition History." In *The Oxford Handbook of Isaiah*, edited by Lena-Sofia Tiemeyer, 37–58. Oxford, UK: Oxford University Press, 2020.

Beeke, Joel R. *The Quest for Full Assurance: The Legacy of Calvin and His Successors*. Edinburgh: Banner of Truth, 1999.

ben Yosef, Akiva. "Pirkei Avot." In *Soncino Talmud*, edited by Isidore Epstein, page range unavailable. London: Soncino, 1973.

Berges, Ulrich. "Farewell to Deutero-Isaiah or Prophecy without a Prophet." In *Congress Volume Ljubljana 2007*, edited by A. Lemaire, 575–95. Leiden, Neth.: Brill, 2010.

Berkouwer, G. C. *Studies in Dogmatics: The Providence of God*. Reprint, Grand Rapids: Eerdmans, 1983.

Bettenson, Henry, and Chris Maunder, eds. *Documents of the Christian Church*. 4th ed. Oxford, UK: Oxford University Press, 2011.

Blenkinsopp, Joseph. *Essays on the Book of Isaiah*. Forschungen zum Alten Testament 128. Tübingen, Germ.: Mohr Siebeck, 2019.

Boettner, Loraine. *The Reformed Doctrine of Predestination*. Phillipsburg, NJ: P&R, 1991.

Bolin, Thomas M. "Nineveh as Sin City." Bible Odyssey (July 2019). https://www.bibleodyssey.org/en/places/related-articles/nineveh-as-sin-city.

Brett, Mark G. "Postcolonial Readings of Isaiah." In *The Oxford Handbook of Isaiah*, edited by Lena-Sofia Tiemeyer, 621–36. Oxford, UK: Oxford University Press, 2020.

Brewer, Debbie, ed. *Quotes of Confucius and Their Interpretations: A Words of Wisdom Collection Book*. Morrisville, NC: Lulu, 2020.

Brown, Francis, et al. *The Brown-Driver-Briggs Hebrew and English Lexicon*. Peabody, MA: Hendrickson, 2006.

Broyles, Craig C., and Craig A. Evans, eds. *Writing and Reading the Scroll of Isaiah: Studies of an Interpretive Tradition*. 2 vols. Supplements to Vetus Testamentum 70. Leiden, Neth.: Brill Academic, 1997.

Brueggemann, Walter. *Disruptive Grace: Reflections on God, Scripture, and the Church*. Edited by Carolyn J. Sharp. Minneapolis: Fortress, 2011.

Bulgakov, Sergius. *The Comforter*. Translated by Boris Jakim. Grand Rapids: Eerdmans, 2004.

Bulkeley, Tim. "Living in the Empire: What Purposes Do Assertions of Divine Sovereignty Serve in Isaiah?" In *Isaiah and Imperial Context: The Book of Isaiah in the Times of Empire*, edited by Andrew T. Abernethy et al., 71–84. Eugene, OR: Pickwick, 1989.

Calvin, John. *Institutes of the Christian Religion: Translated from the Original Latin, and Collated with the Author's Last Edition in French*. Translated by John Allen. 2 vols. Eugene, OR: Wipf & Stock, 2013.

———. *John Calvin's Bible Commentaries on Jonah, Micah, Nahum*. Translated by John King. North Charleston, SC: Createspace, 2017.

Carr, David. "Reaching for Unity in Isaiah." *Journal for the Study of the Old Testament* 57 (1993) 61–80.

Charlesworth, James H., ed. *The Unperceived Continuity of Isaiah*. London: T. & T. Clark, 2019.

Childs, Brevard S. *Isaiah*. TOTL. Louisville, KY: Westminster John Knox, 2013.

Collins, John J., ed. *The Oxford Handbook of Apocalyptic Literature*. Oxford, UK: Oxford University Press, 2014.

Couenhoven, Jesse. "Augustine's Rejection of the Free-Will Defence: An Overview of the Late Augustine's Theodicy." *Religious Studies* 43, no. 3 (Sept. 2007) 279–98.

Couey, Blake J. *Reading the Poetry of First Isaiah*. Oxford, UK: Oxford University Press, 2015.

Date, Christopher, and Ron Highfield, eds. *A Consuming Passion: Essays on Hell and Immortality in Honor of Edward Fudge*. Eugene, OR: Pickwick, 2015.

Davidson, Robert. "Universalism in Second Isaiah." *Scottish Journal of Theology* 16, no. 2 (June 1963) 166–85.

Davis, Paul K. *Encountering Evil: Live Options in Theodicy*. Louisville, KY: Westminster John Knox, 2004.

Dawkins, Richard. *The God Delusion*. London: Black Swan, 2016.

———, and John Lennox. "The God Delusion Debate." Fixed Point Foundation (Feb. 2017). https://www.youtube.com/watch?v=zF5bPI92-50.

Dawson, Dale R. *The Resurrection in Karl Barth*. Reprint, London: Routledge, 2017.

Descartes, René. *Meditations on First Philosophy*. Rev. ed. Translated by John Cottingham. Cambridge, UK: Cambridge University Press, 1996.

de Vera, Nixon. "The Controversy of a Calvinist Theology on Election." Research essay, University of Divinity, 2015.

———. "The God of the Covenant: Karl Barth on Creation Care." *Religions* 12, no. 5 (7 May 2021). https://www.mdpi.com/2077-1444/12/5/326.

———. *The Suffering of God in the Eternal Decree: A Critical Study of Karl Barth on Election.* Eugene, OR: Pickwick, 2020.

De Witt, John R. "The Arminian Conflict and the Synod of Dort." In *Puritan Papers 5: 1968–1969,* edited by J. I. Packer, 3–23. Phillipsburg: P & R, 2005.

Dixon, Leif. *Practical Predestinarians in England, c. 1590–1640.* Surrey, UK: Ashgate, 2014.

Dumbrell, William J. "The Purpose of the Book of Isaiah." *Tyndale Bulletin* 36 (1985) 111–28.

Edwards, Jonathan. *Sinners in the Hands of an Angry God.* Cleveland: Musaicum, 2018. Ebook.

Ellis, E. Earle. *Christ and the Future in New Testament History.* Novum Testamentum Supplements 97. Leiden, Neth.: Brill, 2001.

Ellison, John W. *Nelson's Complete Concordance of the Revised Standard Version of the Bible.* 2nd ed. Nashville: Thomas Nelson, 1985.

Eriksson, Lars Olov. "From Gesenius to Childs: Reading the Book of Isaiah with Two Giants." In *New Studies in the Book of Isaiah: Essays in Honor of Hallvard Hagelia,* edited by Markus Zehnder, 13–30. Perspectives on Hebrew Scriptures and Its Contexts 21. Piscataway, NJ: Gorgias, 2014.

Evans, C. A. "On the Unity and Parallel Structure of Isaiah." *Vetus Testamentum* 38 (1988) 129–47.

Everson, A. Joseph. *The Vison of the Prophet Isaiah: Hope in the War-Weary World; A Commentary.* Eugene, OR: Wipf & Stock, 2019.

Fekkes, Jan, III. *Isaiah and Prophetic Traditions in the Book of Revelation: Visionary Antecedents and their Developments.* Sheffield, UK: Sheffield Academic Press, 1994.

Forsyth, P. T. *The Christian Ethic of War.* Eugene, OR: Wipf & Stock, 1999.

———. *The Cruciality of the Cross.* Eugene, OR: Wipf & Stock, 1997.

———. *Descending on Humanity and Intervening in History: Notes from the Pulpit Ministry of P. T. Forsyth.* Edited by Jason A. Goroncy. Eugene: Pickwick, 2013.

———. *God the Holy Father.* Blackwood, Aus.: New Creation, 1987.

———. *The Justification of God: Lectures for War-Time on Christian Theodicy.* Reprint, South Yarra, Aus.: Leopold Classic Library, 2015.

———. *Missions in State and Church: Sermons and Addresses.* Reprint, London: Forgotten Books, 2018.

———. *Positive Preaching and the Modem Mind.* Kittery, ME: HardPress, 2012.

———. *Revelation Old and New.* Shropshire, UK: Quinta, 2009.

Franke, Chris. *Isaiah 46, 47, and 48: A New Literary-Critical Reading.* Biblical and Judaic Studies 3. Winona Lake, IN: Eisenbrauns, 1994.

Fretheim, Terence, and Karlfried Froehlich. *The Bible as Word of God in a Postmodern Age.* Minneapolis: Fortress, 1998.

Friedman, Richard Elliot. *Commentary on the Torah.* Reprint, San Francisco: HarperOne, 2003.

Gallaher, Brandon. *Freedom and Necessity in Modern Trinitarian Theology.* Oxford, UK: Oxford University Press, 2016.

Gelston, Anthony. "Universalism in Second Isaiah." *The Journal of Theological Studies* 43, no. 2 (Oct. 1992) 377–98.

Gignilliat, Mark S. *Karl Barth and the Fifth Gospel: Barth's Theological Exegesis of Isaiah*. London: Routledge, 2016.

Goldingay, John. *The Theology of the Book of Isaiah*. Downers Grove, IL: InterVarsity, 2014.

Goroncy, Jason. *Hallowed Be Thy Name: The Sanctification of All in the Soteriology of P. T. Forsyth*. London: T. & T. Clark, 2013.

Gowan, Donald E. *Theology of the Prophetic Books: The Death and Resurrection of Israel*. Louisville, KY: Westminster John Knox, 1998.

Grabiner, Steven. *Revelation's Hymns: Commentary on the Cosmic Conflict*. London: Bloomsbury T. & T. Clark, 2015.

Greggs, Tom. *Barth, Origen, and Universal Salvation: Restoring Particularity*. Oxford, UK: Oxford University Press, 2009.

Habets, Myk, and Bobby Grow, eds. *Evangelical Calvinism: Essays Resourcing the Continuing Reformation of the Church*. Eugene, OR: Pickwick, 2012.

Hannay, Alastair. *Kierkegaard: A Biography*. Cambridge, UK: Cambridge University Press, 2003.

Hart, David Bentley. "Church and Israel after Christendom: The Politics of Election." *First Things* (Aug. 2000). https://www.firstthings.com/article/2000/08/church-and-israel-after-christendom-the-politics-of-election.

———. "Providence and Causality: On Divine Innocence." In *The Providence of God: Deus Habet Consilium*, edited by Francesca Aran Murphy and Philip G. Ziegler, 34–56. London: T. & T. Clark, 2009.

———. *That All Shall Be Saved: Heaven, Hell, and Christian Universalism*. New Haven, CT: Yale University Press, 2019.

Hasel, Gerhard F. *The Remnant: The History and Theology of the Remnant Idea from Genesis to Isaiah*. 3rd ed. Berrien Springs, MI: Andrews University Press, 1980.

Hauerwas, Stanley. *Cross-Shattered Christ: Meditations on the Seven Last Words*. Grand Rapids: Brazos, 2011.

Hays, Christopher B. *The Origins of Isaiah 24–27: Josiah's Festival Scroll for the Fall of Assyria*. Cambridge, UK: Cambridge University Press, 2019.

Hegel, G. W. F. *The Logic of Hegel*. Translated by William Wallace. Frankfurt: Outlook, 2018.

Hick, John. *Evil and the God of Love*. New York: Springer, 2010.

———. "An Irenaean Theodicy." In *John Hick's Theodicy: A Process Humanist Critique*, by C. Robert Mesle, xvi–xxxiii. London: Palgrave MacMillan, 1991.

Hildebrandt, Samuel. *Interpreting Quoted Speech in Prophetic Literature: A Study of Jeremiah 2.1—3.5*. Vetus Testamentum Supplements 176. Leiden: Brill, 2017.

Hitchens, Christopher. *God Is Not Great: How Religion Poisons Everything*. New York: Grand Central, 2009.

Hooker, Joy. "Zion as Theological Symbol in Isaiah: Implications for Judah, for the Nations, and for Empire." In *Isaiah and Imperial Context: The Book of Isaiah in the Times of Empire*, edited by Andrew T. Abernethy et al., 107–21. Eugene, OR: Pickwick, 1989.

Hulse, Errol. "The Eschatological Dimensions of Isaiah." *Foundations* 52 (Autumn 2004) 33–40.

Hume, David. *Dialogues Concerning Natural Religion*. Reprint, London: Penguin, 1990.

Hunsinger, George. *Reading Barth with Charity: A Hermeneutical Proposal*. Grand Rapids: Baker Academic, 2015.

Jamieson, Robert, et al. *Commentary Critical and Explanatory on the Whole Bible*. 2 vols. Harrington, DE: Delmarva, 2013.

Jang, Se-Hoon. *Particularism and Universalism in the Book of Isaiah: Isaiah's Implications for a Pluralistic World from a Korean Perspective*. Bern: Peter Lang, 2005.

Johnson, Elizabeth A. *She Who Is: The Mystery of God in Feminist Theological Discourse*. New York: Crossroad, 2002.

Kaminsky, Joel S. "Election Theology and the Problem of Universalism." *Horizons in Biblical Theology* 33 (2011) 34–44.

———, and Anne Stewart. "God of All the World: Universalism and Developing Monotheism in Isaiah 40–66." *The Harvard Theological Review* 99, no. 2 (Apr. 2006) 139–63.

Kaufman, Stephen A. "The Phoenician Inscription of the Incirli Trilingual: A Tentative Reconstruction and Translation." *MAARAV: A Journal for the Study of the Northwest Semitic Languages and Literatures* 14, no. 2 (2015) 7–26.

Kelly, J. N. D. *Early Christian Doctrines*. Rev. ed. New York: Harper & Row, 1978.

Kierkegaard, Søren. *Training in Christianity, and the Edifying Discourse which Accompanied It*. Edited by John F. Thornton and Susan B. Varenne, translated by Walter Lowrie. New York: Vintage, 2004.

Kim, Soo J. "Eschatology in Isaiah." In *The Oxford Handbook of Isaiah*, edited by Lena-Sofia Tiemeyer, 352–76. Oxford, UK: Oxford University Press, 2020.

King, Robert. "The Task of Systematic Theology." In *Christian Theology: An Introduction to Its Traditions and Tasks*, edited by Peter Hodgson and Robert King, 1–34. Minneapolis: Fortress, 1994.

Kook, Abraham Isaac. *Ein Ayah, Berakhot*. Jerusalem: Machon al Shem HaRav Zvi Yehudah Hakohen Kook zt'l, 1990.

LaHaye, Tim and Ed Hindson, eds. *Exploring Bible Prophecy from Genesis to Revelation: Clarifying the Meaning of Every Prophetic Passage*. Eugene, OR: Harvest House, 2011.

Lazar, Rina, ed. *Talking about Evil: Psychoanalytic, Social, and Cultural Perspectives*. London: Routledge, 2016.

Leif, Dixon. *Practical Predestinarians in England, c. 1590–1640*. St Andrews Studies in Reformation History. London: Routledge, 2014.

Lemche, Niels Peter. *The Old Testament between Theology and History: A Critical Survey*. Louisville, KY: Westminster John Knox, 2008.

Levering, Matthew. *Predestination: Biblical and Theological Paths*. Oxford, UK: Oxford University Press, 2011.

Lewis, Alan E. *Between Cross and Resurrection: A Theology of Holy Saturday*. Grand Rapids: Eerdmans, 2003.

Lewis, Clive Staples. *The Weight of Glory*. San Francisco: HarperOne, 2001.

Lindars, Barnabas. "Good Tidings to Zion: Interpreting Deutero-Isaiah Today." *Bulletin* 68 (1985–1986) 473–97.

Lindsay, Mark R. *God Has Chosen: The Doctrine of Election through Christian History*. Downers Grove, IL: InterVarsity, 2020.

Livingstone, Elizabeth A., ed. *Studia Patristica XXII: Papers Presented to the Tenth International Conference on Patristic Studies Held in Oxford 1987*. Leuven: Peeters, 1989.

Ludlow, Morwenna. "*In illud: tunc et ipse filius*." In *Gregory of Nyssa: The Minor Treatises on Trinitarian Theology and Apollinarianism*, edited by Volker Henning Drecoll and Margitta Berghaus. Vigiliae Christianae Supplements 106. Leiden, Neth.: Brill, 2011.

Luther, Martin. *The Bondage of the Will.* Translated by Edward Thomas Vaughan. Kensington, UK: Createspace Independent, 2015.

Mackie, Timothy P. *Expanding Ezekiel: The Hermeneutics of Scribal Addition in the Ancient Text Witnesses of the Book of Ezekiel.* Göttingen, Germ.: Vandenhoeck & Ruprecht, 2014.

Mann, William E. *God, Modality, and Morality.* Oxford, UK: Oxford University Press, 2015.

Mathewson, David. "Isaiah in Revelation." In *Isaiah in the New Testament: The New Testament and the Scriptures of Israel,* edited by Steve Moyise and Maarten J. J. Menken, 189–210. London: T. & T. Clark, 2007.

———. *A New Heaven and a New Earth: The Meaning and Function of the Old Testament in Revelation 21.1–22.5.* Sheffield: Sheffield Academic Press, 2003.

Matz, Robert J., and A. Chadwick Thornhill, eds. *Divine Impassibility: Four Views of God's Emotions and Suffering.* Downers Grove, IL: IVP Academic, 2019.

Maulana, Muhammad. "Hell Is Meant for Purification and Is Not Permanent." The Quranic Compassion (Aug. 2017). https://thequran.love/2017/08/22/ hell-is-meant-for-purification-and-is-not-permanent.

May, Herbert Gordon. "Theological Universalism in the Old Testament." *Journal of the American Academy of Religion* 15, no. 2 (Apr. 1948) 100–107.

McClymond, Michael J. *The Devil's Redemption: A New History and Interpretation of Christian Universalism.* Grand Rapids: Baker, 2020.

McCruden, Kevin. *Solidarity Perfected: Beneficient Christology in the Epistle to the Hebrews.* Berlin: De Gruyter, 2008.

McDowell, John. "Learning Where to Place One's Hope: The Eschatological Significance of Election in Barth." *Scottish Journal of Theology* 53, no. 3 (2000) 316–38.

McKinion, Steven A. *Isaiah 1–39.* Edited by Thomas C. Oden. Downers Grove, IL: InterVarsity, 2004.

Miles, Margaret R. "Violence against Women in the Historical Christian West and in North American Culture: The Visual and Textual Evidence." In *Shaping New Vision: Gender and Values in American Culture,* edited by Clarissa W. Atkinson et al., 11–29. Harvard Women's Studies in Religion 5. Ann Arbor, MI: University Microfilms International, 1987.

Moder, Ally. "Women, Personhood, and the Male God: A Feminist Critique of Patriarchal Concepts of God in View of Domestic Abuse." *Feminist Theology* 28, no. 1 (2019) 85–103.

Molina, Luis de. *On Divine Foreknowledge: Part IV of the "Concordia."* Translated by Alfred J. Freddoso. Cornell Classics in Philosophy. Ithaca, NY: Cornell University Press, 2004.

Moltmann, Jürgen. *The Coming of God: Christian Eschatology.* Translated by Margaret Kohl. Minneapolis: Fortress, 2004.

Moreland, James Porter, and William Lane Craig. *Philosophical Foundations for a Christian Worldview.* Downers Grove, IL: IVP Academic, 2009.

Morgan, Christopher W., and Robert A. Peterson, eds. *Hell under Fire: Modern Scholarship Reinvents Eternal Punishment.* Grand Rapids: Zondervan, 2004.

Moyise, Steve. "Isaiah in the New Testament." In *The Oxford Handbook of Isaiah,* edited by Lena-Sofia Tiemeyer, 531–41. Oxford, UK: Oxford University Press, 2020.

————, and Maarten J. J. Menken, eds. *Isaiah in the New Testament: The New Testament and the Scriptures of Israel*. London: T. & T. Clark, 2007.

Muller, Richard. "Reception and Response: Referencing and Understanding Calvin in Seventeenth-Century Calvinism." In *Calvin and His Influence, 1509–2009*, edited by Irena Backus and Philip Benedict. Oxford, UK: Oxford University Press, 2009.

Musija, Zlatko. "The Eschatological Hope in the Book of Isaiah." *Academia* (May 2011), 1–22. https://www.academia.edu/5533560/Eschatology_in_Isaiah.

Nadler, Steven. *Spinoza: A Life*. Cambridge, UK: Cambridge University Press, 2001.

Nimmo, Paul T. "The Compassion of Jesus Christ: Barth on Matthew 9:36." In *Reading the Gospels with Karl Barth*, edited by Daniel L. Migliore, 67–79. Grand Rapids: Eerdmans, 2017.

O'Day, Gail R., and David L. Petersen, eds. *Theological Bible Commentary*. Louisville, KY: Westminster John Knox, 2009.

Oord, Thomas Jay. *God Can't: How to Believe in God and Love after Tragedy, Abuse, and Other Evils*. Nampa, ID: SacraSage, 2019.

————. *The Uncontrolling Love of God: An Open and Relational Account of Providence*. Downers Grove, IL: IVP Academic, 2015.

Oswalt, John N. *The Book of Isaiah, Chapters 1–39*. TNICOT. Grand Rapids: Eerdmans, 1986.

————. *The Book of Isaiah, Chapters 40–66*. TNICOT. Grand Rapids: Eerdmans, 1998.

————. *The Holy One of Israel: Studies in the Book of Isaiah*. Eugene, OR: Cascade, 2014.

Papaioannou, Kim. *Israel, Covenant, Law: A Third Perspective on Paul*. Eugene, OR: Wipf & Stock, 2017.

Parry, Robin A. *The Biblical Cosmos: A Pilgrim's Guide to the Weird and Wonderful World of the Bible*. Cambridge, UK: Lutterworth, 2015.

————. "Debate over Universalism in Theology and Philosophy." Reforming Hell (Feb. 2020). https://reforminghell.com/2020/02/04/debate-over-universalism-in-theology-and-philosophy-robin-parry/.

————. *The Evangelical Universalist*. 2nd ed. Eugene, OR: Cascade, 2012.

————. "Is Universalism Heretical, Part 3." Theological Scribble (9 June 2010). http://theologicalscribbles.blogspot.com.au/2010/06/is-universalism-heretical-part-3.html.

————. *Lamentations*. THOTC. Grand Rapids: Eerdmans, 2010.

————. "Prolegomena to Christian Theological Interpretations of Lamentations." In *Canon and Biblical Interpretation*, edited by Craig Bartholomew et al., 393–418. Scripture and Hermeneutics 7. Waynesboro, GA: Paternoster, 2006.

————. "Wrestling with Lamentations in Christian Worship." In *Great Is Thy Faithfulness: Reading Lamentations as Sacred Scripture*, edited by Robin A. Parry and Heath A. Thomas, 175–97. Eugene, OR: Pickwick, 2011.

————, and Ilaria L. E. Ramelli. *A Larger Hope?* Vol. 2 of *Universal Salvation from the Reformation to the Nineteenth Century*. Eugene, OR: Cascade, 2019.

Petersen, David L. *The Prophetic Literature: An Introduction*. Louisville, KY: Westminster John Knox, 2002.

Pinnock, Clark H. "The Conditional View." In *Four Views on Hell*, edited by John F. Walvoord et al., 135–66. Grand Rapids: Zondervan, 2010.

Piper, John. *God's Passion for His Glory: Living the Vision of Jonathan Edwards with the Complete Text of the End for Which God Created the World.* Wheaton, IL: Crossway, 2006.

Ray, Darby Kathleen. *Deceiving the Devil: Atonement, Abuse, and Ransom.* Cleveland: Pilgrim, 1998.

Reichenbach, Bruce R. *Divine Providence: God's Love and Human Freedom.* Eugene, OR: Cascade, 2016.

Rice, Hugh. "Divine Omnipotence, Timelessness and the Power to Do Otherwise." *Religious Studies* 42 (2006) 123–39.

Ritschl, Dietrich. *Memory and Hope: An Inquiry Concerning the Presence of Christ.* New York: Macmillan, 1967.

Rizal, José. "Como se gobiernan las Filipinas." Biblioteca Virtual Miguel de Cervantes, Dec. 15, 1890. http://www.cervantesvirtual.com/obra-visor/come-se-gobiernan-las-filipinas-877107/html/701753c4-91c5-493f-94b7-f2865deaf18e_2.html.

Roberts, J. J. M. *First Isaiah.* Minneapolis: Fortress, 2015.

Rollins, Hyder Edward, ed. *The Letters of John Keats,* 1814–1821. Cambridge, UK: Cambridge University Press, 2012.

Roth, John K. "A Theodicy of Protest." In *Encountering Evil: Live Options in Theodicy,* edited by Stephen T. Davis, 1–37. Louisville, KY: Westminster John Knox, 2001.

Ruether, Rosemary Radford. *Sexism and God-Talk: Toward a Feminist Theology.* Boston: Beacon, 1993.

Sanders, John. "A Freewill Theist's Response to Talbott's Universalism." In *Universal Salvation?: The Current Debate,* edited by Robin A. Parry and Christopher H. Patridge, 169–87. Grand Rapids: Eerdmans, 2004.

———. "Why Oord's Essential Kenosis Model Fails to Solve the Problem of Evil While Retaining Miracles." *Wesleyan Journal of Theology* 51, no.2 (Fall 2016) 174–87.

Sawyer, John Frederick Adam. *The Fifth Gospel: Isaiah in the History of Christianity.* Cambridge, UK: Cambridge University Press, 1996.

Schmitt, John J. "Israel and Zion—Two Gendered Images: Biblical Speech Traditions and Their Contemporary Neglect." *Horizon* 18 (Spring 1991) 18–32.

Schopenhauer, Arthur. *Essays and Aphorisms.* London: Penguin Classics, 2014.

Scott, Mark S. M. "Suffering and Soul-Making: Rethinking John Hick's Theodicy." *The Journal of Religion* 90, no. 3 (July 2010) 313–34.

Senior, Donald, and Carroll Stuhlmeuller. *The Biblical Foundations for Mission.* Maryknoll, NY: Orbis, 1989.

Sherlock, Charles. *The Doctrine of Humanity: Contours of Christian Theology.* Edited by Gerald Bray. Downers Grove, IL: IVP Academic, 1997.

Simkovich, Malka. "The Origins of Jewish Universalism: What It Is, and Why It Matters." Lehrhaus (6 Oct. 2016). https://www.thelehrhaus.com/scholarship/the-origins-of-jewish-universalism-what-it-is-and-why-it-matters/.

Sneed, Mark S. *The Social World of the Sages: An Introduction to Israelite and Jewish Wisdom Literature.* Minneapolis: Fortress, 2015.

Sommer, Benjamin D. *A Prophet Reads Scripture: Allusion in Isaiah 40–66.* Stanford, CA: Stanford University Press, 1998.

Spinoza, Benedictus de. *A Spinoza Reader: The Ethics and Other Works.* Translated by Edwin Curley. Princeton, NJ: Princeton University Press, 1985.

Stefanović, Ranko. *Revelation of Jesus Christ: Commentary on the Book of Revelation.* Berrien Springs, MI: Andrews University Press, 2009.

Stromberg, Jacob. *An Introduction to the Study of Isaiah*. T&T Clark Approaches to Biblical Studies. London: T. & T. Clark, 2011.

Stump, Eleonore. *Wandering in Darkness: Narrative and the Problem of Suffering*. Oxford: Oxford University Press, 2012.

Stump, J. B. and Chad Meister, eds. *Original Sin and the Fall: Five Views*. Downers Grove, IL: InterVarsity, 2020.

Sullivan, Meghan. "Problems for Temporary Existence in Tense Logic." *Philosophy Compass* 7, no. 1 (2012) 43–57. https://doi.org/10.1111/j.1747–9991.2011.00457.x.

Sweeney, Marvin A. *The Prophetic Literature*. Interpreting Biblical Texts. Nashville: Abingdon, 2005.

Thompson, Michael E. W. *Isaiah 40-66*. Eugene, OR: Wipf & Stock, 2012.

Tiemeyer, Lena-Sofa, ed. *The Oxford Handbook of Isaiah*. Oxford, UK: Oxford University Press, 2020.

Tomasino, Anthony. "Isaiah 1.1—2.4 and 63–66, and the Composition of the Isaianic Corpus." *Journal for the Study of the Old Testament* 57 (1993) 8–98.

Tull, Patricia K. "God's Character in Isaiah." In *The Oxford Handbook of Isaiah*, edited by Lena-Sofia Tiemeyer, 201–18. Oxford, UK: Oxford University Press, 2020.

Van Winkle, D. W. "The Relationship of the Nations to Yahweh and to Israel in Isaiah XL–LV." *Vetus Testamentum* 35, no. 4 (Oct. 1985) 446–58.

Vincent, Ken R. "The Salvation Conspiracy: How Hell Became Eternal." Christian Universalist Association (2007). https://christianuniversalist.org/resources/articles/salvation-conspiracy/.

Von Balthasar, Hans Urs. *Dramatis Personae: The Person in Christ*. Vol. 3 of *Theo-Drama: Theological Dramatic Theory*. Translated by Graham Harrison. San Francisco: Ignatius, 1993.

Ware, Timothy. *The Orthodox Church: An Introduction to Eastern Christianity*. 3rd ed. London: Penguin, 2015.

Warren, Kate Mary. "Harrowing of Hell." In *Catholic Encyclopedia* 7, edited by Charles G. Herbermann et al., page range unknown. New York: Robert Appleton, 1910.

Watts, Alan, and Al Chung-Liang Huan. *Tao: The Watercourse Way*. London: Souvenir Press, 2011.

Weber, Otto. *Foundations of Dogmatics*. Vol. 1. Grand Rapids: Eerdmans, 1981.

Whybray, R. N. *The Second Isaiah*. T&T Clark Study Guides. London: T. & T. Clark, 2004.

Williamson, H. G. M. *Isaiah 1-5: A Critical and Exegetical Commentary*. International Critical Commentary. London: T. & T. Clark, 2014.

Wingren, Gustaf. *Man and the Incarnation: A Study in the Biblical Theology of Irenaeus*. Translated by Ross Mackenzie. Eugene, OR: Wipf and Stock, 2004.

Wright, N. T. "The Fifth Gospel: Why Isaiah Matters." N. T. Wright Online (May 2020). https://www.ntwrightonline.org/the-fifth-gospel-why-isaiah-matters/.

———. *God and the Pandemic: A Christian Reflection on the Coronavirus and Its Aftermath*. London: SPCK, 2020.

———. *Surprised by Scripture: Engaging Contemporary Issues*. Reprint, San Francisco: HarperOne, 2015.

———. "Tom Wright on Being a Christian during Coronavirus." Premier on Demand (Mar. 2020). https://www.youtube.com/watch?v=tUTD0S9YVuU.

Young, Edward J. *The Book of Isaiah: Chapters 19-39*. Grand Rapids: Eerdmans, 1992.

Yutzy, Elton. *God's Plan for Man and Planet Earth*. Bloomington, IN: Westbrow, 2013.

SUBJECT INDEX

www.ingramcontent.com/pod-product-compliance
Lightning Source LLC
Chambersburg PA
CBHW060333100426
42812CB00003B/979